ICONS OF THE LUSO-HISPANIC WORLD

3

MARÍA DE ZAYAS AND HER TALES OF DESIRE, DEATH AND DISILLUSION

ICONS OF THE LUSO-HISPANIC WORLD

ISSN: 2633-7169 (print)
ISSN: 2633-7177 (online)

The Icons series includes books on a broad range of outstanding individuals – royalty, religious figures, explorers and leaders of indigenous resistance, inventors, scientists, politicians, revolutionaries, activists, authors, artists, musicians, philosophers, film directors, athletes – and occasionally groups of people, who have had a significant impact not only on Spanish- and Portuguese-speaking countries but on a broader, even global, scale. Books in the series offer an expertly researched overview of the impact these icons have made both within and beyond their native regions, considering their achievements, influence on contemporaries, and reception more widely. Focussing on key moments in an icon's life and work, these books trace the acquisition of iconic status. They explore an icon's legacy and image and afterlife(ves), showing how they have been interpreted, appropriated, and at times reimagined. Based on the most up-to-date scholarly research, books in the series explore how and why a Hispanic or Lusophone icon can also be considered an international icon.

Previously published in the series

1. *Federico García Lorca: The Poetry in All Things*, Federico Bonaddio (2022)

2. *Machado de Assis: The World Keeps Changing to Remain the Same*, Mario Higa (2022)

3. *María de Zayas and her Tales of Desire, Death and Disillusion*, Margaret R. Greer (2022)

4. *María Félix: A Mexican Film Star and her Legacy*, Niamh Thornton (2023)

MARÍA DE ZAYAS AND HER TALES OF DESIRE, DEATH AND DISILLUSION

Margaret R. Greer

TAMESIS

© Margaret R. Greer 2022

All Rights Reserved. Except as permitted under current legislation
no part of this work may be photocopied, stored in a retrieval system,
published, performed in public, adapted, broadcast,
transmitted, recorded or reproduced in any form or by any means,
without the prior permission of the copyright owner

The right of Margaret R. Greer to be identified as
the author of this work has been asserted in accordance with
sections 77 and 78 of the Copyright, Designs and Patents Act 1988

First published 2022
Tamesis Books, Woodbridge
Paperback edition 2025

ISBN 978 1 85566 360 2 (Hardback)
ISBN 978 1 85566 422 7 (Paperback)

Tamesis Books is an imprint of Boydell & Brewer Ltd
PO Box 9, Woodbridge, Suffolk IP12 3DF, UK
and of Boydell & Brewer Inc.
668 Mt. Hope Avenue, Rochester, NY 14620-2731, USA
website: www.boydellandbrewer.com

The publisher has no responsibility for the continued existence or accuracy
of URLs for external or third-party internet websites referred to in this book,
and does not guarantee that any content on such websites is, or will remain,
accurate or appropriate

A CIP record for this title is available
from the British Library

Our Authorised Representative for product safety in the EU is Easy Access
System Europe - Mustamäe tee 50, 10621 Tallinn, Estonia,
gpsr.requests@easproject.com

In memory of Robert G. Greer

Who doubts, my reader, that you will be amazed that a woman has the audacity not only to write a book, but to send it for printing, which is the crucible in which the purity of genius is tested…. Who doubts … that there will be many who attribute to madness this virtuous daring to bring my scribblings into light, being a woman, which, in the opinion of some fools, is the same as an incapable thing.

María de Zayas y Sotomayor
Exemplary Tales of Love

Contents

List of Illustrations		x
Acknowledgements		xi
Preface		xiii
Chapter 1	Zayas: Her Life and Times	1
Chapter 2	Exemplary Tales of Love: A Contradiction?	22
Chapter 3	Settings, Styles and Models: Zayas's Literary Context	45
Chapter 4	Turning the Tables on Men in *Exemplary Tales of Love*	61
Chapter 5	Bodies in Pain: *Tales of Disillusion*	79
Chapter 6	Identifying the Subject	93
Chapter 7	I Believe: Religion, Magic, the Supernatural	117
Chapter 8	Zayas on Women	143
Conclusion	Zayas's Afterlives	160
Appendix	Plot Summaries	179
Bibliography		199
General Index		211
Index of Zayas's Works		219

Illustrations

1. *Inés de Zúñiga, Condesa de Monterrey.* © Madrid, Museo Lazaro Galdiano — 3
2. *The Virgin of Montserrat and pilgrims on the road to the monastery.* © Monasterio de Santa María de Montserrat — 123
3. *Infanta Isabel Clara Eugenia and Magdalena Ruíz.* © Madrid, Museo Nacional del Prado — 149

Full credit details are provided in the captions to the images in the text. The author and publisher are grateful to all the institutions and individuals for permission to reproduce the materials in which they hold copyright. Every effort has been made to trace the copyright holders; apologies are offered for any omission, and the publisher will be pleased to add any necessary acknowledgement in subsequent editions.

Acknowledgements

First credit for the existence of this book goes to the enthusiasm and guidance of Megan Milan as commissioning editor for Tamesis Books. She reached out to me early in 2020 with an invitation to write on María de Zayas for their new series, Icons of the Luso-Hispanic World. I was then working on a very different project that was suddenly blocked as we went into lockdown because of Covid, cutting off access I needed to libraries and archives in the United States and Europe. Having written at length on Zayas in previous decades, I could, however, write this introduction to her voice, times, and works for general readers, drawing on my own library and materials accessible online. In fact, doing so proved to be a lifeline that preserved my relative sanity during the pandemic. Heartfelt thanks are also due to Zora O'Neill, accomplished author and editor, who helped me craft the book's chapters for intelligent general readers with her good judgement of how much background information on Zayas's historical, social and literary context to include, and how to avoid excess verbiage and jargon.

My appreciation also for the support and advice of valued friends and colleagues in Early Modern Spanish studies: to Elizabeth Rhodes, co-editor and translator of our anthology of Zayas's stories and author of an illuminating book on Zayas's *Desengaños*, to Laura Bass, expert on Madrid and Spanish art and artists and to Elizabeth Wright, for the breadth and depth of her knowledge of Early Modern Iberian drama and culture. Joyce Zaritsky and other friends suggested recent books as models of good studies for general readers. My thanks as well to new friends made on Zoom and in person through San Francisco Village neighborhood circles and book clubs. And to my son Jim and daughter Emily, who urged me to contact Zora O'Neill and who provide support and sounding boards for my work.

Preface

María de Zayas y Sotomayor was a "rare bird" in Early Modern Spain, a successful published woman author of page-turning tales of love and death. In the overwhelmingly masculine literary tradition of Golden Age Spain, in which women were deemed inferior creatures and enjoined to silence, she defended their worth and rights in two collections of engaging tales that were repeatedly republished through the eighteenth century. Today her stories are drawing – and amazing – a new public. Witness the reaction of one astonished twentieth-century reader I found penciled in the margin of a library copy: "Zayas is a trip!"

That reader's reaction echoed my own when I first read a Zayas story in about 1981. When I was a graduate student in Hispanic literature in the 1970s and 1980s, the only women writers from the early periods on my required reading list were two nuns: Santa Teresa and Sor Juana Inés de la Cruz; I came to admire Santa Teresa and love Sor Juana. When I was finishing my dissertation on another topic, I happened to audit a course by a new professor who had us read a Zayas story. I don't remember which story we read, but I do remember being blown away by its difference and its daring. After a decade of writing on Early Modern Spanish drama, that singular woman's voice drew me to teaching and studying María de Zayas. She herself greets readers with the words that stand as my epigraph.

My purpose is to introduce this icon of the Hispanic world to new Zayas readers, giving a sense of the context in which María de Zayas wrote and how she sought to use her stories to change it for the better for both women and men, entertaining them as she did so. After the first two chapters, readers may want to pick and choose according to their own interests. The first chapter, "Zayas and Her World," sets out what we know of her life and publications and gives a sketch of her sociopolitical context in seventeenth-century Spain. In chapter 2, "Exemplary Tales of Love: A Contradiction," I introduce readers to her tales of love in her first volume, analyzing her paradoxical use of sexual desire to drive her plots while warning of its dangers. I also consider how she treats varieties of love, straight and queer, in the context of the position of Counterreformation Catholicism on sex and marriage. Following that introduction to her storytelling, chapter 3, "Settings, Styles and Models: Zayas's Literary Context," treats Zayas's writing style in prose and poetry and the literary models she reflects and adapts in her works. Chapter 4, "Turning the Tables on Men in *Exemplary Tales of Love*," highlights three stories in the first volume that display her comedic gifts as her female protagonists turn the tables on uncomprehending or abusive men. Chapter 5, "Bodies in Pain, *Tales of Disillusion*," turns to the topic of violence against women and the meaning of the escalating body counts in Zayas's second volume, ending with the question of why she kills women who qualify as good and sometimes delivers earthly rewards to bad actors, both male and female. In chapters 2, 4 and 5, I do not follow all the twists and turns of the plots, for which the reader should see plot summaries in the appendix and the stories themselves, but I explain facets that appear in several tales and those that might puzzle twenty-first century readers. Chapter 6, "I Am Who I Am," explains how a subject's identity was understood in Zayas's day, by gender, class, race (religious "ethnicity" and skin color), family status and wealth, and how Zayas presents important political and religious authorities. Chapter 7, "I Believe: Religion, Magic and the Supernatural," takes up the question of Zayas's presentation of religious belief, convent life, Moors and types of magic and its practitioners. In chapter 8, "An Alliance of Women?" I examine the nature of her proto-feminism, as she set it out in her "To the Reader" preface and as she reveals it in the way she paints her female protagonists and their antagonists. The conclusion, "Zayas's Afterlives," sketches Early Modern reception of her stories in Spain and elsewhere in Europe and summarizes significant critical readings of her works, from her day to ours.

Zayas's first collection, the *Exemplary Tales of Love* (Novelas amorosas y ejemplares), was published in 1637; the second, generally known as the *Tales of Disillusion* (Desengaños amorosos), appeared in 1647. Since this book is written for a general, primarily anglophone audience, I give individual story titles in English, together with their numbers in the corresponding volume. I use the titles of the seven tales included in the anthology translated and edited by Margaret R. Greer and Elizabeth Rhodes,

Exemplary Tales of Love and Tales of Disillusion (indicated henceforth as ETL). For the other thirteen, I give the titles H. Patsy Boyer used in her translations of all the tales, *The Enchantments of Love* (1990) and *The Disenchantments of Love* (1997). In the case of the *Tales of Disillusion* not given titles by Zayas (all but the first one), I use the Greer-Rhodes title for that first tale and enclose Boyer's titles in parentheses after its number for the others. The list, with the stories identified by volume – abbreviated as N or D – and number is as follows, with the original Spanish title in parentheses:

N. 1: Taking a Chance on Losing ETL – (Aventurarse perdiendo)

N. 2: Aminta Deceived and Honor's Revenge B – (La burlada Aminta y venganza del honor)

N. 3: The Miser's Reward B – (El castigo de la miseria)

N. 4: Forewarned but Fooled ETL – (El prevenido engañado)

N. 5: The Power of Love B – (La fuerza del amor)

N. 6: Disillusionment in Love and Virtue Rewarded B – (El desengaño amando y premio de la virtud)

N. 7: Just Desserts B – (Al fin se paga todo)

N. 8: Triumph over the Impossible B – (El imposible vencido)

N. 9: The Judge of Her Own Case ETL – (El juez de su causa)

N. 10: The Deceitful Garden ETL – (El jardín engañoso)

D. 1: Her Lover's Slave ETL – (La esclava de su amante)

D. 2: Most Infamous Revenge B

D. 3: His Wife's Executioner B

D. 4: Too Late Undeceived B

D. 5: Fifth Tale of Disillusion ETL Innocence Punished B

D. 6: Love for the Sake of Conquest B

D. 7: Marriage Abroad: Portent of Doom B

D. 8: Traitor to His Own Blood B

D. 9: Triumph Over Persecution B

D. 10: The Ravages of Vice B

In the chapters that follow, I give citations of Zayas in English, from the Greer-Rhodes anthology or from Boyer's translations, or my own translation, or a hybrid of the two. I follow the translations with the Spanish original, abbreviated if long to its opening and closing phrases, identifying the source in footnotes. Given the ready availability of Zayas's *Novelas* and *Desengaños* in Spanish, readers who want to see the Spanish originals in full can easily locate them.

Chapter One

Zayas: Her Life and Times

MARÍA DE ZAYAS y Sotomayor (1590–ca. 1660?) was indeed a "rare bird" in Early Modern Spain, as a successful published woman author of page-turning tales of love and death. Her tales are lengthy stories of romance, adventure, triumph, violence and loss, involving aristocratic women and their suitors, generally from the same class, although commoners and servants play important roles too. Zayas set them in the frame-tale tradition of Boccaccio's *Decameron* (1353) of stories told by ten young women and men, but rather than fleeing to the countryside from plague-wracked Florence like Boccaccio's storytellers, Zayas's narrators gather around braziers in an elegantly furnished room on cold December nights, to entertain the ailing frame-tale protagonist Lisis. Zayas marketed her two volumes of tales primarily to literate members of an urban lower nobility, who could also read them aloud to a wider, less lettered public. While proclaiming that all were true stories, told directly or by first-person witnesses to her narrators, she seasoned many of them with generous doses of fantasy and magic.

In the overwhelmingly masculine literary tradition of Golden Age Spain, in which women were deemed inferior creatures and enjoined to silence, she defended their worth and rights in two collections of engaging tales, published in 1637 and 1647, that were received with acclaim at the time and repeatedly republished through the eighteenth century. Each volume contains ten lengthy stories of love and death in her aristocratic class, sometimes bringing death to their servants as well. Zayas has them told by male and female narrators, gathered to entertain each other and Lisis, their ailing hostess, in her elegant salon. Lisis is the protagonist of the story that frames both collections. Male writers who were her contemporaries called her "the immortal María de Zayas" worker of "womanly wonders" with her "lively clear talent"; and "sibyl of Madrid" [la inmortal doña María de Zayas /.... / milagros de mujer / ingenio vivamente claro].¹ They also lauded her as "our century's Tenth Muse" [dezima Musa de nuestro siglo], the same title bestowed on the archaic Greek poet Sappho of Lesbos and the Mexican nun Sor Juana Inés de la Cruz. It was, in their praise, a backhanded compliment, one that invited seeing her and other great women writers as isolated, exceptional phenomena.² If male writers could pray for inspiration from the nine muses, (the nine sister-goddesses of the liberal arts and sciences of Greek mythology), women writers seeking to articulate the female experience of the universe needed to have, and be, their own Tenth Muse. Censors charged with approving publications lauded the didactic value of Zayas's stories, one likening her to the "busy, ingenious Bee in her sting, sweetness and worth" [argumentosa Abeja, que en lo picante, dulce, y provechoso, si no la aventaja, la emula].³ Zayas was not of course immortal, either in the flesh or in print; her works faded from view in the nineteenth century, banished along with that of other women writers as mere entertainment of no literary merit. Or worse: critics with Victorian concepts of acceptable discourse by women found some of her stories gross, indecent or sadistic. Changing tastes and views of women brought Zayas back in fashion in the last half of the twentieth century, and her popularity continues to burgeon in the twenty-first.

Of María de Zayas in the flesh, we can assemble at best a patchwork image. The pistol-packing lady in figure 1 is not Zayas, but Iñés de Zúñiga, Countess of Monterrey, painted sometime between 1660 and 1670 by Carreño de Miranda, the most important court painter of the Spanish Baroque after Velázquez. Although Zayas imagines one of her characters having her portrait painted (ETL 4, p. 124, "Forewarned but Fooled"),

1   Lope de Vega, *El laurel de Apolo*, ed. Antonio Carreño, Madrid, 2007, p. 165; "Sibila de Madrid," Castillo Solórzano, *La garduña de Sevilla y anzuelo de las bolsas*, Barcelona, 1644, p. 48.
2   Juan Pérez de Montalbán, *Para todos, exemplos morales, humanos y divino*, Madrid, 1635, f. 353v; On the Tenth Muse title, see Stephanie Merrim, *Early Modern Women's Writing and Sor Juana Inés de la Cruz*, Nashville, 1999, pp. xii, xiii, xl–xl; and Catherine Chung's novel, *The Tenth Muse*, New York, 2019.
3   Fray Vincente Bellmont, in María de Zayas y Sotomayor, *Primera, y segunda parte de las novelas amorosas y ejemplares*, Valencia, 1712. Unnumbered preliminary page. My translation.

Figure 1 *Inés de Zúñiga, Condesa de Monterrey*, by Carreño de Miranda (1660–70) © Madrid, Museo Lázaro Galdiano.

portraiture was generally reserved for royalty and the highest nobility. But the countess's little pistol is a fitting symbol of Zayas's wish to prepare women to defend themselves. In the prologue to D. 4, "Disillusioned Too Late," the narrator argues that men keep women from exercising arms and studying sciences lest women outdo them and take their places; that no woman who wore a sword would allow a man to abuse her. "Men," she contends, "deprive them of learning and arms, as Moors do Christians where there are women, making them eunuchs to be sure of them" [Los hombres de temor y envidia las privan de las letras y las armas, como hacen los moros a los cristianos que han de server donde hay mujeres, que los hacen eunucos por estar seguros de ellos]. Rallying women, she says, "Come on, leave off finery, roses and curls, and let's defend ourselves, some with understanding, others with arms!" [¡Ea, dejemos las galas, rosas y rizos, y volvamos por nosotras: unas con el entendimiento, y otras con las amas!][4]

Zayas was born in the last decade of the reign of Philip II (1556–98), when Spanish dominion over the world's first global empire was at its height. Born to a family of the lower aristocracy, she was baptized in Madrid on September 12, 1590, in the parish of San Sebastián, site of the handsome sixteenth-century church of San Sebastián on Calle Atocha in the center of the city. Her parents were Fernando de Zayas y Sotomayor and María de Carasa; her godparents were Diego de Santoyo and his wife Juana de Cardona. She had one younger sister, Isabel, born in the family's residence on the Calle de la Cabeza and like María, baptized nearby in the parish of San Sebastián in March 1594. Isabel's godparents were Luis Sánchez and Ana López. María had a third sister, Jerónima de Zayas, of unknown age, cited only in an undated lawsuit that María and Jerónima entered after the death of Isabel and her husband, Lucas de Medina, to recover the dowry provided to Medina on the couple's marriage in 1599.[5]

The street in Madrid where the Zayas family lived, the calle de la Cabeza (street of the head), gave rise to a tale as grizzly as some of her stories. Legend has it that during the reign of Philip III, the monarch most frequently referenced by Zayas, a rich priest lived in a house on the street. His servant killed and decapitated him and fled to Portugal with

---

4 Parte segunda del Sarao y entretenimiento honesto [Desengaños amorosos], ed. Alicia Yllera, Madrid, 2021, p. 336. My translation.

5 Manuel Serrano y Sanz misread her mother's name as Barasa in Apuntes para una biblioteca de escritoras españolas desde el año 1401 al 1833, Madrid, 1905, vol. 2, pp. 584–5. Matías Fernández García corrected the name to Carasa, as Martha Elizabeth Treviño Salazar reports in her PhD dissertation, "Estua dio y edición de la Parte segunda del Sarao y entretenimiento honesto (1647) de María de Zayas y Sotomayor," Barcelona, 2018, pp. xvi–xvii. For the third sister, Treviño, pp. xxiv–xxv, cites a document published by Narciso Díaz de Escovar, 1914, p. 24.

the priest's gold. The crime was only discovered when a sacristan from the local San Sebastian parish went to his house to take him receipts from some appointments he held. Finding the door half open, he learned from neighbors that both the priest and his servant had disappeared. He told the authorities, who found the priest "in two pieces" but with no sign of the servant. The crime went long unsolved, until it proved true the saying that assassins always return to the scene of the crime when the murderous servant returned to Madrid dressed as a gentleman. Strolling through the Rastro market, he bought a head of mutton and, not having a servant to carry it, tucked it under his cape. A constable who noticed the trail of blood dripping from it stopped him and asked what he was carrying. He answered that it was a head of mutton he'd just bought, but when he removed the cape, they saw it was the head of the priest. The assassin was so stunned that he confessed on the spot. He was tried, sentenced and hanged in the Plaza Mayor. Legend further relates that on his way to execution in the plaza, the head was borne ahead of him on a silver tray and when the sentence was carried out, it turned back into a head of mutton. Another chapter in the legend says that Philip III ordered a stone-sculpted head of the priest placed on the front of the priest's house, but it so terrified the neighbors that in exchange for their promise to erect a chapel to the Virgen of Carmen, the stone head was removed.[6] Not all the details of the legend are consistent, and María de Zayas never referred to it. Nevertheless, it is a legend whose bloody violence and supernatural turn is akin to scenes Zayas relates in her *Desengaños* – particularly D. 8, "Traitor to His Own Blood."

María's father, Fernando de Zayas, was an infantry captain who was granted the habit of the elite military-religious Order of Santiago in 1628, an order to which María's godfather also belonged. Fernando served as administrator to Pedro Fernández de Castro, Count of Lemos, who was appointed *corregidor* (magistrate) of the Order of Santiago estate of Jérez de los Caballeros in 1638. Zayas's family was also involved in the literary arts. María's paternal grandmother, Luisa de Zayas y Sotomayor, was reported to be an excellent poet and well versed in the humanities. And Zayas's uncle was a well-known Spanish printer, Luis Sánchez, a learned man who was Isabel's godfather. He married Ana de Carasa, sister of María de Carasa, María de Zayas's mother. Luis Sánchez's father, Francisco Sánchez, was one of the best-known Madrid printers in the second half of

---

6 Juan Antonio Cabezas, *Diccionario de Madrid*, Madrid, p. 87; my free translation of the legend.

the sixteenth century, and when his son Luis died in 1627, Ana de Carasa took charge of the Imprenta Real that was the family business until her own death in 1633. With Ana at the head of the printing house, many of the publications were financed by Madrid bookseller Alonso Pérez de Montalban, father of the author Juan Pérez de Montalban.[7] The latter demonstrated his friendship and admiration for our author María in *Para todos*, the miscellany first published in 1632, in which he called her "tenth muse of our century" and said she "has entered poetic competitions with great success, has completed a comedia [three-act play] in excellent verse and has ready for publication a book of eight exemplary novellas in prose and verse" [Zayas, decima Musa ... ha escrito a los Certamenes ... una Comedia ... y ocho Novelas exemplares].[8] María de Zayas thus belonged to a family active in Madrid's literary circles, with significant connections to well-known writers.

That context helps explain how María de Zayas came to be an icon for a restricted group of literate women in Early Modern Spain. In the larger Early Modern European context, very few women wrote anything before the modern era, for several reasons, the first being that they rarely received the education that would enable them to do so. Literacy was higher in urban settings, particularly a court city like Madrid, where approximately 25 percent of the female population was at least marginally literate and able to sign their names, in contrast to some 60 percent of the males. Women's education was more widespread in Spain than in other European countries. Convent schools taught girls to read to enable them to follow basic religious texts; secular women might need to sign contracts and manage complex households.[9] Zayas, like young girls of her class,

---

7 On the paternal grandmother Treviño cites Álvarez y Baena, *Hijos de Madrid, ilustres en santidad, dignidades, armas, ciencias y artes* (1791, vol. 4, p. 48) and on the Pérez de Montalbán connection, Alberto Rodríguez de Ramos ("La biografía de María de Zayas," pp. 244–5) and Agulló y Cobo (*Noticias de impresores*, vol. 2, p. 7). Fernando de Zayas was an executor of the wills of both Luis Sánchez and Ana de Carasa (Treviño, pp. xvii–xxvii).
8 Pérez de Montalbán, *Para todos*, f. 289r. My translation.
9 On women writers in Early Modern Europe, see Margaret L. King and Albert Rabil Jr., "The Other Voice in Early Modern Europe: Introduction to the Series," María de Zayas, *Exemplary Tales*, pp. ix–xxviii. On the Spanish context, see Anne J. Cruz, "Women's Education in Early Modern Spain," *The Routledge Research Companion to Early Modern Spanish Women Writers*, ed. Nieves Baranda and Anne J. Cruz, pp. 27–40, New York, 2018, and S. T. Nalle, "Literacy and Culture in Early Modern Castile," *Past and Present*, 125, pp. 65–96.

would have learned to read at home, being taught either by her mother, another relative or a hired tutor or in a convent school. Although women could not pursue higher studies in colleges or universities, Zayas argues in her "To the Reader" prologue that with access to books and her inclination, women could educate themselves and learn to write as she did. "When I see any book, new or old, I abandon my little lace pillow and do not rest until I skim it over. From this inclination was born knowledge, from knowledge good taste, and from it all the writing of poetry, even writing these novellas" [en viendo cualquiera … no sosiego hasta que le paso. De esta inclinación nació la noticia … hasta escribir estas Novelas].[10]

Whether or not Zayas spent most of her life in Madrid is an open question. The nineteenth-century historian Manuel Serrano y Sanz compiled biographical information about Zayas and other Spanish women writers from the fifteenth to nineteenth century and published some of their writings for the first time, including a Zayas play. He wrote that it was an indisputable fact that Zayas lived in Madrid most if not all her life, although he also thinks the publication of the two volumes of her works in Zaragoza might indicate she lived there for some years.[11] Zayas sets her stories in cities and towns across the breadth of the Iberian peninsula and beyond, and in the absence of reliable information about her, many readers and Zayas critics have fabricated a biography for her from elements in her stories, attributing to her experience the lives and locales she gives to her protagonists. Wise readers, however, resist naïve belief in her reiterated declarations of the truth of her tales and their first-person witnesses. Her descriptions of those cities are quite formulaic and could easily derive from published accounts. With some plausible historical grounding, Agustín G. de Amezúa y Mayo, who published an edition of Zayas's *Novelas* in 1948 and *Desengaños* in 1950, suggested that she might have resided in Valladolid and Naples, having moved with her parents to Valladolid when Philip III and his favorite (*privado*) the Duke of Lerma transferred the court there briefly from 1601 to 1606. Amezúa also suggested our heroine would have lived in Naples if her father moved there with his family while the Count of Lemos was its viceroy (1610–16). Zayas's sketches of Valladolid seem as formulaic as others, but those of Naples and its customs strike me as potentially based on personal acquaintance, particularly in the detailed and fearsome description of the location and dimensions of the chapel where Laura goes to gather body parts of a hanged

10 *Exemplary Tales*, pp. 50–51; *Novelas*, pp. 160–1.
11 Serrano y Sanz, *Apuntes*, vol. 2, p. 584.

man in ETL 5, "The Power of Love." However, Alicia Yllera, editor of the *Desengaños*, finds her description of Naples in that tale too conventional to witness personal experience.[12] Zayas adds similarly precise detail in recounting how Marcos is enticed by the demonic character to hang himself in N. 3, "The Miser's Reward," a rewriting of a Cervantes novella. She probably knew, as do modern authors of fantastic fiction, that such precision lends verisimilitude. The only locale other than Madrid we can be sure Zayas knew personally is Barcelona, where she took part in a poetic competition in 1643. But to explain her surprising presence there, we first need to trace her publishing career.

Preliminaries to books published in Early Modern Spain usually included complimentary poems contributed by friends of the author and other writers. Miguel de Cervantes parodied this tradition by prefacing the first part of *Don Quixote* (1605) with poems he attributes to characters from the novels of chivalry that were his target. Zayas's publishing ventures began with this type of poetic homage to writers Miguel de Botello, Pérez de Montalbán and Francisco de Quintana, as she published sonnets, *décimas* and songs in their works in 1621, 1622, 1624, 1626 and 1632. She would also contribute poems in tribute to Lope de Vega and Juan Pérez de Montalbán after their deaths in 1636 and 1639 respectively. The latter, as well as praising her talents and her success in literary contests in his *Para todos*, penned a preliminary sonnet for her *Novelas amorosas*, as did her fellow writer of novella collections, Castillo de Solórzano, and Ana Caro de Mallén, the successful dramatist from Seville.

While Zayas was contributing preliminary poems to other writers' works in the 1620s, she was also composing her own first collection of stories. Pérez de Montalban declared that Zayas had eight novellas ready for publication by 1632. Yet her first volume, the *Novelas amorosas y ejemplares*, was not published until 1637, not in Madrid but in Zaragoza, where her second volume would also appear ten years later. Despite Serrano y Sanz's speculation that publication in Zaragoza might indicate residence there, there is no other indication of such residence. Two factors were likely to have shifted publication of her first volume to that city in 1637. One, the connection with the Imprenta Real of Madrid headed by her uncle Luis Sánchez and then by his widow, Zayas's maternal aunt, ended with the

---

12 Alicia Yllera, "Introducción," María de Zayas y Sotomayor, *Parte segunda del Sarao y entretenimiento honesto [Desengaños amorosos]*, Madrid, 2021, p. 22; Salvador Montesa Peydro concurs, in *Texto y contexto en la narrativa de María de Zayas*, Madrid, 1981, p. 23.

latter's death in 1633. The other factor, of greater immediate importance, was the block on publication of novellas and plays in the Castilian realm from 1625–34. This was a part of the reform project of Philip IV and his favorite, the Count-Duke of Olivares, and the Junta de Reformación created when Philip IV ascended to the throne in 1621. That combination of authorities proposed that the Council of Castile should cease authorizing publication in its realms of any volumes of plays, novellas or similar works, judging them prejudicial to the manners, education and morality – particularly sexual morality – of the public. Some authors and publishers tried to circumvent this suspension by falsifying documents of approbation and dates or publication location, but the council later published an edict prohibiting those subterfuges. As the Cervantes scholar and eminent bibliographer Jaime Moll interprets the documents authorizing publication of her *Novelas*, Zayas indeed had a volume of eight novellas ready for publication in 1626, and ecclesiastical approval of Joseph de Valdivielso, which is dated June 4, 1626, was secured. Then, in light of the suspension of civil licenses in Castile, the Aragonese bookseller and publisher Pedro de Esquer took her manuscript to Zaragoza and, with the addition of two more novellas, secured the approvals of Juan Domingo Briz and Pedro Aguilón for publication in that realm, the Aragonese approval carrying the date of May 6, 1635.[13] It was published with the title *Novelas amorosas y exemplares compuestas por doña María de Zayas y Sotomayor, natural de Madrid* (Amorous and exemplary novellas composed by doña María de Zayas y Sotomayor, native of Madrid), in Zaragoza, in the printing house of the Hospital Real y General de N. Señora de Gracia, financed by Pedro Esquer, bookseller. A second edition with the same title with the addition "Newly corrected and modified by the author" appeared the same year. Two further editions by Esquer said to be from the same printer appeared in 1638, and one in Barcelona in 1646.[14]

Zayas's second volume was also first published by Pedro Esquer in the same Zaragoza printing house in 1647, bearing the title *Parte segunda del Sarao y entretenimiento honesto* (Second part of the Soiree and honest entertainment), although it is generally referred to as the *Desengaños amorosos*,

---

13 "Diez años sin licencias para imprimir comedias y novelas en los reinos de Castilla: 1625–1634," *Boletín de la Real Academia Española* 54, 1974, pp. 97–9; and "La primera edición de las *Novelas amorosas y ejemplares* de María de Zayas y Sotomayor," *Dicenda: Cuadernos de filología* 1, 1974, pp. 177–9.

14 See details and images in Julián Olivares, "Introducción," *Novelas amorosas*, Madrid, 2000, pp. 113–50.

as the ten tales it contains are labeled *desengaños* (disillusionments). Over the course of the first volume of tales, Lisis, the protagonist of the frame tale, had become disillusioned in her hope of winning the love of Juan, who prefers her cousin Lisarda, and had promised to become engaged to another man. "Desengaños" describes the import of the tales, all of whose protagonists suffer disillusionments. On yet a third level, it evokes the general philosophy of Counterreformation Spain, one of *desengaño*, or disillusionment with secular life. This second volume appeared without the usual laudatory verses by other authors. Their absence gives credence to the idea that she was then living outside Madrid and away from its literary circles. On the other hand, the second part of Cervantes's *Don Quixote* omits any such verse as well, carrying only a dedication to his patron, the same Count of Lemos who employed Zayas's father. Zayas's *Desengaños* were prefaced by a dedication to the Duke of Hijar, signed by Inés de Casamayor, the widow of the bookseller Matías de Lizau, who financed the production.[15] Her combative dedication recommends its publication and seeks the duke's protection from

> envious backbiters who, in the manner of nocturnal shades, are horrified that our sex should have merited such generalized applause, been crowned with such well-earned laurels and earned itself lasting fame with honors so high in such a shining, immortal talent. As if these profitable distinctions were linked only to males and some fiery sword blocked or forbade entrance to the paradise of letters to feminine discourse, or some dragon reserved the golden fruit of learning for men only.
>
> [las sombras de envidiosos maldicientes que a fuer de fantasmas nocturnas hacen espantos de que nuestro sexo haya merecido tan generales aplausos … o algún dragón solo para los hombres reservara la fruta de oro de las ciencias.] [16]

This dedication thus repeats Zayas's assertion of women's writerly capacities and rights in the "To the Reader" prologue to the *Exemplary Tales*.

Pérez de Montalbán stated that Zayas had successfully participated in literary contests, and a "Prologue by a Dispassionate Reader" in her *Exemplary Tales* declares that the learned Academies of Madrid have applauded and celebrated her. While there is no evidence of her membership

---

15 Julián Olivares, "Introducción," María de Zayas y Sotomayor, *Honesto y entretenido sarao (Primera y segunda parte)*, Zaragoza, 2017, p. xli.
16 María de Zayas y Sotomayor, *Honesto y entretenido sarao (Primera y segunda parte)*, ed. Julian Olivares, Zaragoza, 2017, vol. 2, p. 429. My translation.

in the private and thoroughly male-dominated "learned Academies" of Madrid, she may have been invited to participate in poetic competitions they sponsored.[17] She was a full participant in a competition sponsored by the Academy of St. Thomas Aquinas in Barcelona in 1643. Such contests were relatively open to women, particularly those held in Catalonian-Aragonese locations.[18] The poetry that she and other participants contributed has not survived, but the manuscript of the *Vejámen* (Vexation) or poetic "roast" that Francesc Fontanella wrote to conclude it was published in 1987. Such poetic roasts regularly satirized the poetic or personal failings of the participants, and the St. Thomas roast was no exception. It was cast as an allegorical dream in which Apollo appears fully armed and furious because poets, his followers, have been enclosed in a hospital for the insane. But while it took aim only at the poetic flaws of the male poets, it mocked Zayas both as a poet and in the flesh. Fontanella plays on her gender by capitalizing on her name, Zayas, writing it as "sayas," the word for skirts. He portrays her as a bewhiskered woman who may look like a man but lacks a sword under her skirts:

> I saw Doña María of the Skirts with a manly face, who although she has "skirts," twirls a haughty mustache. She looked like a gentleman, but it will be discovered that a sword can hardly be hidden under feminine skirts. In the third *décima*, she was unfortunate at glossing and she has a poor procuress if she wants to win a prize. Oh, Lady Dame Skirt, to reward your good desires, you will have a charming crown [made of] the hoop of your farthingale.
>
> [Doña María de Sayas / viu ab cara varonil, / que a bé que "sayas" tenia, / bigotes filava altius./... de sèrcol de un guardainfant / tindrà corona gentil.][19]

To the wordplay on her name, skirts and face, Fontanella adds a sexual wordplay on the meaning of "third" (*tercera*) as a sexual go-between or procuress as well as an ordinal number. He then makes a linguistic

---

17 Willard King, *Prosa novelística y academias literarias en el siglo XVII*, Madrid, 1963, p. 54. See also Anne Cruz, "Las academias: Literatura y poder en un espacio cortesano," *Edad de Oro* 18, 1998, pp. 49–57.

18 See Inmaculada Osuna Rodíguez, "Literary Academies and Poetic Tournaments," Baranda and Cruz, *Routledge Research Companion*, pp. 153–67.

19 Kenneth Brown, "Context i text del *Vexamen* d'Academia de Francesc Fontanella," *Llengua i Literatura Catalanes* 2, 1987, vv. 725–40. Belén Atienza helped me translate the Spanish-infected Catalán verse text.

dive under her skirts to make a crown of the hoop of her farthingale, the petticoat that held women's skirts in the belled shape fashionable in seventeenth-century Europe. Fontanella may have felt entitled to mock Zayas with jokes of questionable taste because of the friendship between the Fontanella brothers and Zayas. Publication of a second edition of her *Desengaños* in 1649 was approved by Fray Pío Vives of the Barcelona convent of Santa Catalina Mártir, where the academy met, and by Francesc Fontanella's older brother, Josep, who signed as "Fontanella Regens. 23 septemb. 1648."

The possible Zayas-Fontanella friendship does not resolve other questions raised by her presence in Barcelona and by this burlesque portrait of Zayas as a mustached woman with a manly face and deportment but lacking a "sword" under her skirts. We do not know what she looked like, whether she was a pink-cheeked lady like the image of Iñés de Zuñiga (fig. 1), who dressed in skirts belled out wide by a farthingale, or a bit of a butch in appearance as well as her sometimes aggressive tone. Unquestionably, Fontanella paints her as sexually ambiguous, in an era and culture that exhibited women with beards and mustaches as freaks of nature. The most famous such image, José de Ribera's painting of Magdalena Ventura, now in the Collection of the Duchess of Lerma in Toledo, displays a balding, bearded woman nursing her baby with her similarly bearded husband fading into the background behind her. Saint's tales and legends also circulated about bearded women like Saint Paula of Avila, called Santa Paula Barbada, a beautiful young woman in a medieval hamlet near Avila who asked to be bewhiskered to free herself from men's desire.[20] The frequently maligned figure of the duenna, a governess, companion or chaperone of girls, is often pictured in Early Modern Spanish literature as a woman whiskered by age who can only satisfy her continuing sexual urges by acting as a go-between for the young women in her charge. Fontanella's joke about Zayas needing a better "tercera" than her poetry to win the prize she desires implies sexual as well as literary frustration.

In her own work, Zayas portrays with outrage a homosexual relation between men in D.7, "Marriage Abroad, Portent of Doom." In the previous tale, D.6, "Love for the Sake of Conquest," the possibility of lesbian love espoused by the character known as Estefanía proves to be a male ruse that ends tragically after Estefanía reveals himself as Esteban. Zayas appears to have shied away from identification with Sappho, the

---

[20] "Leyenda de Santa Paula Barbada," *Casas Gredos* (blog), January 3, 2016, https://casasgredos.wordpress.com/2016/03/01/leyenda-de-santa-paula-barbada.

gifted female lyric poet from the Greek island of Lesbos. Although the list of foremothers she cites in "To the Reader" closely aligns with Lope de Vega's comparison of her to famous women writers in *Laurel de Apolo*, Zayas omits mentioning Sappho and Lesbos, which head Lope's list. Love between women in Early Modern Spain escaped attention in a way that male homosexuality did not, and in a patriarchal culture, labeling a woman as "varonil" (manly) was frequently employed to praise her brilliance or courage. Fontanella's burlesque portrait of her in his *Vejamen* of secessionist Catalonian sympathies could therefore be read as a double-edged strategy to both praise and mock this Castilian friend/interloper.

The *Vejamen* does illuminate one topic, the possibility suggested by various readers and scholars that Zayas might have joined a convent. Fontanella addresses Theodora Molera, one of the women welcomed as marginal participants in the competition, as a nun, "sor Theodora Molera" (verses 965, 1145) but calls Zayas "doña María" or "Senyora Doña Saya" (verses 725, 735). She could have been living as a secular resident of a convent, however.

But why was Zayas, a native of Madrid, in Barcelona in that year, when Catalonia was rebelling against the Spanish crown and French and Spanish troops fought outside Barcelona for control of Catalonia? One possibility is that she might have been residing in Barcelona or elsewhere in the larger realm of Aragón, perhaps in Zaragoza (where both volumes of her stories were published). As I have noted, one explanation for the absence of laudatory poems in her 1647 *Disillusionments* could be that she was far from her Madrid's literary circles when it was published. Might she have lived in Barcelona or Zaragoza until her death? One theory is that she lived in Barcelona in 1643 and continued living there until her death in an epidemic of the plague and was buried in a common grave.[21]

We have no death certificate for a María de Zayas, a fairly common name, that can conclusively be identified with our author, although Serrano y Sanz published two death certificates for women so named. One of them could be our writer, a María de Zayas, widow of Juan de Valdés, who died in the Madrid parish of San Sebastián on January 11, 1661. This María de Zayas had also worked for a number of years for the Marquise of Malagón, Magdalena de Ulloa, whose will at her 1618 death left Zayas

---

21 Kenneth Brown, "María de Zayas y Sotomayor: Escribiendo poesía en Barcelona en época de guerra (1643)," *Dicenda: Cuadernos de filología hispánica*, Complutense, no. 11, 1993, p. 360, cited in Treviño, p. xlii; Olivares, "Introducción," p. xlviii, n. 76.

one and a half reales a day as long as she lived. Documents of 1631 to 1633 in Valladolid show that this María de Zayas and Juan de Valdés were resident in that city when they sued the marquise's heirs for payment of what the marquise left María in her will. Juan de Valdés died sometime between 1633 and 1644; another document of 1644, a receipt for payment of 220 reales for payment of part of the 3,833 reales owed to her, was signed by María de Çayas, widow of Valdés, whose signature is very similar to that of a María de Zayas in 1617. That year, María de Zayas and Juan de Valdés signed a petition for papal recognition of the Immaculate Conception of the Virgin Mary.[22]

When this María died in 1661, she left all her possessions to Bartolomé de Zaragoza and his wife, Laura Grasa, in whose house on the calle del Olivar she had lived the last year of her life. The bequest included the right to collect from the heirs of the Marquise of Malagón the daily real and a half she had left Zayas, which had not been paid for the last five years. This Zayas requested that her body be buried in her parish, that of San Sebastián, and said that although she knew how to read, she had a witness sign the documents because her illness and vision loss made it impossible for her to sign them. The calle del Olivar intersects the calle de la Cabeza where the author María de Zayas and her younger sister Isabel had lived, just two blocks south of the San Sebastián church where they were baptized, between the present-day subway stops Tirso de Molina and Antón Martín. If the María de Zayas who died there in 1661 was the writer, she ended her life in the same neighborhood in which it began, after living at least a few years in Valladolid.

This hypothesis is at best suggestive, however. Other evidence casts doubt on the identification of the author with the signer of those documents.[23] First, Zayas the writer gives great weight to aristocratic identity and the importance of marrying according to one's status in the social hierarchy, so it seems doubtful that she, or her family, would have wished her to marry a servant such as Valdés. Nor does the writer Zayas ever mention a relationship with or affection for the Marquise of Malagón, as she

---

22 Isabel Barbeito Carneiro, *Mujeres del Madrid barroco: Voces testimoniales*, Madrid, 1992, pp. 166–7.

23 See Alberto Rodríguez de Ramos, "La biografía de María de Zayas: Una reo visión y algunos hallazgos," *Analecta: Revista de la Sección de Filología de la Facultad de Letras, Universidad de Málaga*, 37, 2014, pp. 246–53; I thank Ely Treviño for bringing this to my attention.

does for the Countess of Gálvez and the Countess of Lemos. Failing the discovery of more evidence, we should leave the question open.[24]

Recent investigations have turned up new scraps of information about Zayas, including two wills made in Naples in 1656 and 1657 by a moderately well-off widow named María de Zayas, resident in Naples, who died there on April 9, 1658. She was the widow of a Spanish captain, Francisco de Vargas Machuca; her son and grandchildren died in a terrible wave of plague that devastated Naples in those years. Donatella Gagliardi, who published the wills, thought this María might be the novelist, but we would need other confirmation to advance that claim.[25] Thus, we are left with more questions than answers about her life and death. What we can say, however, is that in the ten years that separated the publication of her *Novelas* and *Desengaños*, her tone changed. In the second collection, her invective against the abuse of women is more pervasive and strident, and the violence she has her protagonists suffer reaches grotesque proportions. Some readers have attributed the change to personal experience, perhaps a disappointment in love such as that she gives her frame protagonist Lisis, but this is an unsubstantiated, naïve approach. I think it much more probable to ascribe it to the pessimistic mood that enveloped Spain as the seventeenth century advanced, as the monarchy suffered a series of defeats overseas and economic and political crisis at home, culminating in the revolt of Catalonia and Portugal in 1640, which brought war home to the peninsula.

Zayas was born near the end of the reign of Philip II (1557–98), at the height of the power of the Spanish empire.[26] Her stories reflect the extent of that empire in their settings not only in major cities of the empire, but also in the Canary Islands, Naples, Sicily, Flanders, its North African toeholds in Fez, La Mamora (Mehdya) and Tunisia, as the Hapsburg monarchy contested Islamic power over the Mediterranean world.[27] She lived and wrote during the reign of Philip III (1598–1621), the monarch most named in her stories, and Philip IV (1621–65). Maintaining

---

24 Rodríguez de Ramos, "Biografía," pp. 247–53; Treviño, pp. xliii–xliv.
25 Donatella Gagliardi, "Dos testamentos inéditos de María de Zayas (Nápoles, 1656 y 1657)," *eHumanista* 40, 2018, pp. 561–86.
26 See Thomas James Dandelet, "The Impact of Spanish Imperial Political Culture in Iberia and Europe, 1500–1700," Cacho Casal and Egan, *Routledge Hispanic Studies Companion*, pp. 16–17.
27 For a table listing all those settings, see Margaret R. Greer, *Maria de Zayas Tells Baroque Tales of Love and the Cruelty of Men*, University Park, 2000, appendix 3.

those possessions and defending the Catholic faith involved the monarchy in far-flung wars and financial hemorrhaging: the Eighty Years' War against Dutch rebels in the northern Netherlands (1568–1648), intermittent conflict with England and France, periodic battles in Italy, and the enormous human and economic costs of commitments in central Europe before and during the Thirty Years' War (1618–48) waged to contain Protestant advances and sustain the Spanish-Austrian Hapsburg alliance. These conflicts had strapped the monarchy's resources even during the height of the silver and gold shipments from American mines in the sixteenth century. English and Dutch inroads on the monopolies the monarchy tried to maintain on trade with its colonies, piracy and the costs of debt financing also took a financial toll. The monarchy was forced to declare bankruptcy and devalue its currency several times. Inflation caused by the influx of American wealth had the long-term effect of impoverishing Spain, as cash was exported to repay loans from foreign bankers and incipient Spanish industries failed, unable to compete with cheaper imports. Depopulation caused by war, plagues, emigration to the colonies, and internal migration from farming communities to cities meant that agricultural self-sufficiency, always difficult because of the lack of water in large areas of the peninsula, could not regularly be sustained.

This economic upheaval and the accompanying social and political change could not help but affect Zayas and her family, although their relatively comfortable status in the lower nobility presumably afforded them significant protection from its immediate effects. Zayas's parents were living when she published her first volume, and her father was still alive in 1642, the year of her mother's death, when he served as executor of her will.[28] That same year, however, another man replaced him as administrator of the Jérez de los Caballeros estate of the Order of Santiago.[29]

Zayas inserts a few indicators of economic distress in three of her stories in the first volume. Two stories register the migration of poor *hidalgos* – the lowest rank of the nobility, literally, "sons of something" – from the mountainous regions of northern Spain to cities to improve their lot. The northern provinces were depicted in fiction and on stage as populated by old Christians (that is, not converts from Judaism or Islam), possessing titles of nobility but little other wealth. In ETL 3, "The Miser's Reward," Zayas describes Marcos as

> A gentleman from Navarre ... a man of lofty aspirations but humble earthly possessions, for stepmother fortune had endowed him with the

[28] Rodríguez de Ramos, "Biografía," p. 245.
[29] Yllera, "Introducción," p. 15.

single possession of a meager bed on which this young man, whom we will call don Marcos, and his old father retired to sleep at night and sat on to eat on during the day.

[un hidalgo, tan alto de pensamientos como humilde de bienes de fortuna, ... este mozo, a quien llamaremos don Marcos, y un padre viejo.][30]

When he is twelve years old, Marcos secures a position as page in a prince's house, where he learns all the tricks of the trade, particularly that of miserliness. In ETL 10, the migrant from the north who arrived in Zaragoza on business is Carlos, who will play a key role in this miracle tale. Lisis's mother, the narrator, describes him thus:

A gentleman from the mountains happened to come to Zaragoza for business during this period, wealthier in goods of nature than in those of fortune, a man of thirty or thirty-six years of age, gallant, discreet, and of highly agreeable qualities, named Carlos ...

Our Carlos found himself poor and expatriated because, although he overflowed with nobility, what he lacked in riches was sufficient to prevent him from asking for her [Constanza's] hand, sure his request would not be granted.

[Sucedió en este tiempo venir a algunos negocios a Zaragoza un hidalgo montañes, más rico de bienes de naturaleza que de fortuna ... seguro de que no se la habían de dar.][31]

The third instance of poverty is that of Clara, a supposedly wealthy merchant's beautiful daughter whom Fernando marries after accumulating huge gambling debts. Once they are married, however, the merchant, unable to pay the dowry promised, takes all his money and departs for the Indies, leaving Clara in poverty and reduced to working as a servant for Fernando and his sorceress-mistress (see chapter 7). All these instances, however fictitious, do register economic truths of Early Modern Spain.

---

30 *Novelas*, p. 253. My translation, modifying that of Boyer, who alters the passage, changing what Zayas wrote to make it appear that Marcos migrated to Madrid twelve years after the death of this father, rather than his mother. Between the first edition of 1637 and the second, corrected edition of the same year, this phrase referring to the old father was eliminated: "era mendigo tan viejo que hasta los más empedernidos le tenían lástima y daban limosna" [He was a beggar so old that even the most hard-hearted felt sorry for him and gave him alms]. *Novelas amorosas*, p. 253. Despite eliminating that phrase, the following sentence refers to the death of the mother, not the father.
31 ETL, pp. 179–80; *Novelas amorosas*, pp. 520–1.

Despite the much greater weight of economic and political problems weighing on Spain by the time Zayas published her second volume, Zayas voices through her narrators more concern for deceptive self-presentation and social climbing, along with increasing emphasis on male abuse of women, physical and verbal. In D. 6, the first song performed by "Estefanía" is a ballad s/he sings about the descent from the truth and abundance of the Golden Age to the reigning Age of Iron in which wealth is wasted on silks and brocades, as "France has stolen / Spain's valor / and the Spanish have taken French frippery" [Que (los españoles) a sus trajes vuelvan / y vuelvan a Francia / los que le han hurtado / que parece infamia],[32] and a tax should be imposed on the title "don" for the relief of the poor. The irony, of course is that Esteban is a carpenter's son pretending to be noble but poor, who is cross-dressed as Estefanía to pursue the beautiful and wealthy young girl Laurela. In the following story, D. 7, "Marriage Abroad: Portent of Doom," Zayas gives the widowed doña Luisa a lengthy comic tirade against the use of "don" and "doña":

> In those lands [Flanders], as in Italy, they don't use the title "don," except sometimes for priests, because nobody flaunts titles like "don" as much as in Spain. This is particularly true nowadays when vanity has reached such an extreme that even coachmen, lackeys, and kitchen maids use the title. The cursed "don" is so degraded that tavern maids and fruit-sellers call themselves doña "Serpent" and doña "Tigress." If I had my say, through that's not likely to happen, no proper person would ever use the title "don." A couple of days ago I heard a little lapdog called doña Jarifa and a kitty called don Morro. If His Majesty (may God preserve him) would put a tax on each "don," he would earn more than one percent because there are houses in Madrid, and I myself know them, that teem with as many "dons" as a grave teems with worms. I was told as a true story that not long ago a jolly working woman from Vallecas came downtown to sell bread. Each time her burro moved, she would say: "hold still, don Dapple." When she wanted to move on, she'd say "don Giddyup" and when she wanted to stop, "don Whoa."
>
> [En aquellos países, ni en Italia, ninguno se llama "don," si no son los clérigos ... Y queriendo partise, empezó a decir "don Arre," y queriendo pararse, "don Jo."][33]

---

32 Zayas, *Disenchantments*, trans Boyer, p. 212; *Desengaños*, p. 428.
33 Zayas, *Desenchantments*, p. 255; *Desengaños*, pp. 485–6.

Zayas seems to have perceived a greater threat to noblewomen's identity from social mobility than economic pressures, as wealthy members of the bourgeoisie married impoverished aristocrats or purchase titles of nobility from a cash-strapped monarchy. She was not, however, fully consistent in this. In D. 8, she condemns the greedy patriarchal father for refusing to allow Enrique to marry Mencía because his grandparents were commoners.

Despite the economic and sociopolitical upheaval of her era, there were other, more propitious forces at work for Zayas and other Early Modern Spanish fiction-writers and dramatists. One was the continuing effect of the sixteenth-century expansion of education, in which Spain – or at least Castile – preceded northern Europe. The development of absolute monarchy and the growth of the Spanish empire spurred that expansion, as staffing their expanding bureaucracies required *letrados*, men educated in law and other disciplines. It was also fed by the cultivation of Renaissance humanism and the demand for a better-educated clergy that might indoctrinate the populace and defend against heresy and competition from other faiths in religion-divided Europe.[34] Women, as Zayas complains, were excluded from filling such offices, however. Hand in hand with the revolution in education went the development of the printing press, which increased the availability of books and made them affordable to a wider, if still limited, literate public. Madrid, once made the stable center of the court, became the primary center for the publication and distribution of literary works, but printing houses and booksellers produced and sold books in other cities as well.[35]

Equally propitious for writers was the development of an urban, low- to mid-level nobility such as that to which Zayas belonged. Nieves Romero-Díaz provides an excellent analysis of the relationship between this urbanization and the popularity of novellas by Zayas and others. That development was particularly marked in Madrid, after Philip II made it the capital of Spain in 1561, stimulating the growth of its population from forty-five hundred in 1528 and around twenty thousand when it was made the capital, to around eighty thousand by the last decade of the sixteenth century. A wave of plague then reached the city, but the population rebounded to between seventy and one hundred thousand during Philip

---

34 Richard L. Kagan, *Students and Society in Early Modern Spain*, Baltimore, 1974, p. xiii–xv, 79–87.
35 Jaime Moll, "Escritores y editors en el Madrid de los Austrias," *Edad de Oro* 17, 1998, p. 101.

IV's reign.[36] Similar developments occurred in other cities as well, most notably in Seville, which numbered some sixty to seventy thousand about 1500, lost population to plagues and emigration thereafter, but then became a sixteenth-century boom town, with a population of around one hundred fifty thousand by 1588.[37] As we will see, Zayas's self-identity, and that of most of her protagonists, depended on belonging to the nobility, but to a portion of the nobility in the process of self-definition in its urban residence. Traditionally, the aristocracy defined its nature and purpose – and justified its tax-exempt status – through military service, as the defense of the realm, and in theory regulated itself in accord with a chivalric ethos. For the urban nobility, however, other types of service to the monarchy or the local polity might take the place of military service and provide an alternative path to social distinction and authority. Critical issues for the urban elite's self-definition would be the compatibility of commercial activity with nobility and the role of money in maintaining or achieving noble status, as cash-strapped monarchs sold possession of lucrative positions and titles of nobility.

While we should not look for realism in Zayas's stories, we can find in them reflections of these conditions. In the first place, the development of an urban, low- to mid-level noble class, who reside in relatively close proximity, sometimes with several families living in the same multifamily edifice. Zayas displays this in the gathering of friends to entertain the ailing Lisis, and Mariana de Carvajal, who followed Zayas's model in writing novellas, makes this proximity yet more evident in her stories. Whereas Boccaccio in the *Decameron* gathers his narrators in the countryside, fleeing plague-devastated Florence, Zayas brings hers together in Lisis's Madrid *estrado* (domestic receiving space). Zayas often makes the engagement of a gallant in a war an obstacle to love or dispatches a faithless or abusive man to die in battle. Frequently, this involves combat in Flanders, as in ETL 1 and ETL 8, but it may also be in Italy or North Africa, where the protagonist Jacinta's beloved dies in a shipwreck on the way to try

---

36 Nieves Romero-Díaz, *Nueva nobleza, nueva novela: Reescribiendo la cultura urbana del barroco*, Newark, 2002, pp. 35–6; population estimates vary. I take these from J. H. Elliott, *Imperial Spain, 1469–1716*, London, 2002, p. 315 and Ruth McKay, *Life in a Time of Pestilence: The Great Castilian Plague of 1596–1601*, Cambridge, 2019, p. 49, n. 17. See also Laura R. Bass, "Staging Madrid: Urban Comedy for a New Court Capital," *The Routledge Hispanic Studies Companion to Early Modern Spanish Literature and Culture*, ed. Rodrigo Cacho Casal and Caroline Egan, London, 2022, pp. 323–42.

37 Elliot, *Imperial Spain*, p. 186.

to put down a rebellion against Spanish control of La Mamora. Other love affairs begin when the gallant accompanies monarchical officials or the king himself to another city or realm. The role of money is evident in the suitors whom fathers accept or reject, as is the reluctance to accept children of merchants or commoners as appropriate spouses. ETL 10, "The Deceitful Garden," gives a glimpse of the effects of the system of primogeniture (*mayorazgo*) that worked to sustain the position of the aristocracy by preventing the fragmentation of their estates, as the eldest son inherited the vast majority of a family's holdings, affording only a small allowance to younger sons, making it difficult for them to compete in the marriage market. A number of her stories also show us fathers (or an uncle standing in for a deceased father) who resisted devoting family resources to providing the dowries that daughters needed to make a successful match. In D. 8, "Traitor to His Blood," a father first pressures his daughter Mencia to become a nun because the dowry a girl required on becoming a nun was smaller than that she would have needed in marriage, then turned down Enrique, who wanted to marry her without a dowry, because his grandparents were commoners.

In sum, what we know of Zayas's life and times affords us a sense of when and where she was born and spent her childhood, the comfortable status of her family, part of the urban lower nobility, and her connections to the publishing world. We know that she secured an adequate education, partly from the self-education she could derive from access to books, perhaps through her aunt and uncle's printing house. We can glimpse her connections to the Madrid literary world in preliminary poems contributed to her own and other writers' works, and their accolades to her as a rare, feminine icon in that male-dominated enterprise. However one interprets its sexual innuendos, Fontanella's burlesque roast concluding the 1643 Barcelona competition reveals the resistance she encountered, as does Inés de Casamayor's fiery dedication to the 1647 publication of Zayas's *Desengaños*. If our author was indeed the María de Zayas whose death certificate registered her death in 1661, she was married to Juan de Valdés for a number of years and may have lived with him in Valladolid but was a widow in 1644 and resident again in Madrid. Perhaps further research may help us piece out a more complete image of her life. In the meantime, we should resist extrapolating into her biography the experiences Zayas gives to the characters in her stories. Both the inventive wit of her first volume and the dark violence of the second are our best evidence of Zayas's lively imagination and writerly gifts.

Chapter Two

Exemplary Tales of Love: A Contradiction?

"EXEMPLARY" IS NOT a word we use much in the twenty-first century, except perhaps to refer to the "exemplary behavior" – or the absence thereof – of a child or a public figure. But in the early seventeenth century, both Miguel de Cervantes and María de Zayas called their novella collections "exemplary." Cervantes called his, published in 1613, simply *Novelas ejemplares* (Exemplary Novellas). "People are not always in churches" or "attending to their affairs," Cervantes writes in the prologue to the collection, but need "times of recreation, when the afflicted spirit can rest" [no siempre se está en los templos; ... no siempre se asiste a los negocios ... Horas hay de recreación, donde el afligido espíritu descanse]. And he adds, "If it happened somehow that the reading of these *Novels* could encourage the person reading them to any evil desire or thought, I would rather cut off the hand that wrote them than make them public" [por si algún modo alcanzara que la lección estas *Novelas* pudiera inducir a quien las leyera a algún mal deseo o pensamiento, antes me cortara la mano con que las escribí, que sacarlos en público].[1] These were not empty words, since Cervantes had lost the use of his other hand fighting the Ottomans in the battle of Lepanto in 1571. In an age when exploration and conquests in the New World, Africa, the Near and Far East expanded

---

[1] *Exemplary Novels*, trans Edith Grossman, ed. Roberto González Echevarría, New Haven, p. 4; *Novelas ejemplares*, ed. Julio Rodríguez-Luis, Madrid, 1994, pp. 84–5. For more on the topic of exemplarity in the fifteenth to seventeenth centuries, see Greer, *María de Zayas*, pp. 331–4, 445–6, nn. 21–5.

knowledge of far-flung lands and cultures, amid religious division between Catholics, Jews, Protestants, Christians and Muslims, and political, social and economic change propelled by competition for power, writers used examples as devices to model reality in such a way as to achieve shared belief and to modify behavior. At the end of chapter 1, I listed a few of the ways those pressures are reflected in Zayas's stories, and I will point out others in subsequent chapters. Although she writes in the genre of the love story, few of her tales follow the pattern we expect in that genre, of lovers who overcome obstacles to be happily united at the end in marriage to their first beloved. That is why I analyze in this chapter the ways in which she adjusts the love story to make it exemplary of the hazards that men and women should avoid.

The question for writers and their readers in Zayas's era was in what kind of texts examples should appear, and by whom and how they should be read. Reading of vernacular prose fiction was distrusted by authorities, who condemned its consumption with arguments that originated in Plato's expulsion of poets from his ideal Republic. Rather than our classifications of fiction and nonfiction, Early Modern Spanish critics classified texts as History or Poetry. B. W. Ife summarizes the categories:

> Fact, or whatever went under the guise of fact, was the realm of History. Unashamed fiction went under the banner of poetic truth and was the province of Poetry... . The natural medium for Poetry (things which aren't true but ought to be) was verse, and for History (things which are true but perhaps ought not to be), the proper medium was prose, preferably Latin prose.[2]

Vernacular prose fiction swept away that distinction. Fictions written in everyday language, without the mediation of Latin, the language of scholars, or the artificial structure of verse, were denounced as dangerous poisons, "lies" that seduce the unwary. The case against fiction rested both on moral and metaphysical arguments. The moral argument was that literary fiction sets bad examples and encourages vicarious experience, particularly in love affairs, leading readers to seek to emulate them in their own lives. In metaphysical terms, as Ife explains, the objection was that fiction is a counterfeit form of reality and that convincing fictions undermine the authority of truth.

---

2   *Reading and Fiction in Golden-Age Spain: A Platonist Critique and Some Picaresque Replies*, Cambridge, 1985, p. 10. Ife's discussion of the metaphysical objections to fiction is on pp. 24–5.

The Spanish humanist Juan Luis Vives (1492–1540), while supporting the education of women and use of the vernacular, inveighed forcefully and repeatedly against the reading of literary fiction in *The Education of a Christian Woman* (1523, revised 1538). Vives left Spain at 17 to avoid the Inquisition, and after studying in Paris, he wrote his work in Latin at Oxford and dedicated it to Catherine of Aragon, who had commissioned it for the instruction of her daughter Mary I of England. Vives opposed Henry VIII's divorce of Catherine, was subjected to house arrest for that for six weeks in 1527, then left for the Netherlands, where he spent the rest of his life. Nevertheless, his treatise on the education of women was "rooted in a Spanish reality."[3] Translated in short order into English and Spanish and repeatedly republished, it would influence multiple treatises on the education and proper conduct of women in the sixteenth and seventeenth centuries, in Spain and in England. Vives wrote that "a woman's only care is chastity"; accordingly, she should be "edified by chaste tales," reading the New Testament, saints' lives, devotional works, and writings of philosophers devoted to moral improvement. He condemns as a pestilence works in the vernacular that treat nothing more than love and war, pernicious books like the chivalric and sentimental romances popular in Spain, Ovid's *Art of Love*, and the *Decameron*, judging them full of lies and stupidity, written by men who were slaves of vice and filth. He did not condemn learning or learned women, maintaining that ignorance was more likely to breed evil. But he wrote that "in a woman, no one requires eloquence or talent or wisdom or professional skills or administration of the republic or justice or generosity; no one asks anything of her but chastity. If that one thing is missing, it is as if all were lacking to a man."[4]

Developments I mentioned in chapter 1 – the increased availability of printed books, the expansion of education, increased urbanization, and the growth of an urban nobility and of literacy among some commoners – probably contributed to the frequency and virulence of such attacks against literary fiction by moralist critics. Greater availability of literary fiction in the vernacular exposed more of the populace to it. Ife maintains too that a change in the way literary fiction was experienced

---

3   Emilie Bergmann, "The Exclusion of the Feminine in the Cultural Discourse of the Golden Age: Juan Luis Vives and Fray Luis de León," *Religion, Body and Gender in Early Modern Spain*, ed. Alain Saint-Saëns, San Francisco, 1991, pp. 124–36.
4   Vives, *The Education of a Christian Woman*, ed. and trans. Charles Fantazzi, Chicago, 2007, Book I, paragraphs 3, 10, 19–20, 31, 34, 44.

might contribute to its effect on readers; that is, that silent, private consumption of a tale, without the mediating effect of a visible narrator or someone present reading aloud, and without the correcting effect of reactions of other listeners, could induce readers to identify with morally dubious characters and events.[5] Cervantes displays that fear to comic effect with the madness of his aging knight in Don Quixote. And in his prologue to his Novelas ejemplares, he introduces his tales as relaxing and salutary, with no evil effects.

María de Zayas intended the titles of her collections as the first line of defense against moralist critics of fiction. She wanted the title of her first volume to be *Honesto y entretenido sarao* (Honest and entertaining soirée). This would have side-stepped its immediate classification as literary fiction in general, and more particularly, would have avoided the questionable reputation of the Italian *novella*, rife with accounts of sexual desire, licit and illicit, and depraved friars and priests. But her market-minded publisher Pedro Esquer, surely well aware of the popularity of Italian novellas and of Cervantes's *Novelas ejemplares*, changed the title to *Novelas amorosas y ejemplares* (Exemplary Tales of Love). Zayas's second volume was published in 1647 with her chosen title, *Parte segunda del Sarao y entretenimiento honesto* (Second part of the Soiree and honest entertainment).

The majority of Cervantes's novellas are also stories of amorous desire, successful or tragic, but not all of them. All of Zayas's novellas are tales of love, or at least of sexual desire – precisely the type of story that drew moralists' condemnation. The contradiction I propose in this chapter's title is therefore that between the terms "exemplary" and "love." In her two volumes, Zayas's narrators tell twenty-one stories of sexual desire, reiterating repeatedly in nearly all of them, in the story or its introductory frame or both, that their purpose is to warn their audience against the power and danger of that desire. In the *Novelas amorosas*, she gives her readers the entertainment of fictional love stories, wrapped in exemplary moralizations. To misquote Mary Poppins, "a little bit of medicine makes the sugar go down."

Lisarda, the narrator of the first story, explains its title, "Taking a Chance on Losing," by declaring that telling it will show

> how neither the models of good behavior nor the models of bad behavior suffice to alter the doom of a woman when her stars incline her to it. But to hear it would serve well to caution them against throwing themselves into the sea of their unbridled desires, trusting in the small

---

5 Ife, *Reading and Fiction*, pp. 3–10.

boat of their weakness, fearing that not only the weak powers of women might drown therein, but also the illustrious and heroic understanding of men, whose deceits they should indeed fear.

[cómo para ser una mujer desdichada, cuando su Estrella la inclina a serlo, no bastan ejemplos ni escarmientos; ... los claros y heroicos entendimientos de los hombres, cuyos engaños es razón que se teman.][6]

If desire is to be so feared, then readers can well ask, why tell all these stores of desire? The all-encompassing contradiction in Zayas's tales is her designation of sexual desire as the enemy, even as she uses that same desire as the motor, the driving force of her plots. As an author, she is anything but unique in this; desire and narrative are all but inseparable, desire not just for an object, but for meaning, for the ordering force that narrative gives our existence, for both hearer and teller. In that first tale, when Fabio finds Jacinta cross-dressed as a shepherd singing sadly by a mountain stream, she hesitates to "waste his time" with her long, sad story. "On the contrary," replies Fabio, "you have caused me such concern and desire to know it that, if I believed I might turn into a savage dwelling among these rocks, as long as you were among them I will not abandon you until you relate it to me and until I remove you, if I can, from this life'" [Antes—replicó Fabio—me has puesto en tanto cuidado y deseo de saberla que, ... y te saque, si puedo, de esta vida].[7] Fabio's desire is not sexual but philosophical: a desire for meaning. He wants to understand how a lovely young woman came to be hiding on a wild mountainside in men's clothes, and then, in the end, he wants to see her enclosed in one of the few spaces considered appropriate for respectable women in their patriarchal society – a home under the supervision of a father, husband or brother or in a convent.

The desired object in Zayas's stories is not just love and sexual satisfaction, as we will see in this and following chapters; her characters also value friendship, family ties, financial gain, fame, social status, honor and justice, particularly the justice due women abused both in the flesh and by men's words. And they fervently hope to meet a "good death," with their souls cleansed by confession and in hope of heaven. The complications she builds in her plots arise from conflicts between two or more of those

---

6   ETL, p. 61; *Novelas*, p. 173.
7   ETL, p. 66; *Novelas*, pp. 178–9. On the role of desire in narrative, see Peter Brooks, *Reading for the Plot: Design and Intention in Narrative*, New York, 1985.

desired objects. In the first novella, the conflict is between Jacinta's search for love, marriage practices in her patriarchal society, and family honor.

Jacinta tells Fabio that she and her brother were born "to my father's house, he for its eternal sadness and I for its dishonor" [nacimos en casa de mi padre un hermano y yo, él para eterna tristeza suya, y yo para su deshonra].[8] Jacinta uses "casa" (house) in the same figurative meaning as English "house" – that is, not just the physical abode, but also the patriarchal clan in which she was born. Civil law in seventeenth-century Spain gave parents the right to arrange their children's marriages based on their judgment of the family's sociopolitical and economic interests, but this could conflict with the church's insistence that marriage was a sacrament that the marital partners assumed of their own free will.[9] Lovers who could not secure parental (usually paternal) consent could seek permission of a vicar or other ecclesiastical authority to marry, a practice Zayas invokes later in this first novella, when Jacinta and her lover secure it from the pope himself.

At sixteen, with her mother dead and her father not paying attention to arranging a marriage for her because he cares only about her brother, Jacinta dreams a lover to life. In her dream, when she pulls back the cape covering the face of a handsome man she sees walking through a forest, he stabs her in the heart with a dagger. She wakes up screaming with pain and totally in love with the dark Narcissus of her dream. He materializes as Félix, a neighbor on her street who had long been away at war, and he is equally lovestruck when he sees her on a balcony. More commonly in other Zayas novellas, a noble gallant falls in love on seeing his lady at Mass, one of the few ways closely guarded, respectable noblewomen were allowed in public in the stories set in Spain. Usually, the young woman whose sight strikes desire in the man's heart is unmarried, but in N. 7, "Just Desserts," one of the tales in which Zayas's narrator turns the tables to laugh at men, she is married. In most Zayas tales, the lovers' courtships follow early modern rituals, with the man strolling by the windows of his lady's house, sometimes strumming a guitar and singing to her, sometimes exchanging love notes and poetry smuggled to each other with servants' help and conversing at night through barred windows on the ground floor. According to amorous protocol, the lady should resist his suit and hide her desire, but the first time Jacinta and

8   ETL, p. 67; *Novelas*, p. 179.
9   See Alfredo Martín García, "Divorce and Abuse in 16th, 17th and 18th century Spain," *Procedia: Social and Behavioral Sciences* 161, 2014, pp. 184–94.

Félix talk through a ground floor window, she tells Félix that she loved him even before she saw him in the flesh.

But conflicting family ties complicate Jacinta and Félix's romance, in the person of his cousin Adriana. Early Modern families often arranged marriages between cousins not just to sustain emotional ties but also to keep familial property intact, rather than dividing it to provide daughters' dowries as well as sons' inheritance. Believing he will be able to work things out with Jacinta before Adriana and her mother can secure the papal dispensation that is necessary for marriage between first cousins, Félix humors Adriana and plays along with the arrangement. But this provokes Jacinta's jealous fury, and to appease her, he bribes her servant Sarabia to let him into her house, and in Sarabia's presence, he promises to marry her. In response, she gives him possession of her body and soul. Such wedding vows, if exchanged in the presence of a witness (as they also are in N. 8 and in D. 8, "Traitor to His Own Blood"), were binding in an ecclesiastical court.

Adriana takes revenge on the lovers by writing a letter to Jacinta's father saying that someone was staining his honor; she then commits suicide. Her skin turns black from the poison she took, marking her as a mortal sinner, who, according to Catholic tenets, should not be buried in sacred ground. There are other suicides in Zayas's tales, all of them characters she marks negatively; in one version of N. 3, "The Miser's Reward," that of a man who loves money more than women; in N. 6, "Disillusionment in Love and Virtue Rewarded," a sorceress who stole the heroine's husband; in D. 1, "Her Lover's Slave," a Moorish woman rival; and a frustrated attempt at suicide by a cruel husband in D. 4, "Too Late Undeceived."

Jacinta's father tries to avenge his offended sense of honor with his own hands; only a barking dog and the watchful servant Sarabia allow the lovers to escape when her father and brother attack with swords and pistols. The lovers take refuge in a convent where two of Félix's aunts were nuns. A church or convent was then a refuge from human justice – or injustice, as the case might be – although secular officials sometimes tried to have those seeking it removed from that protection. Félix kills Jacinta's brother when father and brother attack him again, and when he goes to Naples and from there to serve with Spanish forces in Flanders, her father's false letter announcing Félix's death persuades Jacinta to become a nun. When he reappears six years later, disregarding her vows, they sleep together in a cell in the convent, trusting that she can secure a papal dispensation. Jacinta's first pledge to wed Félix took priority over her profession as a nun, a bride of Christ, and they travel to Rome to secure that dispensation. The pope absolves them, for a hefty fine and a promise that they will not live together for a year. While Félix goes off to help put down a Moorish rebellion in Mehdya, or Mamora, a harbor on the coast of Morocco, Jacinta goes back to Spain, staying with relatives of Félix, a widowed aunt and her daughter Guiomar. And there, she wakes up screaming from another dream, one that foretells Félix's death. In her words, "Since fortune gave me don Félix in dreams, it wanted to take him from me in the same fashion" [Porque como la fortuna me dio a don Félix en sueños, quiso quitármele de la misma suerte].[10]

Félix's death is not, however, the end of Jacinta's story of love. Fearing both her vengeful relatives and the scandal she brought her former sister-nuns, Jacinta does not return to her convent but stays with Guiomar and her mother. Friends advise her to marry again, fairly common for women as well as men in Zayas's era, as people often endured the early death of a partner, whether from illness, in war, or in childbirth. Jacinta tells Fabio that in three years of mourning, "I found no other don Félix who satisfied my eyes nor filled the emptiness of my heart" [Yo no hallaba otro don Félix que satisficiese mis ojos ni hinchiese el vacío de mi corazón].[11] Celio, who was a frequent visitor in Guiomar and her mother's house, however, does then fill that emptiness, awakening her interest and dazzling her sight and mind through their competitive exchange of poetry and his boasts of disdaining another woman's love. Celio celebrates Jacinta's cleverness and beauty until she says, "I did not remember don Félix at all" and "with Celio alone were my senses occupied" [ya de todo punto no me acordaba de don Félix; solo en Celio estaban empleados mis sentidos].[12] But once she confesses her love and her desire to give him all she owns in marriage, Celio tells her he plans to be a priest, an object for which he has been studying for years. He then begins to neglect her and to pursue other women. In the midst of this second episode of love and its loss, Zayas's narrator protests, "Woe is me, for when I consider the strategies and tactics with which men overwhelm women and do combat with their weakness, I say they are all traitors, and love is war and a pitched battle, in which love fights honor, castellan of the soul's fortress, with blood and

---

10 ETL, p. 87; *Novelas*, p. 200. The prominent role of dreams in this novella led me to a psychoanalytic reading of Zayas narratives, as I explain in the introduction to *María de Zayas*, pp. 8–9.
11 ETL, p. 88; *Novelas*, p. 201.
12 ETL, p. 91; *Novelas*, p. 204.

fire" [¡Ay de mi!, que cuando considero las estratagemas y ardides con que los hombres rinden ... donde el amor combate a sangre y fuego al honor, alcalde de la fortaleza del alma].[13] No blood is shed, but in the fire of passion, when Celio leaves for a year in Salamanca, Jacinta decides to follow him there, accompanied by a man Guiomar and her mother know. But instead of going to Salamanca, her escort leads her toward Barcelona and robs her. As Jacinta finishes her tale, Fabio tells her that he knows Celio, that he treats all women that way, that "his star inclines him to love where he is abhorred and abhor where he is loved" [Su estrella le inclina a querer donde es aborrecido, y aborrecer donde le quieren].[14]

With this second episode in her lead-off novella, Zayas makes an argument that surfaces in many of her tales: contrary to the cliché of feminine inconstancy, she shows men as less true and faithful than good women. Zayas's narrators advance this argument implicitly in other plots, when men seduce or marry the protagonist only to shift their desire to other women. Nise states the argument more firmly in N. 5, "The Power of Love," saying of the young wife Laura, "What did Laura lack to be blessed? Nothing, except having trusted in love and believing that it was powerful enough to overcome the greatest impossibilities, which is what it is to ask a man to be faithful" [¿Qué le faltaba a Laura para ser dichosa? ... pedir a un hombre firmeza].[15]

I have found in teaching that some traditionally romantic readers are initially uncomfortable with this second episode in Jacinta's story, thinking that when she allows herself to be seduced and betrayed by Celio, it casts doubt on the sincerity of her love for Félix. Yet as students continue reading Zayas's tales, they no longer voice that discomfort. I consider this evidence that Zayas at least partially succeeds in her goal of having her tales reeducate women and men about the nature and dangers of desire, although her second volume will also demonstrate over and over that women had few ways of avoiding that danger in the patriarchal culture of Early Modern Spain, other than by retreat to a convent.[16]

---

13   ETL, p. 90; *Novelas*, p. 203.
14   ETL, p. 93; *Novelas*, p. 207.
15   *Novelas*, p. 353; my translation.
16   See Edward Friedman, "Enemy Territory: The Frontiers of Gender in María de Zayas's *El traidor contra su sangre* and *Mal presagio casar lejos*," *Ingeniosa invención: Essays on Golden Age Spanish Literature for Geoffrey L. Stagg in Honor of His Eighty-Fifth Birthday*, ed. Ellen M. Anderson and Amy R. Williamsen, Newark, 1999, pp. 41–68.

Jacinta accedes to Fabio's wish that she return to her convent but only partially, because, she says,

> my love prohibits me from accepting a husband, and to belong to God, being Celio's, because, although what I would win with each is different, to give my will over to such a divine Spouse I would needs be very free and available. Well I know what I win in light of what I lose, which is heaven or hell, for of such is my passion… I am a phoenix of love. I loved don Félix until death took him from me; I love and will love Celio until it triumphs over my life. I made the choice to love and with that choice I will die. And if you arrange for Celio to see me, I am content with this.

> [Para admitir esposo, me lo estorba mi amor, y para ser de Dios, ser de Celio; …Y si tú haces que Celio me vea, con eso estoy contenta.]¹⁷

Jacinta is but one of many phoenixes of love in Zayas's stories, creatures burned to death but reborn from the flames of passions that reduced their love to ash. Zayas uses the motor of desire to drive her tales from the first to the last, repeatedly warning of its dangers but never fully closing the door against it, even as the frame-tale protagonist Lisis, like Jacinta, withdraws to a convent at the end of the second volume, where she too will live as a secular resident. After Lisis and the narrator conclude the frame tale, Zayas adds a final paragraph, addressing Fabio in her own authorial voice. She writes:

> Now, most illustrious Fabio, to satisfy your request that this story not have a tragic ending, the lovely Lisis remains in the cloister, fearful lest some deceit undeceive her, not forewarned by her own misfortunes. This is not a tragic ending, but rather the happiest possible, since, wealthy and desired by many, she subjected herself to no one. If your desire to see her continues, seek her out with chaste intention, with which you will find her as much yours, with a will as firm and chaste as she promised, and as much your servant as ever, and as you deserve, for even in recognizing this she is outdone by none.

> [Ya, ilustrísimo Fabio, por cumplir lo que pedistes de que no diese trágico fin a esta historia, la hermosa Lisis queda en clausura, … que hasta en conocerlo ninguna le hace ventaja.]¹⁸

---

17 ETL, p. 95; *Novelas*, pp. 209–10.
18 ETL, pp. 325–6; *Desengaños*, p. 688. For other critics' readings of Fabio, see Greer, *María de Zayas*, pp. 342–3.

Readers and Zayas scholars propose various identities for this Fabio, from a narrative trick, a kind of magic rabbit pulled out of a hat, to a personal friend of the author. I think Zayas means to link him with the Fabio who found Jacinta on Montserrat, listened to her tales, and took her back to her convent. Doing so lets us understand the entire, two-volume collection as one long multi-episodic exemplary story of the education of Jacinta/Lisis told to Fabio from beginning to end. In Zayas's collection, the dream of love and sexual satisfaction is a fantasy that must be lived through in some form, but marriage is more often a way station than a final destination in her women's lives. Love fades, or is serialized, as Jacinta experiences; in the *Disillusionments*, however, love often brings death in its wake. The crux of Zayas's tales is how – and whether – women survive love.

Zayas invents many variations on that theme, however. A few of the women in her first volume turn the tables on men. In the third, fourth and seventh tales in the first collection, a series of women makes fools of their suitors, as we will see in chapter 4. In N. 2, "Aminta Tricked, Honor's Revenge," the protagonist, Aminta, insists on taking revenge on a man who seduced her with the help of his lover, Flora. The man, who calls himself Jacinto, has taken Aminta to the house of a widow he knows and abandoned her there. The widow's son Martín falls in love with Aminta on sight, and when she learns that Jacinto is in fact named Francisco and is already married, he keeps her from committing suicide. Martín would like to marry her, but she insists first on taking her revenge personally. After working for Jacinto and Flora for a month in Valladolid, disguised as a page, she stabs Jacinto in the heart as he sleeps, then stabs Flora in the throat, proclaiming, "Traitor, Aminta punishes you and avenges her dishonor!" [¡Traidora, Aminta te castiga y venga su deshonra!]¹⁹ By changing from their attire as a page and a mule driver into aristocratic garments, she and Martín escape and live happily wed under assumed names in Madrid. In this second novella, Aminta's vengeance reads as a call to arms for women, and that call is even louder in Zayas's second collection. In D. 4, "Too Late Undeceived," the narrator calls for women to defend themselves with wit and weapons and calls on men to allow them the exercise of both.

In Zayas's first volume of stories, all the more or less respectable female protagonists survive, and most do marry, although not necessarily with

---

19 María de Zayas, *The Enchantments of Love. Amorous and Exemplary Novels*, trans. H. Patsy Boyer, Berkeley, 1990, p. 73; *Novelas*, p. 245.

their first love. And although Jacinta refuses to renew her vow as a nun in N. 1, Zayas does not discount the refuge of the convent in later stories. Laura, the young wife in N. 5, "The Power of Love," resorts to the promises of a sorceress and the equivalent of grave robbing in hopes of luring back the love of her fickle husband, Diego. But she is so terrified by that experience that when she is rescued, she chooses to go to a convent. A repentant Diego begs her to return to live with him, but she refuses and when he is killed in battle, she becomes a nun. We will see more of Zayas's treatment of religious belief and convent life in chapter 7, "I Believe."

Our iconic tale-spinner María de Zayas was quite unique in her century, if not in ours, in seriously addressing the existence of what we now call queer love. She did not take a satirical approach, as Fontanella did in his burlesque dream sequence that suggested Zayas was butch in appearance but had no "sword" under her skirts. Nor did she treat it comically, as dramatists do in the short burlesque plays of the same period starring the much-loved comic actor Cosme Pérez (alias Juan Rana), well known to be gay.[20] On the contrary, Zayas centers the possibility of lesbian and gay sexual desire in two stories in her second volume, the *Disillusionments of Love*, both of which end tragically.

D. 6, "Loving Only to Conquer," is a full-fledged prefiguration of the 1982 romantic comedy *Tootsie*, albeit ending in tragedy. Esteban, the young rogue who is Zayas's equivalent to the character played by Dustin Hoffman in the film, falls in love with Laurela, the youngest of three daughters in a rich, noble household. Cross-dressed and calling himself Estefanía, he secures a job as a ladies' maid in her household, and with his musical talents, he wins the love of all – not just Laurela, but a male servant or two, and Laurela's father. Once Esteban proclaims himself to be Estefanía, Zayas consistently adopts feminine pronouns *ella* (the subject pronoun she) and *la* (direct object pronoun her) for Estefanía, who proclaims love for Laurela over and over. Others in the household laugh at Estefanía's defense of true love as a proposition of the soul, not limited by the gender of a body, and at her fits of jealousy over other suitors for Laurela's hand. When Laurela's father announces that his daughter is to be engaged to Enrique, a neighboring gentleman, Esteban tells her he is not Estefanía, but Esteban, a poor but noble gentleman from Burgos whose only hope was to win her love disguised as a woman. Seeing Laurela, who never suspected his deceit, regard him with horror, Esteban replies, "Is it

---

20 See Peter E. Thompson, *The Triumphant Juan Rana: A Gay Actor of the Spanish Golden Age*, Toronto, 2006.

possible that you've been so blind that you haven't seen in my love, in my jealousy, in my sighs and tears, in the feelings expressed in my songs and poems, that I really am what I say and not what I seem? Who's ever seen a woman fall in love with another woman?" [Es posible que has estado tan ciega ... ¿quién ha visto que una dama se enamore de otra?][21] He threatens to kill himself with his dagger if she does not reward his love, and then he stops her from turning the dagger on herself to save her honor, calming her down by telling her it was a joke.

During a sleepless night Laurela agonizes over the dangers from her father and fiancé and the lure of loving her/him as Esteban. By morning, she has a high fever, and her unsuspecting family allows "Estefanía" to care for her during the month of her recovery. Esteban persuades her that if they marry, her father will accept it, and they exchange marriage vows. Laurela leaves a letter of explanation for her father and she and "Estefanía" steal away at night to a room Esteban's friend lends them where "they went to bed with great pleasure, Laurela believing don Esteban to be her husband" [donde se acostaron con mucho reposo, Laurela creyendo que con su esposo].[22] At this point, we depart the gender-swapping rom-com for Zayas's uniquely twisting tragedy. The next morning, Esteban tells her he is not noble nor from Burgos, but the son of a carpenter and already married. He leaves her at a nearby church and disappears, taking the money and jewels she had brought with her. Her uncle sees her crying in the church, she confesses to him, and he takes her home and tells her father, who leaves her there for a year. Then, with the cooperation of the uncle and aunt, they weaken a wall in the house and pull it down on Laurela and a maid, killing both.

Just as Laurela is left to wrestle with Estefanía's comments on lesbian love and Esteban's partial confession, the reader also must assess just how explicitly Zayas is narrating a tale of love between women. Various critics explain how Zayas has indeed narrated the possibility of lesbian love.[23] As

21 *Desenchantments*, p. 227; *Desengaños*, pp. 448–9.
22 *Disenchantments*, p. 231; *Desengaños*, p. 324.
23 See Mary Gossy, "Skirting the Question: Lesbians and María de Zayas," *Hispanisms and Homosexualities*, ed. Sylvia Molloy and Robert McKee Irwin, Durham, 1998, pp. 19–28; Lisa Vollendorf, "The Future of Early Modern Women's Studies: The Case of Same-Sex Friendship in Zayas and Carvajal," *Arizona Journal of Hispanic Cultural Studies* 4, 2000, pp. 265–84; H. Patsy Boyer, "The War between the Sexes and the Ritualization of Violence in Zayas's *Disenchantments*," *Sex and Love in Golden Age Spain*, ed. Alain Saint-Saëns, New Orleans, 1996, pp. 123–45; and Sherry Velasco, "Listening to

I have previously suggested, the method Laurela's father used to kill her is richly symbolic.[24] Laurela is punished for showing up the cracks in the imperfectly built walls both between two supposedly unique, stable genders and between socioeconomic classes. By juxtaposing the Estefanía and Esteban statements on love between women in the same tale, however, Zayas can have it both ways. She can discount lesbian love, as she avoided the association Lope de Vega made between her and Sappho, while piling more vituperation on the deceits of men. Of most men, that is; she spares the neighbor fiancé Enrique, who wanted to marry Laurela even after she was seduced by Esteban.

Zayas leaves no such ambiguity in her rejection of male homosexual love in D. 7, "Marriage Abroad: Portent of Doom." She makes it the climax of a story of four daughters of a great Spanish lord, all brought to death through their marriages to foreigners in Portugal, Italy and Flanders, combining homophobia with xenophobia. The third sister, Blanca, is promised by her brother to a Flemish prince. She consents to the marriage on the condition that he come to Spain and court her for a year as if their marriage were not already arranged. He does so to the satisfaction of all, but when they are married and go to Flanders, his attention to her wanes and her father-in-law makes abundantly clear his hatred of her and all Spanish women. Her only consolation is close friendship with the prince's sister, Marieta. Marieta's manservant is stabbed to death within the palace, and not long afterwards, Marieta is strangled to death and her father-in-law summons Blanca to witness the spectacle. Knowing that she is likely to be his next victim, Blanca distributes her jewels to her childhood companion María and the other Spanish women who accompanied her to Flanders and then writes to her brother of the events.

The prince has a page, Arnesto, whom, people tell Blanca, he loves more than he loves her. Blanca goes to the prince's room one day expecting to see him in a tryst with another woman but instead finds him in bed with Arnesto. She has the bed taken out in the patio and sets it on fire. The next day, the father-in-law has Arnesto bleed Blanca to death. Anticipating her execution, Blanca calls her Spanish confessor and after confessing, tells him to flee immediately. María manages to get word to Blanca's brother, just arrived in Antwerp. The other Spaniards are all locked in the palace tower, where they are held as prisoners for four years.

Lesbians in Early Modern Spain," Cacho Casal and Egan, *Routledge Hispanic Studies Companion*, pp. 584–600.
24 Greer, *María de Zayas*, pp. 222–8.

Despite her absolute rejection of the sexual relationship between the prince and Arnesto, Zayas does paint the prince with some sympathy, not only in his courtship of Blanca in Spain but also in his protests against his father's cruelty to her. Her condemnation falls most ferociously on his Hispanophobic father and on the page Arnesto. The narrator of D. 7, a woman named Luisa, observes that the cruel reprisals of the Duke of Alba in Flanders were revenge for Blanca's murder, then says that she is granddaughter of Blanca's companion María, and she heard the story told by her parents and grandparents.

In sum, Zayas's attitude toward queer love in D. 6 and D. 7 is at best a halting, limited recognition of lesbian and gay love, one she wraps in negative hues and develops in tragic plots. Nevertheless, I find evidence in these two tales of her awareness of patterns that persist yet today in the nature of social and familial reactions to homosexuality. Without ever acknowledging patriarchy as the originating evil, Zayas pins primary guilt for the abuse and death of women on one or more male culprits. In D. 6, Esteban seduces not only Laurela, but her father as well. Hearing of the new maid who had been hired and of her charms and abilities,

> he said he wanted to see her, so Estefanía came in and engagingly kissed her master's hand. He, quite taken with her, praised her beauty so lavishly that Estefanía realized he'd fallen in love with her. This didn't bother her a great deal, although she was afraid that he might chase her.
>
> [diciendo la quería ver, vino Estefanía, y con mucha desenvoltura y agrado besó a su señor la mano, ...aunque temió verse perseguida de él.][25]

Don Bernardo her father does just that:

> every chance he got. He kept promising to marry her off well if she would only accede to his desire. She tried to protect herself by saying she was a virgin. To keep him from becoming overbold and discovering her deception, she didn't dare remain alone in the house when he was home.
>
> [en todas las ocasiones que se ofrecían la perseguía, ... se descubriese la maraña.][26]

I suggest that we see don Bernardo's year-long delay of punishment and hopes to catch and punish Esteban as well as Laurela, alongside the

---

25 *Disenchantments*, p. 215; *Desengaños*, p. 432.
26 *Disenchantments*, pp. 217–18; *Desengaños*, pp. 435–6.

body-crushing method he chooses, as akin to the passionate homophobia of certain men who have themselves felt the lure of "queer love."

In D. 7, Zayas makes Blanca's Flemish father-in-law the primary force behind her death, along with Arnesto. From the day she arrived in Flanders, both voice their hostility to her and to all Spaniards. Historically, the intermarriage of Spaniards with the local nobility was a factor that sustained the Spanish empire. But with Spanish power declining and the monarchy confronting rebellions or the threat of uprisings in Portugal, Catalonia, Sicily and Naples by the mid-seventeenth century, Zayas in this tale paints Spanish women as victims of resented alliances. Arnesto and the bullying, cruel father-in-law together bleed Blanca to death. She faints and the prince, moved by her beauty, protests and pleads with them to stop, drawing this angry reaction from his father:

> Shut up, you womanish coward, you traitor! Beauty affects you more than your affront! Shut up, I tell you, and let her die! One less enemy! If you don't have the courage, then conceal your weakness by leaving. Get out, don't watch, but a man who faints just from watching a woman die will ill defend himself or suffer offense from other men. I only wish I had all Spanish women in the same position I have her in.
>
> ["Calle, cobarde, traidor, medio mujer, …Así tuviera a todas las de su nación como tengo a ésta."]²⁷

Thus, Zayas's tale points up the complex dynamics of the power hierarchy, sex and gender identity in the colonizer-colonized relationship. Technically, Flanders was not a Spanish colony, but a part of the inheritance of Charles V, and in fact Flanders would remain Catholic and loyal to Spain when the Peace of Münster and the Treaty of Westphalia of 1648 put an end to the Eighty-Years War (the Dutch Revolt). Hostilities ended the very year that the *Desengaños* was published in 1647. In chapter 5, on that second volume, we will see how Zayas also accuses Spanish men of being insufficiently manly in defending their women and homeland.

In the last three stories of her first volume, Zayas offers up happy endings to tales of love. In one of her most iconic adventure tales, however, the protagonist of N. 9, "The Judge of Her Own Case," upends the

---

27 *Disenchantments*, p. 268; *Desengaños*, pp. 502–3. For a political Freudian reading of colonizer-colonized relations, see José Piedra, "Nationalizing Sissies," *¿Entiendes? Queer Readings, Hispanic Writings*, Durham, 1995, pp. 370–409. On the Peace of Münster and the Treaty of Westphalia, see Geoffrey Parker, *Europe in Crisis 1598–1648*, 2nd. ed., Oxford, 2001, pp. 199–209.

gender-power hierarchy in a way that distresses some readers. Estela is a beautiful young woman from Valencia who is betrayed, kidnapped and all but raped. Cross-dressed as a soldier, she then leads Spanish troops to victory, earning the favor of the emperor Charles V and ever more distinguished posts, culminating with that of viceroy of Valencia. As viceroy, she subjects her beloved Carlos to prolonged scrutiny before revealing her identity and marrying him. Estela is the only daughter of wealthy parents in Valencia, courted by the young and rich noble Carlos. While she has many suitors, she comes to prefer Carlos. But complications multiply. Another woman enamored of Carlos, Claudia, dresses as a man and calls herself Claudio to become Carlos's favored page. And a wealthy young Italian count arrives in Valencia and falls in love with Estela, whose parents arrange her marriage to him. Estela and Carlos plan to elope. Then comes the intervention of another man who has eyes for Estela, Amete, whom Zayas describes as "a genteel and gallant Moor who had belonged to Carlos's father and, having been ransomed, was just about to go to Fez, where he had been born" [Un gentil y gallardo moro ... no aguardaba sino pasaje para irse a Fez, de donde era natural].[28] Amete and Claudia/o kidnap Estela and take her to Fez, where Amete's caresses turn to abuse when she refuses him, while Claudia marries Amete's brother and converts to Islam. Then she and Amete conspire again to help him force Estela to yield, but her screams bring to the rescue Jacimín, the very gallant son of the king of Fez. He would help her return to Spain, but she cross-dresses to go to Tunis to help Charles V there and in other campaigns. Among the Spanish soldiers she finds Carlos, who was jailed after having been accused of her kidnapping and presumed murder. Still posing as a man, Estela makes him her secretary, grilling him repeatedly about his love for her and condemning his suspicion that she betrayed him with Claudio. Her harshest interrogation comes when he is put on trial for her disappearance in her court in Valencia. Finally revealing her identity, she declares herself Carlos's wife, apologizing to the Italian count and begging her parents' agreement. Charles V makes her a princess and transfers her titles, wealth, and viceregal position to Carlos.

The length of the ordeal to which Estela subjects Carlos makes many readers uncomfortable. One male critic called it a "sadistic and horrifying story," and others concur at least partially. Even Emilia Pardo Bazán, the eminent nineteenth-century novelist who published a collection of Zayas novellas, calls it "a very weak and entangled tale" [muy endeble y asaz

---

28 ETL, p. 156; Novelas, p. 492.

embrollada fábula].²⁹ However, if we pay attention to the identity of the narrator to whom Zayas assigns this tale, we can see why she structured it as she did, and what that tells us about her understanding of gender relationships. The tale is told by don Juan, the man whom Lisis loves but who prefers Lisarda yet resents don Diego's courtship of Lisis. Zayas has him tell his audience in the introductory frame:

> I considered it a joke, discreet listeners, to have to tell a story, so I didn't have one prepared. But last night the beautiful president of this assemblage commanded that I obey, so I took pen in hand and wrote out several drafts, products of my feeble wit. Letting your wit fill in for my faults, I shall begin like this.
>
> [Por burla había tenido, discreto auditorio, ... supliendo los vuestros mis faltas, digo así:]³⁰

Applying our wits as don Juan asks us to do, we will note that this story is presented to the reader as fiction, not the declaration of truth that opens or closes others. Zayas further marks the unreality of the tale with a linguistic marker of Spanish fairy tales as Estela is made viceroy, writing, "Ve aquí a nuestra Estela Virrey de Valencia" [Lo and behold, now how our Estela is viceroy of Valencia]. "Ve aquí" is a marker of surprise and the unreality of fairy tales with which Zayas has don Juan undercut his own narrative. The fairy tale Zayas has him tell is one in which a woman overcomes multiple hurdles to reach unparalleled success and then hands it all over to a man while she resumes the traditional role of wife – his princess. Zayas/don Juan finish it with a classic fairy tale ending, writing that "the new lovers, laden with riches and honor [...] celebrated their wedding, regaling the city with delight once more, their estate with lovely heirs, and historians with reason to write this tale of wonder" [Con que los nuevos amantes, ricos y honrados, ... motivos para escribir esta maravilla].³¹

The other two "happy ending" stories with which Zayas concludes her first volume are miracle tales of love: N. 8, "Triumph over the Impossible" and N. 10, "The Deceitful Garden." Miracle stories are modeled on those related in the New Testament that serve to witness Jesus's divine power

---

29 My translation of Ludwig Pfandl's view that it is a "sádica y espeluznante hisP toria," *Historia*, p. 369; M. Chevalier partially concurs. Pardo Bazán, pp. 14–15; all cited in Greer, *María de Zayas*, p. 205.
30 ETL, p. 151; *Novelas*, p. 485.
31 ETL, p. 173; *Novelas*, p. 511.

to heal the sick, raise the dead, and to defeat the devil by exorcising demons.[32] In N. 8, the triumph is over death; in N. 10, over the effects of sibling jealousy and the devil's magic trick. Don Lope narrates N. 8, in which Rodrigo's prayer to Christ brings his beloved back to life, as Jesus brought his friend Lazarus back to life in John 11:1–44. Leonor and Rodrigo have grown up as neighbors in Salamanca, loving each other since childhood. But because Rodrigo is a younger son, not in line to inherit the family estate, Leonor's parents reject his suit and promise her to another man, Alonso, which causes an enmity between the two neighboring families akin to that between the Montagues and the Capulets. Rodrigo's parents send him to serve in Flanders, where his actions so please the Spanish governor there, the Duke of Alba, that he is awarded a substantial income and membership in the military-aristocratic Order of Santiago.[33] Before leaving, Rodrigo swore to Leonor that he would not wed for three years, but he is detained by events in Flanders for four years. Leonor's parents, overhearing her laments, send a false letter to Rodrigo's parents with the news that he has married a rich Flemish woman; then they persuade their daughter to marry Alonso. When Rodrigo returns unmarried, she falls in a faint and is declared dead; she is buried in a large, underground vault. Grief-stricken, Rodrigo bribes his way into the vault, embraces her cadaver, then kneels and prays for her life before a life-sized figure on a nearby altar of Christ crucified. As he prays, with a weak, "Ay," Leonor stirs back to life, and Rodrigo smuggles her out of the vault. They publish the banns and are married in the presence of Alonso and Leonor's parents in their church. The parents, knowing her dead and buried, assume the banns refer to another woman of the same name, until her mother recognizes her at the end of the marriage ceremony. Alonso and Rodrigo plead their cases with civil and ecclesiastical authorities, and the case is brought to a famous professor of canon law at the University of Salamanca. He presents

---

32 See "miracles," *HarperCollins Bible Dictionary*, revised ed., Paul J. Achtemeier, general ed., San Francisco, 1996, pp. 687–9.
33 The Alba in question in this story as in D. 7, "Marriage Abroad: Portent of Doom," is presumably the third Duke of Alba, Fernando Álvarez de Toledo, named commander of Spanish troops in the Netherlands in 1567 and responsible for brutally repressive tactics against Flemish leaders. For more on the convoluted story of Alba and his son's love life and military and political service, see Greer, "María de Zayas and the dukes of Alba," in *"Los cielos se agg otaron de prodigios": Essays in Honor of Frederick A. de Armas*, ed. Kerry Wilks and Christopher Weimer, Newark, 2017, pp. 225–34, and Geoffrey Parker, *The Army of Flanders and the Spanish Road, 1567–1659*, Cambridge, 1972.

the suit to his students, who acclaim unanimously, "Give her to Rodrigo, give her to Rodrigo, she belongs to him" [Dénsela a don Rodrigo, dénsela a don Rodrigo, que suya es].[34] However unsound as a legal procedure, the students' judgment did accord with Catholic marriage law, as Leonor testifies to the bishop:

> She'd given him her promise, which she'd been unable to keep because her parents forced her into marrying don Alonso by means of threats and the false information that don Rodrigo had married. Under these circumstances, she had perforce given her consent. Don Alonso himself could support this as he'd never succeeded in getting her to consummate the marriage.
>
> [Ella le había dado palabra, ... jamás había podido acabar con ella que consumasen el matrimonio.][35]

While divorce in Zayas's Spain was exceedingly rare, nonconsummation of marriage was then as now grounds for annulment.[36] In any case, Leonor tells the bishop that she had really, truly died, furnishing corroborating details that Zayas does not relate. She does add the happy ending, that Leonor and Rodrigo live happily wed for many years and have one son, although evidence of Leonor's passage through the valley of death persisted in her lasting pallor.

Leonor and Rodrigo's dedication to their first vows might seem dramatic but it is corroborated by the real-life marital history of the seventeenth-century Spanish actors Luisa de Robles, Juan de Labadia and Alonso Olmedo Tufiño. Actress Luisa's first husband, Labadía, was either on a ship on his way to visit his parents in France, or on one near Vélez Málaga (there are two different accounts) that was scuttled by Moors who took Christian passengers captive. Another passenger survived clutching a floating plank; he escaped drowning and took news of the shipwreck to Luisa and others in Spain. Having had no news of Labadía despite seeking it, Luisa later married the Spanish actor and theater company owner Alonso Olmedo. Two or three years after their marriage, Labadía, having been released from captivity, appeared in Granada while they were having dinner. Olmedo recognized him immediately, stood up from the table and said, "My lady, this is your husband; it is my poor fate that, loving you so much, your husband has come to undo our marriage. Take half my

---

34 *Novelas*, p. 482. My translation.
35 Zayas, *Enchantments*, p. 269; *Novelas*, p. 481.
36 See Martín García, "Divorce and Abuse," pp. 184–94.

clothing for your husband and half our money and linens. I will go to live elsewhere."[37] Neither Labadía nor Olmedo subsequently lived with Luisa de Robles, but the three remained good friends – a harmonious agreement that caps Zayas's other miracle tale of love, N. 10, "The Deceitful Garden."

Zayas has Lisis's mother Laura narrate "The Deceitful Garden," a rewriting of Boccaccio's *Decameron* X.5. In Zayas's mother-narrated tale, another mother plays a crucial role in helping her two daughters to a happy ending. Whereas Zayas subtly undercut the truth value of don Juan's narration of N. 9 implicitly, Laura prefaces her story with a lengthy, explicit caution:

> I do not wish (discrete audience) to sell you as proven truths the events of this story, although all of them are of the quality that could well be so, since for one brother to kill another, for a sister to be a traitor to her sister, the one driven by jealousy and the other by love and envy, is not a new occurrence. [...] That poverty teaches cunning and more so if it is accompanied by blind fondness, is nothing either. Nor is it for a lover to risk the loss of his soul to achieve what he desires. No less would it be that a woman, if she wants to protect her honor, should search for or do impossible things. Nor do I find it so great that the devil, in order to take captives to his fearful and horrible prison, should give men to understand with false appearances that he is pleased to do what they desire. What is most amazing is that there should be any good work in him, as will be seen in my tale of wonder. But there can be other secret causes for that of which we are ignorant. In this, I do not oblige you to believe more than what pleases you, since my telling it is only to give an example and a warning to protect yourselves from risks.
>
> [No quiero, discreto auditorio, venderos por verdades averiguadas los sucesos de esta historia; … el decirla yo no es más de para dar ejemplo y prevenir que se guarden de las ocasiones.][38]

Laura then paints for us a perilously deceptive competition for love between a pair of brothers and sisters in Zaragoza. The older brother, Jorge, loves and courts the elder sister, Constanza, while his younger brother

---

37 See the entries for Luisa de Robles, Labadía and Alonso Olmedo y Tufiño in *Diccionario biográfico de actors del teatro clásico español*, ed. Teresa Ferrer Vals, Kassel, 2008, and Luis Vélez de Guevara, *La mayor desgracia de Carlos V*, ed. William R. Manson and C. George Peale, Newark, Delaware, 2002, p. 68, n. 43.

38 ETL, p. 174; *Novelas*, pp. 512–13.

Federico loves her sister, Teodosia. Teodosia secretly abhors Federico and loves Jorge so passionately that she tells Jorge that Constanza's modest response to his courtship stems from love for Federico. Jorge slays Federico, running him through with his sword outside the city, unseen by anyone, then flees to Barcelona and on to Naples. On the heels of this tragedy, the girls' father dies, leaving them with great wealth in the care of their mother, Fabia. Some two years later, Carlos, a man Zayas describes as "wealthier in goods of nature than in those of fortune" but "gallant, discreet and of highly agreeable qualities" [más rico de bienes de naturaleza que de fortuna ... galán, discreto y de muy amables partes],[39] comes to Zaragoza on business. Taking up residence across the street, he is dazzled by Constanza, he strikes up a friendship with Fabia, and with kindness and gifts, he wins the good will of all. Feigning dire illness, he makes a will leaving everything to Constanza and reveals to Fabia his love for her daughter and his wish to leave her all his estate for her dowry. This done and accepted, he recovers and proves such a good husband to her that no one minds the deceit. But four years later, Jorge reappears and renews his pursuit of Constanza. She avoids contact with him until Teodosia falls dangerously ill of the melancholy of frustrated love. Fearing for Teodosia's life, Constanza summons Jorge while Carlos is away hunting and begs him to accept Teodosia as his wife. He rejects her plea. Whereupon Constanza jokingly proposes this pact:

> If you create for me, in this small plaza at the front of my house, between now and morning, a garden so adorned with beds and scented flowers, trees and fountains, that neither in its refreshing air nor beauty, nor in the diversity of birds in it, it be no less than the famous hanging gardens of Babylon that Semiramis made above its walls, I shall put myself in your power and will do for you whatever you desire. And if not, then you must abandon this pretension, granting me in payment becoming my sister's husband.
>
> [Como vos me hagáis en esta placeta que está delante de mi casa, de aquí a mañana, un jardín ... otorgándome en pago el ser esposo de mi hermana.][40]

---

39 *Novelas*, p. 520; my translation.
40 *ETL*, p. 184; *Novelas*, p. 527. The hanging gardens of Babylon created by the Assyrian queen Semiramis were one of the great wonders of the ancient world. For the legends of her beauty and perverse cruelty, see the plays about her by Cristóbal de Virués, *La gran Semíramis*, and *La hija del aire*, Parts I and II, by Pedro Calderón de la Barca.

The devil finds a distraught Jorge wandering outside the city and, putting paper and a lap desk in his hands, has Jorge draw up and sign a document giving him possession of his soul in exchange for creating that marvel. Next morning Carlos calls Constanza to view the fabulous garden. She faints and when she revives, telling Carlos what happened, she begs him to kill her; Carlos pulls out his sword but as he puts its point not to her breast but to his own, Jorge grabs the handle and releases Constanza from her word, whereupon the devil, not to be outdone, returns Jorge's document to him saying, "I want no soul of one who knows how to conquer himself so well" [No quiero alma de quien tan bien se sabe vencer] and vanishes in a huge explosion of smoke.[41] Jorge and Teodosia are married, and both couples live long lives and have many children.

When Teodosia dies, she leaves behind an account in her own writing telling the story of her deceit and Jorge's killing of Federico. While Zayas and her narrators regularly claim first-person testimony as the basis of their tales, she does not do so in this case. Zayas inherited the basic elements of the magic garden story from Boccaccio and a sixteenth-century Spanish writer, Juan de Timoneda. But Zayas transforms the magician into the devil himself and adds a Faustian pack for Jorge's soul, as well as a Cain-and-Abel rivalry between the brothers.

Zayas brings most of the love stories in her first volume to a happy ending, while leaving a few in a more-or-less neutral space between love and loss. The ratio of happiness to unhappiness is more than reversed in her second volume, in which we would have to make the balance that between survival and death. I think the subtitle of that volume could well be "101 Ways to Kill a Woman." In both volumes, this iconic female narrator of love, loss and cruelty offers her hearers and readers a diversity of melodramatic tales with a wealth of colorful details at which my brief summaries can only hint. I suggest we read Laura's preface to N. 10 as Zayas's rejoinder to the contradiction between "Exemplary" and "Love" that heads this chapter. She lists ways that love and desire can go dangerously wrong but concludes by saying that she offers readers an example and a warning to protect themselves against risk.

---

41 ETL, p. 189; *Novelas*, p. 532.

Chapter Three

Settings, Styles and Models: Zayas's Literary Context

ZAYAS INVITES READERS of her *Exemplary Tales of Love* into the long-familiar scene of storytelling to entertain or instruct friends. Well-known examples besides Boccaccio's *Decameron* are Chaucer's *Canterbury Tales* and *One Thousand and One Nights*. Painting such a scene was not Zayas's invention, however, nor the only model available to her. Other literary or proto-literary models that we can identify as influences in her writing include oral storytelling, poetry, hagiography, popular novellas, Greek romance, and picaresque tales. Before analyzing more of her stories and her influence on other writers, we should look at the literary models on which Zayas could build, as I do in this chapter.

Scenes of oral storytelling bridged the lengthy transition from oral culture to one consumed in print, either read aloud to listeners, or silently for the reader's private enjoyment. Given her voracious reading, Zayas probably read at least a partial version of the *Decameron* in Spanish translation and, if she did live for some time in Italy, might have read it in Italian. She is likely to have experienced as oral tales told among friends or cited in sermons the genre of Middle Eastern advice tales, brief stories that in later centuries were gathered in *One Thousand and One Nights* and similar collections. Some Early Modern story collections recreated that oral scene. The title of Antonio de Eslava's *Noches de invierno* (Winter Nights) (1609) evoked the simple pleasure of friends exchanging stories around a fire on a cold night. Zayas's narrator don Miguel conjures up a firelit image in N. 7, "Just Desserts." The story's protagonist Hipólita prefaces telling it to don García: "My story would amaze anyone who heard it. When you hear it from the beginning, it will really astound you. It's so strange you'll think it's one of those fabulous tales people tell in the winter by the fireside instead of a real story" [mis cosas admiren ... cuando sepais desde principio mi historia ...los inviernos a las chimeneas que caso sucedido].[1] Throughout her two volumes, Zayas has her narrators establish the physical setting of the storyteller and audience as each begins his or her tale.

In the introduction to her first volume, Zayas describes a gathering of aristocratic urban women: "noble, wealthy, beautiful and friends ... living in the same house–although in different rooms" [nobles, ricas, hermosas y amigas ... vivir todas juntas en una casa, aunque en distinto cuartos] around a kindled brazier on a cold December evening.[2] Zayas sets an aristocratic story-telling scene in detail, with the women sitting on cushions and the men in chairs in her *estrado* (receiving space), while the ailing Lisis reclines on a luxurious couch. Musicians play songs and ballads, and both men and women organize games and theatrical performances and dance as well as telling stories. Each evening is capped by a delicious supper. Zayas intended to title her collection *Honesto y entretenido sarao* (Honest and entertaining soiree), the title in the Madrid approval and license, rather than *Novelas amorosas y ejemplares* (*Exemplary Tales of Love*). Covarrubias's 1611 dictionary defined "novedad" (novelty) as "a new and unaccustomed thing. It is usually dangerous for bringing a change in ancient customs" [Cosa nueva y no acostumbrada. Suele ser peligrosa por traer consigo mudança de uso antiguo]. Novela, deriving from the same root word, could carry the same negative aura; one of the meanings cited in the 1811 *Diccionario de autoridades* is "fiction or lie in any matter" [ficción o mentira en qualquier materia].[3] Zayas's publisher Pedro Escuer changed the title of the first volume, anticipating a better market for it, but the second volume did appear with the variant of her first title, "*Honest and entertaining* soiree." Within the first volume, the stories were titled *Maravillas* (Wonders) and in the second, *Desengaños* (Tales of Disillusion). Women and men alternate in the *Exemplary Tales of Love* while only women narrate the *Tales of Disillusion*. Surrounding the combined two volumes of twenty stories, the frame narrative itself is in effect a twenty-first tale, as Lisis, schooled by the examples of men's verbal and physical abuse of women, opts at the end of the *Tales of*

1   *Enchantments*, p. 217; *Novelas*, p. 416.
2   *ETL*, p. 54; *Novelas*, p. 167.
3   Sebastián de Covarrubias Orozco, *Tesoro de la lengua castellana o española*, Madrid, 1984; *Diccionario de autoridades*, ed. facsímile of the Real Academia Española, vol. 2, Madrid, Editorial Gredos, 1964.

Disillusion to enter a convent rather than marrying either Juan, her first love, or Diego, her faithful suitor.⁴

Lisis, reclining on her luxurious couch by the brazier, surrounded by her friends, is suffering from quartan fever, a fever that recurs every fourth day, with two intermittent days. Although now associated with malaria, it was understood throughout Early Modern Europe as a psychosomatic condition, a kind of melancholy caused by lovesickness, specifically provoked by jealousy or frustration in love as well as climatic or other environmental conditions. Her ailment is not unique in literature from the period: the first tale in Eslava's *Noches de invierno* illustrates the possible economic effects of lovesickness with a story of how one of its frame participants lost a ship due to the immoderate passion of its young captain. Hippocratic medical and Ovidean literary traditions converged in interpreting the condition as an imbalance in the sufferer's four basic bodily humors – blood, phlegm, black bile and yellow bile – an imbalance that could be corrected by erotic satisfaction, distraction, or renouncing the resisting love object. Lisis's very name, Ingrid Matos-Nin points out, underlines both the condition she suffers and the role that the storytelling is intended to serve. "Lisis" in the *Dictionary of the Real Academia Española* derives from the Greek word for "solution," meaning in medicine, "the slow, favorable ending of an illness" [terminación lenta y favorable de una enfermedad].⁵ Elena Casey proposes that as well as merging the medical and literary-metaphorical value of *cuartanas* (quartan fever), Zayas makes them creative, as enabling a collective, authorial female agency through her narratives. Ending the first collection Lisis apparently adopts the most drastic solution, renouncing the faithless Juan and promising engagement to Diego on the first day of the year, significantly, the Feast of the Circumcision. When that provides no more than a brief remission, she suffers a nearly fatal relapse brought on by Juan's preference for Lisarda and her ill-considered engagement. Her relapse is relieved by the company of Zelima/Isabel and resolved with Lisis's final decision to choose life as

---

4 On Zayas's title, see Yllera, "Introducción," pp. 92–3; Olivares, "Introducción," pp. lxiiii–lxviii; Romero-Díaz, *Nueva nobleza*, pp. 11–12, n. 1.

5 *Diccionario de la Real Academia Española*, "Terminación lenta y favorable de una enfermedad," consulted July 24, 2020. My translation. Matos-Nin, "Lisis o la remisión de la enfermedad del amor en las novelas de María de Zayas y Sotomayor," *Letras femeninas* 32.2, 2006, p. 102; Casey, "The *Cuartanas* of Lisis: The Remissive Etiology of the *Novelas amorosas y ejemplares* by María de Zayas y Sotomayor," *eHumanista* 32, 2016, pp. 571–4.

a secular resident in a convent. Whether she had planned it in advance or, more likely, arrived at this two-movement resolution with advancing years and Spain's darkening political situation, Zayas makes the frame tale work to her declared didactic purpose.

The vision of women and men taking turns telling stories to a group of listening friends is a fictional image of direct human communication unmediated by writing and print publication. As well as following tradition with this fictional vision, Zayas chose a wise strategy for a woman writer inserting herself in a masculine literary world. Writing and publication was considered improbable or unseemly for women at that time, but storytelling to family and friends in a domestic setting was not. Zayas deviates from this ruse of orality in only two instances: the introduction to ETL 9, in which the designated fictional male narrator don Juan says, "I took up my pen and wrote a few pages" [Tomé la pluma y escribí unos borrones] the night before his storytelling turn; and in Lisis's concluding harangue to her listeners: "if what has been written does not undeceive you" and "if my written defense is insufficient" [si no os desengaña lo escrito; si mi defensa por escrito no basta].[6] Moreover, the vision of oral narration is consistent with Zayas's writing style. She writes in long, looping sentences, often linking them beyond the occasional full stop/period by beginning the following sentence with "and," a marker of orality – although in a second corrected edition, the opening "y" (and) was often excised. To deflect critique from male "listeners" Lisis opens the last Disillusion by affirming that she does not put on airs in language, but rather speaks (that is, writes) plainly. She avows:

> And, since I do not pretend to canonization for my intelligence but rather for my ability to undeceive, I have certainly never sought out rhetorical nor overly cultivated reasoning in what I say or in what I will say because, aside from being a type of language I abhor to all possible extreme, I would like for everyone to understand me, those who are educated and those who are not ... And thus I have attempted to speak in the language that my nature teaches me and I learned from my parents.

> [No traigo propósito de canonizarme por bien entendida ... [y no] he buscado razones retóricas ni cultas.... he procurado hablar en el idioma que mi natural me enseña y deprendí de mis padres.][7]

---

6 ETL, p. 151; Zayas, *Novelas*, p. 485; ETL, p. 324; *Desengaños*, p. 686.
7 ETL, p. 285; *Desengaños*, p. 636.

Particularly in the frame sections and the beginning of the stories, however, she deploys a challengingly complex Baroque syntax. She does so, I believe, to endow the scene with the aristocratic atmosphere she sought to convey. That aristocratic design is especially marked in the Introduction of each volume, as she describes Lisis reclined on her daybed throne in her richly furnished receiving area hung with "costly Flemish tapestries whose woodlands, flowers and knolls appeared to be the forests of Arcadia or the hanging gardens of Babylon" [costosos paños flamencos, cuyos boscajes, flores y arboledas parecían las selvas de Arcadia o los pensiles huertos de Babilonia].[8]

Lisis has her narrators tell their stories from a deluxe version of a storyteller's perch, in a luxurious salon. That scene of narration for a listening public fits the age in which Zayas wrote, when luxury conferred prestige; she paints it richly to appeal both to people who can read and listeners who can't. Although even in Madrid, only 25 percent of the female population might be literate and 60 percent of the males, Zayas's audience was not restricted to those numbers: a literate person could easily read the stories aloud, thanks to their plain language, so that listeners could enjoy their juicy plots. Cervantes shows this known practice in chapter 32 of *Don Quixote*, Part I, as the innkeeper, his family, servants and guests talk about the kinds of pleasure they take from after-supper story reading when there is a literate guest to read a novel of chivalry – or the Cervantine novella left in an old suitcase there, "The Man Who Was Recklessly Curious." Zayas's scene of oral narration is not a rustic inn, but an urban, multifamily dwelling of noble friends and their servants (*criados*). Her narrators regularly speak of servants, mostly as background helpers, sometimes as objects of vituperation for accepting bribes, gossiping about or abetting the failings of their masters and mistresses. Servants are sometimes performers as well, like Diego's servants, who perform *entremeses* (comic skits) and dances in the *Exemplary Tales of Love* frame tale. We should thus imagine a wider community of nonreaders, including servants hovering in the background, listening intently to her stories, as told to guests within her work and read aloud to other audiences.

8   ETL, p. 56; *Novelas*, p. 169. In the Greer-Rhodes translation, we have tried to reproduce the texture of Zayas's prose by retaining her syntax, but we simplify it somewhat in her opening sentences. Boyer broke Zayas's sentences down for twentieth-century readers, producing a very readable text, albeit with some sacrifice of accuracy and without notes explaining historical or mythical figures and places Zayas names.

Zayas's close Spanish predecessor Cervantes eschewed using a frame tale in his *Novelas ejemplares* (Exemplary Tales). But it's worth noting that if Zayas did not follow his steps with her frame, she does take his lead in crafting stories much longer than the Italian novellas of Boccaccio, Bandello and Cinzio and their Spanish follower, Juan de Timoneda in his *Patrañuelo* (1567). The episodes that comprise her lengthy tales are often quite loosely connected. A particularly striking example is D. 10, "The Ravages of Vice." The first episode has a young Spanish nobleman Gaspar, while in Lisbon with Philip III, making nightly visits to one of four sisters in a distinguished residence and finding a dead but still moaning body in the cellar. He then falls in love with Florentina, the younger of two beautiful sisters, who lives in such seclusion that he cannot approach her until he finds her in the street one night, moaning and nearly dead from sword wounds after her affair with her brother-in-law has provoked a massacre in her residence. Other than successive episodes in the young gentleman Gaspar's life, Zayas creates no explicit links between the two sequences. I suggest that to understand their deeper meaning, readers should look for key terms that can link elements of her stories that she leaves unspoken in order to negotiate a tension between her two identities – with women as a group, and with the nobility as a class. In this tale, I consider the key "the enemy within": the Portuguese who hate Spaniards and were rebelling against the Spanish monarch; servants who are indispensable enemies in aristocratic households; sisters who are not true blood sisters but rivals in love; and finally, treacherous desire as enemy within the body of women.[9]

A soiree in Madrid such as the one Zayas creates would have included the recitation of poetry by the story tellers, and to mimic this effect, Zayas interspersed poetry throughout all of her tales but one, ETL 10. Her two volumes include a total of eighty poems. Writing and reciting poetry was considered an appropriate activity for the cultured gentleman and for a sufficiently educated woman as well. That did not make writing secular poetry unproblematic for women writers, however. In Renaissance and Early Modern poetry, women are figured as silent beautiful objects of masculine desire, the pretext for exploring and displaying the male poet's soul and exhibiting his poetic skill in a literary dialogue with his primarily male audience. Expression of independent feminine desire was then viewed as unseemly, sinful and culturally destabilizing, a position

---

9 See chapters 5 and 6 and Greer, *María de Zayas*, pp. 309–15.

that Zayas does not share, despite her concern for its dangers.[10] Women writers of love poetry therefore followed three strategies, as outlined by Olivares and Elizabeth Boyce: acceptance, adaptation or subversion of the masculine tradition.[11]

Zayas's use of the three strategies depends on the fictional context in which she inserts the poems. She most closely follows the masculine codes of courtly love and the Petrarchan love discourse of icy fire and pleasure in suffering for love when giving voice to a masculine character, such as Félix's sonnet "To Love the Day" in ETL 1, "Taking a Chance on Losing" as its first quatrain demonstrates:

> To love the day, to abhor the day,
> to call to the night and disdain it later,
> to fear fire and approach the flame
> to have pain and happiness at once,
> [Amar el día, aborrecer el día, / llamar la noche y despreciarla luego, / temer el fuego y acercarse al fuego, / tener a un tiempo pena y alegría][12]

In that same tale, when speaking in Jacinta's voice, however, as in the décima "I Adore What I See Not," she opts for adaptation, that of addressing a concept, thereby at least theoretically masking the gender of both the object and the poetic speaker:

> I adore what I see not
> and do not see what I adore;
> I know not the cause of my love
> and desire to find the cause.
> Who can manage to understand
> my confused delirium?
> For without seeing I have come to love
> out of mere imagining,
> my affection inclining
> to a being who has no being.

I say "theoretically" for two reasons: first, because hearing or reading the poem in its narrative context lends an implicitly gendered voice to the poetic speaker and that speaker's desired object. And secondly, masking

---

10 See María Jesús Fariña Busto, "A propósito de algunos sonetos incluidos en las *Novelas y Desengaños amorosos*," *Monographic Review* 13, 1997, p. 59.
11 Julian Olivares and Elizabeth S. Boyce, *Tras el espejo la musa escribe: Lírica femenina de los Siglos de Oro*, Madrid, 1993.
12 ETL p. 72; *Novelas*, p. 184.

gender can be challenging in both English and Spanish because of their patterns of gendered pronouns. Avoiding them can create awkward poetic lines.[13] Hiding gender can be particularly difficult in Spanish, in which it inflects adjectives as well as pronouns. In some instances, Zayas may have worked hard to mask it; in others, she seems to enjoy and to heighten the confusion or dissonance between the gender of the character and the poetic discourse he or she employs. A good example is the sonnet in D. 1 that Isabel says don Manuel sang, explaining that they called each other Belisa and Salicio. The concluding tercet spreads serene sunshine over the melancholy images of the tragic heroines Philomena and Procne:

> The earth, condemned to a great flood,
> as totally submerged in its rage,
> her eyes were rivers overflowing,
> because the clouds turned into angry seas.
>   The sweet retiring Philomena, since she cannot see the sun's red rays,
> does not sing him songs of abandonment,
> seeing herself disconsolate without his light.
>   Procne laments, the nightingale does not sing,
> the flowers have lost their beauty and perfume
> and everything is likewise sorrowing,
>   until, with such great light as to shock the sun,
> all wisdom, grace, and love,
> Belisa came forth and everything became serene.
> [A un diluviio la tierra condenada, / …salió Belisa, y serenose todo.] [14]

But both Manuel's angry reaction after she sings the sonnet and the ending of the story reinstate the sad relevance of the Philomena and Procne images.

In other poetic inserts, Zayas narrators have both feminine and masculine fictional voices invoke mythical heroes and heroines: Tantalus as symbol of their frustrated desire, Icarus and Phaeton as images of their dashed pursuit of amorous satisfaction, and suicidal Dido's lament for Aeneas's abandonment. The song "Oh Sovereign Goddess" that the cross-dressed Estefanía/Esteban sings in D. 6 piles on the mythical references and also illustrates Zayas's heightening of gender–voice dissonance as s/he invokes Endymion and Diana, Europa and the white bull, Midas's treasure,

---

13 Compare the Greer/Rhodes and Boyer renderings of the decima in ETL pp. 69–70, and *Enchantments*, pp. 19–20 to the Spanish original in *Novelas*, pp. 181–2.

14 *Disenchantments*, pp. 47–8; *Desengaños*, pp. 213–14.

Phoebus's chariot, Jason and the golden fleece, Narcissus and Echo, Venus and Adonis, Persephone and Pluto, Hermaphrodite and other mythical lovers. Zayas also uses the conventions of pastoral poetry, which provide a gender-equal space for expressing both male and female desire.[15] As these examples show, it is hard to classify some of her poetic choices as clearly acceptance, adaptation or subversion of masculine poetic discourse, because one shades into the other.

I would, however, consider a clear subversion of masculine poetic conventions Zayas's repeated emphasis on masculine fickleness and female constancy, thereby reversing the common complaint in love poetry of male authors. She gives this strategy to Lisis in a ballad in the opening frame section, "Listen woodlands, to my weeping," in which she distances her jealousy over Juan's preference for Lisarda by singing a ballad that laments the ingratitude of Celio, Jacinta's second love object in *ETL* 1.

> Listen, woodlands, to my weeping,
> hear, for I complain once again,
> for never does contentment
> endure more for the unfortunate.
>   Once again I made
> your elm and ash trees
> and your pure glass
> witnesses of Celio's ingratitude.
>   [...]
>   And I, for I love you,
> weep over your abandon and feel your disdain.
> [Escuchad, selvas, mi llanto, / ... lloro tu olvido y tus desdenes siento.][16]

She positively delights in cross-dressing the poetic narrative voice as well as the sartorially cross-dressed subject Claudia/Claudio in the sonnet, "May the One Who Has Had His Will" [Goce su libertad el que ha tenido] in ETL 9, "The Judge of Her Own Case."[17] She performs a more subtle subversion in yet another sonnet in the first novella, "In the Clear Crystal of Disillusion." Jacinta, believing herself disillusioned with love, admires herself in the mirror and takes pride in her independence. Then Celio inserts himself in her mirrored gaze and both Celio and Jacinta enter into

---

15 On pastoral discourse, see Elizabeth Rhodes, "Skirting the Men: Gender Roles in Sixteenth-Century Pastoral Books," *Journal of Hispanic Philology* 11.2, 1987, pp. 131–49.
16 ETL, pp. 58–9; *Novelas*, pp. 171–2.
17 ETL, p. 154; *Novelas*, p. 490.

a complex game that reflection displays: that passion on both their parts is as much the desire to be desired as it is love for their chosen object.[18]

Zayas also adapted the formal structure of poetry as well as its content. While she composed in a number of traditional poetic forms: sonnets, ballads and romancillos (ballads with six- or seven-syllable lines), décimas (ten-line octosyllabic stanzas) and madrigals, she frequently added an estrambote: extra verses – appended to sonnets, a form also known by the label "tailed sonnet."[19] Sometimes only three verses, as in the sonnet "Scarcely Did I Take My First Step in Love" [Apenas en amor di el primer paso] that Carlos sings to Octavia in D. 2, "Most Infamous Revenge," one of the principal forms of the burlesque sonnet that emerged in fourteenth-century Italy and would be adopted in Spain, where it would thrive while the form declined to decadence in Italy. In this variety of tailed sonnet, the first verse in the coda rhymes with the last line of the last tercet, and the last two verses are a rhymed couplet. Zayas handles the form skillfully, as one can see even in Boyer's English translation, which does not try to imitate the rhyme scheme:

> My hope has died, but at least it was mine;
> She pays me falsely while I worship constant;
> If I follow Cupid, I discover jealousy.
>   Oh love, sweet enemy!
> Oh cruel tyranny!
> Ruling and loving permit no sharing.
> [Apenas en amor di el primer paso, ... tropiezo en celos, si a Cupido sigo. / ¡Oh amor, dulce enemigo! / ¡Oh cruel tiranía! / Reinar y amar no quieren compañía.][20]

Sometimes the *estrambote* is much longer, as in Carlos's next sonnet, "Alas How I Imitate Tantalus in My Pain" [¡Ay, cómo imito a Tántalo en la pena], which adds more than fifty verses. This form was known as a *capitolo* or sometimes as an epistle or elegy. It was usually in linked tercets, but Zayas begins its "tail" in such tercets, then continues it with other rhyme schemes. That Zayas included both forms of the tailed sonnet in this story set in Milan, Italy, might be a subtle recognition of their Italian

---

18 ETL, p. 89; *Novelas*, pp. 202–3.
19 See Adrienne L. Martín's study *Cervantes and the Burlesque Sonnet*, Berkeley, 1991, p. 21.
20 *Disenchantments*, p. 88; *Desengaños*, p. 265. On the *capitolo*, see Valerie Masson de Gómez, "The Vicissitudes of the *Capitolo* in Spain," *Pacific Coast Philology* 16.1, 1981, 57–65.

origin, or perhaps of its extension and renovation by Spanish poets. In any case, both types of additions work against the fundamental challenge of the sonnet form, that of expressing complex emotion in a condensed, formal structure. When male poets added an estrambote, they commonly did so to comic effect, for reasons well analyzed by Adrienne Martín. Zayas does not follow them in this comic intent, however, nor did Pérez de Montalban, in the sonnet with estrambote he contributed to the preliminaries for her *Novelas*.

Nor did Zayas aim at parody in having Isabel, accompanying herself on a guitar, follow Florentina's tale in D. 10 by singing a long ballad of twenty-four quatrains in *esdrújulo* verse; that is, a succession of verses all accented on the antepenultimate syllable, not the usual stress in Spanish. It became relatively popular with certain Spanish poets in the early seventeenth century, including Lope de Vega and Góngora.[21] In Isabel's ballad, lines 2 and 4 in each quatrain have an assonantal rhyme scheme á-o (with varying intervening unstressed vowels between the accented "a" and the final unstressed "o"). Verses 1 and 3 in each quatrain also end in *esdrújulos* (proparoxytones). Assonantal rhyme is standard in Spanish ballads, but the rhythm imposed by the *esdrújulos* in the long song "In the meadow amidst rustic thorns" [Al prado, en que espinas rústicas] she assigns to Isabel is anything but standard, although it became a common form of their use about 1650. Such rhymes could lend a pompous or a comic tone. Lope used it to both effects, in religious poetry, and in plays; he employs it to comic effect in the drama *Los comendadores de Córdoba*, having the braggart lackey Galindo sing a ridiculous sonnet-serenade in *esdrújulo* rhyme for the kitchen slave girl Esperanza he courts.[22] I find Zayas's long romance forced; it is surely an impressive display of her wit and the range of her rhyming vocabulary, but it is hard to focus on her message rather than the bravura of her mode of delivery. English translations communicate the message, not the mode, impossible in English verse. Elizabeth Rhodes argues that Zayas's intent in her second, more Baroque volume was to make readers work to understand her message to the nobility, to make sense of the contradictions in its delivery. Read with that view, one could say that this final poem suits her intent.

21 Antonio Alatorre, "El verso esdrújulo en el siglo XVII," *Anuario de Letras* 38, 2000, pp. 427, 436–7.
22 ETL, pp. 315–18; *Desengaños*, pp. 675–8; Lope de Vega, *Los comendadores de Córdoba*, ed. José Enrique Laplana Gil, Act I, vv. 932–45.

In fact, we should probably view her poetry as her entry in a literary dialogue with the primary masculine tradition, whether she accepts, adapts or subverts masculine models. Reading this way gave me a new appreciation of the sonnet Fadrique sings to Serafina in ETL 4, "Forewarned but Fooled." It repeats "eyes" (ojos) and words ending in "ojos," twelve times, in all but two verses. Even conceding that the consonantal rhyme in "ojos" might sound better read aloud in Spanish, such hyperbolic repetition strikes my ear with a comic effect.

> That I should die, tyrant, for your eyes
> and that your eyes take pleasure in killing me;
> that I should want with your eyes to console myself
> and that your eyes give me a thousand annoyances;
>   that I surrender my eyes as spoils
> to your eyes, and they, instead of loving me,
> being able in my annoyances to bring me happiness,
> turn flowers into burrs;
>   that your eyes kill me with disdain,
> with rigor, with jealousy, with indifference,
> when my eyes for your eyes die;
>   O sweet ingrate! who in your eyes have
> as much ingratitude as beauty,
> against eyes that adore your eyes.
> [Que muera yo, Tirana, por tus ojos / … contra unos ojos que a tus ojos quieren.]²³

Boyer's translation is smoother than the Greer/Rhodes literal rendering, and rhyming "prize" with "eyes" she works into it an analogy to the "ojos / enojos / despojos / abrojos /" rhyme in the original. Both, however, seem comic. This may serve as an ironic commentary on Fadrique's incapacity to see what was right before his long-suffering "eyes": that Serafina was not only in love with his rival Vicente but also carrying his child. Isabel's comments in the frame-tale section of the Third Night in the *Desengaños* support such an ironic reading, inviting us to see not Fadrique's supposedly sincere lyric devotion but his blindness, or perhaps both at the same time.

> I feel sure that not all poets really feel what they write; rather, I imagine that they write about what they don't feel. I have intentionally sought to console the gentlemen by singing about a loyal man to give them courage and hope as they face the jury this final night, and to wish them good luck.

---

23 ETL, p. 116; *Novelas*, p. 296.

[Y tengo por sin duda que no todos los poetas sienten lo que escriben; ... buen suceso de su parte.]²⁴

Other than poetic traditions, the most important model for Zayas was obviously the novella, framed or unframed in collections, or included in a longer narrative form like *Don Quixote*. Apart from the frame convention, we can trace parts of some Zayas stories back to Boccaccio, Bandello and other Italian novella writers, and to their remodeling by Cervantes. She rewrites the Cervantine novella I referred to earlier, "The Man Who Was Recklessly Curious" in D. 3, "His Wife's Hangman" but has the narrator Nise defend her procedure saying:

> You may think you've heard before some of the disenchantments already told or yet to tell, maybe because I or the other storytellers have heard a similar story, but not with the detail that adorns them in this setting. Certainly they've not simply been taken from any old sources as some invidious critics stated about the first part of our entertaining soirees.
>
> Telling a true case not only entertains but educates as well.
>
> [Si acaso pareciere que los desengaños aquí referidos, ...a contar un caso verdadero, que no solo sirva de entretener, sino de avisar.]²⁵

Zayas crafted her version of Cervantes's ninth Exemplary novel *The Deceitful Marriage* in ETL 3, "The Miser's Reward," and in D. 3, her version of the novella "The Man Who Was Recklessly Curious" inserted in his *Don Quixote*, Part I, chapters 32–4. At least part of the inspiration for the character of Zaida in D1, "Her Lover's Slave," is probably the role of Zoraida in "The Captive's Tale" in the first part of *Don Quixote*. In all three cases, however, despite sharing basic elements, her stories are very different from those male-authored stories. Zayas also reshaped a Lope de Vega novella from his *Stories for Marcia Leonarda* (*Novelas a Marcia Leonarda*), "The Fortunes of Diana" in her ETL 9, "The Judge of Her Own Case." And basic elements of D. 4, "Too Late Undeceived," can be traced from Apuleius's *The Golden Ass* to versions narrated by Boccaccio, Bandello and Marguerite de Navarre. Despite Nise and other narrators' claims only to tell true stories, never previously told in such detail, elements of other stories may well be inspired by the novellas of Pérez de Montalbán and Castillo Solórzano, and by plays of Lope and Calderón, as motifs were freely interchanged between novellas and plays in her day,

---

24 *Disenchantments*, p. 309; *Desengaños*, p. 557.
25 *Disenchantments*, p. 113; *Desengaños*, pp. 297–8.

well before the advent of copyright laws. As the Covarrubias definition of *novedad* (novelty) cited above indicates, in premodern eras, writers and their readers looked for talent and originality less in invention of a radically new theme or plot than in the ingenious reworking of traditional forms, themes and tales. Few of the diverse collection of stories Chaucer relates in *The Canterbury Tales* were his own invention. His translator Nevill Coghill observes that "it was not considered the function of a teller of stories in the fourteenth century to invent the stories he told, but to present and embellish them with all the arts of rhetoric for the purposes of entertainment and instruction."[26] Nor was novelty the function of the storyteller in Early Modern Spain. What makes Zayas an iconic figure lies in the detail she added to her version of the stories, the evidence of her own voice and talents, their value in defending the women's worth, and their model for the women writers who followed her.

Hagiography, the stories of the lives of saints, was another narrative genre that shaped Zayas's stories. Saints' lives were approved reading for women readers, advocated by Juan Luis Vives in *The Instruction of a Christian Woman* (1523), which Catherine of Aragón commissioned for the instruction of her daughter, Mary Tudor. Saint Teresa of Avila reflects the influence they had on readers' lives, relating in glowing terms how she and a brother were inspired by them to want to seek martyrdom in Muslim lands.[27] Narratives of saints' lives and related legends played a vital shaping role in Zayas's second volume, the *Tales of Disillusion*. This is most obvious in D. 9, "Triumph over Persecution," narrated by a nun, which is Zayas's version of the romance legend of Queen or Saint Beatriz of Hungary recounted in the second *Flos sanctorum*. The episodic structure of Zayas's stories is akin to that of hagiographic tales, which were by their very nature episodic, as they relate episodes in the saint's life that qualify him or her for sanctification. Patricia Grieve and Elizabeth Rhodes both analyze how Zayas manipulated male-authored hagiographic discourse to make it a woman-writer's vehicle to express women's situation and concerns. Grieve and Rhodes read Zayas's objective in that manipulation differently, however.[28]

---

26 Nevill Coghill, "Introduction," Geoffrey Chaucer, *The Canterbury Tales*, trans. Nevill Coghill, London, 1977, pp. 17–18.
27 *The Life of Saint Teresa of Ávila by Herself*, trans J. M. Cohen, London, 1957, pp. 23–4.
28 See Rhodes, *Dressed to Kill*, p. 87, on the derivation of D. 9 from the *Flos sanctorum*, published in Spanish as *Leyenda de los santos* (Legend of the Saints,

The model for the Heliodoran or Greek Romance was the *Aethiopica* of Heliodorus of Emesa, translated to English with various title combinations as the *Ethiopian Story* or *The Adventures of Theagenes and Chariclea: A Romance*. Europeans first encountered this third-century Byzantine romance in a manuscript discovered when the Ottomans sacked the royal palace in Hungary in 1526. It was then published in many languages. Zayas could have read it in either one of two translations into Spanish, the first of which was based on the 1547 French translation of Jacques Amyot and published anonymously in Antwerp, the second translated by Fernando de Mena and published with the title *La historia de los leales amantes Theágenes y Chariclea* (The story of the loyal lovers Theagenes and Chariclea) in 1587, 1614 and 1616.[29] Cervantes, joining multiple Renaissance writers in their admiration of that work, promised that in his forthcoming "epic in prose," *Los trabajos de Persiles y Sigismunda* (The trials of Persiles and Sigismunda), he dared to compete with Heliodorus. Cervantes's protagonists Persiles and Sigismunda, like Theagenes and Clariclea, are devoted, chaste lovers separated by fortune who undergo multiple adventures and face dangerous competitors over a wide-ranging geographic and cultural landscape as they seek to reunite and marry. Elements of that model may have influenced Zayas's plotting of her ninth novella, "The Judge of her Own Case," and D. 1, "Her Lover's Slave," both of which take the protagonists from Spanish locales to Muslim lands in North Africa. In "The Judge of Her Own Case," the besieged lovers are happily united in marriage, but Zayas gives them a very different ending in "Her Lover's Slave." Manuel, the faithless lover of the narrator, Zelima/Isabel, repeatedly refusing to marry her after having raped her, is killed by her faithful suitor Felipe, Isabel vows to become a nun, and Felipe goes to war and is killed.

And the influence of picaresque fiction? The label itself derives from the Spanish word *pícaro*, an astute, ingenious, low-born person with no

---

1497); Patricia Grieve, "Embroidering with Saintly Threads: María de Zayas Challenges Cervantes and the Church," *Renaissance Quarterly* 44, 1991, pp. 86–106.

29 See Forcione, *Cervantes's Christian Romance*; Michael Armstrong-Roche, *Cervantes' Epic Novel: Empire, Religion, and the Dream Life of Heroes in Persiles*, Toronto, 2009; and Boruchoff, "Competir con Heliodoro: Cervantes y la crítica ante una leyenda," in *USA Cervantes: 39 Cervantistas en Estados Unidos*, ed. Georgina Dopico Black and Francisco Layna Ranz, Madrid, 2009, p. 202.

assigned job who might work in a kitchen for leftovers.[30] The original literary picaro was Lazaro, or Lazarillo, the protagonist of the anonymously-authored *La vida de Lazarillo de Tormes, y de sus fortunas y adversidades* (The Life of Lazarillo de Tormes: His fortunes and adversities) (1554). The genre closely associated with the rebirth of the novel was native to Spain and was consolidated with the publication of Mateo Alemán's *Guzmán de Alfarache* (parts 1 and 2, 1599, 1604), from which its influence spread across Europe. James Mabbe published in 1623 a version modified to English tastes, *The Rogue, or the Life of Guzman de Alfarache*. As Mabbe's title "The Rogue" underlines, picaresque works relate the adventures of a character of low social origins who struggles to live by his or her wits in a corrupt society. Francisco de Quevedo expanded it with a satirical version of the genre, *El buscón*, published in 1626 after circulating in manuscripts for some two decades. Its publication continued, sometimes linked to Lazarillo, and in English versions titled *The Swindler, The Scavenger,* or *The Grifter*. Cervantes added picaros to the novella tradition in his Exemplary novels with the tale of "Rinconete y Cortadillo" and "The Deceitful Marriage," the latter inspiring Zayas's own version, ETL 3, "The Miser's Reward." Francisco López de Úbeda created a feminine variety in *La pícara Justina* (1605), a pseudo-autobiographical confessional narrative which John Stevens would translate a century later as *The Spanish Jilt* (1707), anticipating the kindred spirit Daniel Defoe created in *Moll Flanders* (1722).[31] Other pícaras would be crafted in Justina's wake, including *La hija de Celestina* (1612; Celestina's daughter); and *La garduña de Sevilla* (The stone marten of Seville) (1642). The gifted Spanish woman writer and critic Emilia Pardo Bazán wrote in the nineteenth century that Zayas created a new subgenre, a picaresque literature of the aristocracy.[32] Zayas's aristocratic pícaras exercise their wits successfully in ETL 4, "Forewarned but Fooled," and ETL 7, "Just Desserts"; only in ETL 3, "The Miser's Reward," is the principal female rogue reduced to begging at the end. No classic picara appears in Zayas's second volume. Other than saints' tales, sources for Zayas's "dark poetics" in that second volume are not evident.

---

30 See Robert A. Folger, "From Lazarillo to 'otro Lazarillo': The Picaresque Novel in Golden Age Spain," Cacho Casal and Egan, *Routledge Hispanic Studies Companion*, pp. 291–304.
31 Edward Friedman, *The Antiheroine's Voice: Narrative Discourse and the Transformations of the Picaresque*, Columbia, 1987, pp. 121–39.
32 Emilia Pardo Bazán, "Introducción," pp. 12–15. See chapter 8: "Conclusion: Zayas's Afterlives."

Chapter Four

Turning the Tables on Men in *Exemplary Tales of Love*

In her "To the Reader," Zayas names the primary challenge she faced in publishing her novellas: simply to be taken seriously as a woman writer. Her "audacity" in doing so, she asserts, ought to be attributed to "virtuous daring" rather than madness. Another challenge was that of defending women vigorously without alienating male readers, who made up far and away the largest body of the literate public in her day. Zayas qualifies as fools those who think women are incapable, adding that "anyone ... [who is] no less than a good courtier, will neither find it a novelty nor gossip about it as idiocy" [Pero cualquiera, como sea no más de buen cortesano, ni lo tendrá por novedad ni lo murmurará por desatino].[1] In concluding the preface, she amplifies her demand for masculine courtesy:

> There is no rivalry with women; the one who fails to esteem them is a fool, because he needs them, and the one who insults them is an ingrate, for he lacks the respect due the hospitality that women gave men in their first journey. And so, then, you must not wish to be discourteous, idiotic, base, or ungrateful. I offer you this book very sure of your gallantry and confident that, should it displease you, you will be able to pardon me because I was born a woman, not with obligations to write good novellas but with a great desire to succeed in serving you. Farewell.
>
> [Con mujeres no hay competencias: quien no las estima es necio, ... con muchos deseos de acertar a servirte. Vale.][2]

---

[1] ETL, p. 47; *Novelas*, p. 159.
[2] ETL, "To the Reader," p. 51; *Novelas*, p. 161. The "first journey" is pregnancy.

I imagine Zayas standing tall to deliver this straightforward demand, reminding men that they are all born of women and are obliged both by human biology and by codes of gentlemanly conduct to respect them. And then softening her sermon with a graceful closing curtsey to her audience.

In her first volume, the *Novelas*, Zayas performs a balancing act, alternating fictional lessons and exhortations to women with others to men. She does so by switching between female and male narrators, having some of them preface their tales with warnings to members of their own gender. In N. 2, "Everything Ventured," Matilde, the narrator, introduces her tale saying she will follow Lisarda's example in ETL 1. Where Lisarda gave tribute to women's constancy in love, Matilde will tell "how we women are obliged not to let ourselves be deceived by men's trickery. Foolishly and without thinking, we fall into their snares, when we should be learning how to avenge ourselves, since honor stained can be cleansed only with the blood of the offender" [a lo que estamos obligadas, que es a no dejarnos ... mancha del honor sólo con sangre del que le ofendió sale].[3] That is precisely what the heroine of Matilde's tale, Aminta, does, avenging her seduction and abandonment by killing her seducer Jacinto and his lover, Flora, with her own hands.

After the first two stories narrated by women, Zayas has men narrate the next two, and continues this alternation: ETL 5 and 6 are narrated by women, 7, 8 and 9 by men, and 10 by a woman. Don Álvaro narrates N. 3, Zayas's version of Cervantes's novella "The Deceitful Marriage," which she entitles "El castigo de la miseria" (The Miser's Reward). Don Álvaro makes no reference to women in his warning preface; rather, he cautions men against miserliness: "Avarice is the most pernicious vice a man can have. When a man is greedy then he's foolish, boorish, irritating, and hateful to everyone" [Es la miseria la más perniciosa costumbre que se puede hallar en un hombre, pues en siendo miserable, luego es necio, enfadoso y cansado, y tan aborrecible a todos].[4] But the theme of deception of the first two stories continues, in the deceitful marriage into which the protagonist is lured by his avarice. Except for the deceitful marriage, Zayas rewrote Cervantes's novella almost completely. In Cervantes's collection, it serves as a kind of preface or frame for the following tale, the "Colloquy of the Dogs," a tale the male protagonist of the double deceit says he overheard recounted by two miraculously talking dogs while he was in a hospital being treated for syphilis, caught from the woman he married.

---

3 *Enchantments*, pp. 45–6; *Novelas*, p. 212.
4 *Enchantments*, p. 79; *Novelas*, p. 251.

Zayas keeps only the core point of the greed-based marriage, adding her own twist by replacing the dogs with a cat.

Zayas, in fact, gives us two versions of this story. Or one, with a confusing opening paragraph and a significantly rewritten ending. The protagonist is Marcos – or don Marcos, as Zayas calls him consistently, awarding him the honorific due the nobility although he is only twelve years old when she introduces him. She makes him an *hidalgo* (gentleman), the lowest noble rank, giving him this title despite his poverty and miserly nature. Through don Álvaro's narration, she later deploys a sarcastic retraction of that honorific, one the Boyer translation skips, presumably because the joke in it doesn't work in English.

The opening confusion has to do with how Marcos came to migrate from somewhere in Navarre to Madrid, with or without his father, and which parent died twelve years before. The tangle shows, as readers of the Spanish original can appreciate, the challenge Zayas's looping sentence structure presents to translators. The sentence in italics is omitted in the second, corrected edition of the *Novelas* and in the Boyer translation:

> A gentleman from Navarre came to serve a grandee at court, a man (*un hidalgo*) of lofty aspirations, but humble earthly possessions, for stepmother Fortune had endowed him with the single possession of a meager bed on which this young man, whom we will call don Marcos, and an old father went to sleep at night and sat on *to eat*, a father so old that his many years provided the income to sustain them, because his age softened even the hardest hearts: *he was a beggar so old that even the hardest hearts had pity on him and gave them alms*. Don Marcos was twelve years old when he came to this honorable pastime and earned the position of page in a princely house, almost the same number of years having passed since he lost his father *(mother)* from a sudden pain in the side.

> [A servir a un grande de esta Corte vino de un lugar de Navarra un hidalgo, … era mendigo tan viejo que hasta los más empedernidos le tenían lástima y daban limosna. Era … mereció en casa de este príncipe la plaza de paje.][5]

I do not think the initial confusion affects the meaning of the tale in this case, although the loss of a mother, which is what Zayas originally wrote, has clear repercussions for Zayas's heroines. The alternate ending, however, does impact the message the story transmits, as we will see.

---

5 *Novelas*, p. 253; my translation, modifying that of *Enchantments*, p. 80.

If don Álvaro's opening description creates some sympathy for the twelve-year-old Marcos, he quickly dispels it. As a page in that princely house, he tells us that Marcos becomes expert in the picaresque habits of pages: knavery, squalor and miserliness. He particularly excels in the last of these practices. "He willfully condemned himself to a penury more extreme than any hermit would endure," saving almost all the coppers he earned "at the expense of his own stomach and his companions' meals" [Condenándose él mismo de su voluntad a la mayor laceria que pudo padecer un padre del yermo … a costa de su estómago y de la comida de sus compañeros].[6] Zayas has don Álvaro employ the type of humor that Spanish picaresque authors like the anonymous creator of *Lazarillo de Tormes* and Mateo Alemán employ to describe the social conditions and arrangements that turn adolescents into rogues, but don Álvaro has Marcos consciously turn those practices against himself. On occasion, the narrator even adopts the kind of dehumanizing humor wielded by Francisco de Quevedo in the *Buscón*: "Don Marcos was of medium height, and with his parsimonious eating habit, he turned from a man into a stalk of asparagus" [Era don Marcos de mediana estatura, y con la sutileza de la comida se vino a transformar de hombre en espárrago]. One of these jibes is evidence of the difficulty of translating humor. His master eventually promotes Marcos from the position of page to "gentilhombre." The early eighteenth-century *Diccionario de autoridades* defines "gentilhombre" as "the subject who is noble by birth" as well as a designation of various positions of service to the king. Zayas has don Álvaro comment that "don Marcos came to merit passing from page to *gentilhombre*, his master thereby making of him what heaven did not" [Vino a merecer don Marcos pasar de paje a gentilhombre, hacienda en esto su amo en él lo que no hizo el cielo], i.e., a gentleman.[7]

As an adult, earning considerably more and having his own house, Marcos only "knotted his purse more tightly," don Álvaro tells us. He had light in his house only if he found a candle stub the butler had overlooked, and even when he had one, he would undress just inside the door so as to snuff out the candle as soon as he got to his room. When he hired a servant, he gave him just a mat to sleep on and two coppers for food, or he just hired an errand boy to empty the recycled honey jar he used in lieu of a chamber pot. He ate only cheap bread and cheese except on holidays,

---

6 *Enchantments*, p. 80; *Novelas*, p. 253.
7 *Novelas*, p. 254; my translations. *Diccionario de autoridades*, facsimile ed., Real Academia Española, 3 vols., Madrid, 1979.

but when he found his fellow servants eating, he would praise the wonderful aroma of the stew they were eating, then help himself to a chunk from each of their plates. Nor do these tricks exhaust the methods for sponging that Álvaro relates, which earned Marcos the reputation throughout Madrid "as the world's most temperate man. He was also chaste for, as he was wont to say, no woman is beautiful if she costs money and no woman is ugly if she's free" [ya era conocido en toda la Corte ... y en siendo en balde no la hay fea].[8]

By the time he was thirty years old, Marcos was considered a rich man, because with his penny-pinching ways, he had managed to save six thousand ducats. He was offered various opportunities to marry but he avoided them, fearing a bad outcome. Finally, though, the cunning male marriage broker Gamarra proposed he marry doña Isidora, "a lady who, although she'd never married, was considered a widow. A woman of good taste who, while a little older, disguised her age with artful makeup and dress" [una señora que no había sido casada, ... con las galas, adornos e industria].[9] Marcos was told her wealth was more than fourteen thousand or fifteen thousand ducats, and Isidora said that her late consort had been one of the finest gentlemen of Seville. Our narrator then tells us that Isidora had promised Gamarra a good reward if he could arrange the match.

Wasting no time, Gamarra arranges for Marcos to visit Isidora's house that very afternoon. Astonished at its many beautifully furnished rooms, "he thought it looked more like the house of a titled noble than an everyday house" [que más parecía una casa de una señora de título que de particular].[10] Isidora has two good looking maidservants, Marcela and Inés, and serves Marcos a rich meal, shown off on handsome china and table linens. While Marcela plays a guitar and sings, Isidora and Inés serve the repast to Marcos and to a handsome young man, Agustín, whom she introduces as her nephew. As Marcos fills his stomach, so little accustomed to such sustenance, he pays no mind to her attentions to Agustín. Walking back home after supper and more entertainment, more enamored of her wealth than of Isidora, he even tells Gamarra that if he and Isidora should not have children, he would be content with Agustín if the young man respects him as his father. Any reader of Zayas's era or ours, of course, needs no other ironic clues to Marcos's innocence to know what will transpire. No summary does justice to all the comic notes in this tale. But

---

8 *Enchantments*, p. 82; *Novelas*, pp. 255–6.
9 Zayas, *Enchantments*, pp. 82–3; *Novelas*, p. 256.
10 Zayas, *Enchantments*, p. 83; *Novelas*, p. 257.

when Marcos is invited back the next day to dine and sign the marital papers, Álvaro recounts one particularly humorous exchange. After dinner, Isidora suggests a card game called *jugar al hombre* (to play the man). Missing the wordplay, Marcos rejects it as a threat to his money, saying,

> not only did he not know how to "play the man," but he didn't know a single card, and he truly found on his account that not knowing how to play saved him many ducats a year.

> "Well don Marcos," said doña Isidora, "is so virtuous that he doesn't know how to play, although I keep telling Agustinico that it is what is best for one's soul and pocketbook."

> [pues no tan solamente no sabía jugar al hombre, ... mejor al alma y a la hacienda.]¹¹

With this exchange, Zayas has don Álvaro impugn Marcos's virility; she is also laughing at his innocence and miserliness. In a society in which generosity and virility as well as control of the women in one's care was expected of noblemen, it's an excellent strategy for Zayas to set her critique in the fictional voice of an aristocratic male narrator.

On Marcos and Isidora's wedding night, she puts a supposedly ailing Agustín to bed with loving care while Marcos locks the doors and windows, distressing the maids who are used to late night flirtations and lucrative partying. Inés goes to console Agustín and Marcela runs away through a back gate to keep a date, taking the wedding finery Marcos bought for Isidora with her, as well as a valuable gold chain. The following morning, Inés's screams wake up Marcos, who finds himself in bed with "a phantom, a deathly ghost" [un fantasma, o imagen de la muerte],¹² seeing that Isidora's wrinkled face without makeup is closer to that of a woman of fifty-five than the thirty-six years she'd noted in her dowry papers. Her hairpieces are lost in the bedcovers and her false teeth too, except those caught in his mustache. Dressing and reapplying her makeup, she looks again like the woman he thought he was marrying. But then two servants of the Lord Admiral arrive telling Isidora to return all the silver service and china she had borrowed. Some days later, the owner of her borrowed furniture and the landlord arrive to evict them from the flat Marcos thought she owned. While Marcos is contracting a cheap

---

11 *Novelas*, p. 266; my translation.
12 Zayas, *Enchantments*, p. 100; *Novelas*, p. 288.

apartment, Isidora, Agustín and Inés abscond with all his belongings and savings and leave for Barcelona.

As a despairing, impoverished and indebted Marcos walks toward his master's house he encounters Marcela, who persuades him that Isidora arranged all his misfortunes, but that she knows a magician who could help him learn where Isidora has gone with his money and belongings. The "magician" is in fact Marcela's boyfriend, who says that for the right price he can summon a devil to reveal their whereabouts. His magic consists of training a cat with torture and launching it with its fur aflame through a tiny window so that it lands, screeching and clawing, on Marcos's head. The racket made by the yowling cat and the screams of a terrified Marcos draw neighbors and a constable, who find Marcos in a dead faint and hold Marcela and the "magician" in custody until Marcos revives the following day. When the enchanter reveals the details of his "magic" and the police locate the dead cat, the case is dismissed with a warning to Marcos not to be so gullible. Mortified, he goes home to find a letter from "Doña Isidora the Vengeful" to "Mister Miser Marcos" saying he deserved his punishment for his miserly mistreatment of his own body and others. She offers to return to live with him if he saves up another six thousand ducats. The letter makes Marcos so angry that he falls ill from a high fever.

When Marcos recovers, he encounters a man he recognizes as the marriage broker, Gamarra. Gamarra sympathizes with Marcos and says he is going to hang himself rather than face execution for gambling with jewels entrusted to him by his employer, the Duke of Osuna. A man overhears their conversation and seeing two nooses rigged up in a tree, goes running to alert the mayor. They find don Marcos hung with one noose, the other hanging empty. When the Duke of Osuna says he knows nothing of a Gamarra or such jewels, they conclude that the second man must have been the devil whose lies drove Marcos to despair. Marcos's master arranged the funeral and, the narrator adds, "He got permission for him to be buried in holy ground, giving as excuse that his despair had driven him crazy. Such is the vanity of the world that it honors the body of a man even though the poor wretch's soul was probably burning in hell" [Dieron de todo cuenta a su amo de don Marcos, ... el alma esté donde la de este miserable].[13] That is how the story ends in the first version.

A second version of this novella appeared in a second edition published the same year as the first, 1637, bearing the added subtitle "Newly Corrected and Amended by Their Author." That second version was

---

13 Zayas, *Enchantments*, p. 112; *Novelas*, pp. 289–90, n. 56.

republished twice in 1638 and appears in virtually all subsequent editions in Spanish. Although Boyer bases the rest of her translation on the second, corrected edition, she chose to use the first ending of this story. In the second version, Marcos dies "miserably" [miserablemente] from the fever provoked by the shock of Isidora's letter – the adjective "miserably" serving to mark both his suffering and his miserly nature.

Why would Zayas have made this change? I leave that larger question for chapter 7. With apologies to cat-lovers, I turn instead to what I see as the reason for her use of the punishment visited on Marcos by a tortured cat. I see it as a clever and suggestive element of her rewriting of Cervantes's novella "El casamiento engañoso," and of an episode in *Don Quixote*, Part II, chapters 44 and 46.

In "El casamiento," the supernatural element is its narration in a hospital by two dogs marvelously gifted with speech, albeit a marvel whose veracity Cervantes hedges about with doubts. The centuries-long relationship of interdependence between humans and dogs is encapsulated in the common saying "a dog is man's best friend" (a universalizing use of the masculine gender as dog-loving women know). Cats, however, have long been associated both with magic and with women. Analyzing the cultural context of the assassination of a Parisian printer's wife's beloved cat in the 1730s in *The Great Cat Massacre*, historian Robert Darnton illustrates the fascination that cats have had for men over the centuries, from ancient Egypt to modernity. Darnton and students of that fascination attribute it to the animals' mysterious bearing and inscrutability, which invites the human imagination to attribute magic qualities to them. The use of a cat in the magic séance may seem bizarre to a contemporary reader, but for Marcos it would have been predictable, as since the tenth century cats had regularly been associated with witchcraft. Hundreds were burned as witches in disguise; in the fourteenth and fifteenth centuries, the Inquisition prosecuted owners of cats, and by the end of the fifteenth, the devil was often painted as a cat.[14] Darnton provides horrific details of how their demonic character was imagined:

> Witches transformed themselves into cats in order to cast spells on their victims. Sometimes, especially on Mardi Gras, they gathered for hideous sabbaths at night. They howled, fought, and copulated horribly under the direction of the devil himself in the form of a huge tomcat. To protect yourself from sorcery by cats there was one, classic remedy:

---

14 Seymour Menton, "El gato emblemático," *La Gaceta* (Fondo de Cultura Económica) no. 232, p. 37; Robert Darnton, *The Great Cat Massacre and Other Episodes in French Cultural History*, New York, 1984, pp. 93–4.

maim it. Cut its tail, clip its ears, smash one of its legs, tear or burn its fur, and you would break its malevolent power.

Apart from the context of witchcraft, cats have also been intimately associated with female sexuality. Although the sexual double meaning that "pussy" has in English does not exist in Spanish, the association of women and cats in sexual contexts certainly does. Lope de Vega, who said that a generic characteristic of women is having the soul of a cat, wrote a mock-heroic epic, *La gatomaquia,* on the ill-fated love of a poor Roman cat for a beautiful feline who abandons him for a rich rival tomcat.

Cervantes plays on the association of cats with magic and female sexuality in the *Don Quixote* episode. While the old knight is a guest at the Duke and Duchess's country estate, in one of the tricks played on him, Altisidora, a mischievous serving maiden to the Duchess, pretends to be in love with Don Quixote and woos him with a ballad she sings by his bedroom window. The next night, as he sings his response declaring his fidelity to his beloved Dulcinea of Toboso, Altisidora and her accomplices empty out by his window a sack full of cowbells and cats with bells tied to their tails. One terrified cat jumps through Don Quixote's window, leaps at his face, and sinks his claws and teeth into the old knight's nose. Hearing the racket, the Duke opens the door to find Don Quixote struggling to remove the cat, which he calls a demon, a wizard and enchanter. The Duke manages to uproot the "demon" and Altisidora bandages his wounds, whispering to him that his hardness of heart is the cause of his misfortunes. Don Quixote is confined to bed for five days in cat-inflicted suffering, though it is still considerably less severe than that which Zayas's narrator Álvaro inflicts on Marcos for his ill-considered marriage to Isidora.

In giving Doña Isidora a name etymologically similar to that of Altisidora, Zayas creates a first link between the two women. As Henry Sullivan points out, there was a sizeable family of women's names ending in *-dora,* derived from the Greek noun *doron,* meaning gift. Sullivan posits that Cervantes's invention of the name "Altisidora," or "Gifts of the Most High" is not just a cruel joke like those she visited on Don Quixote, but in fact the cat attack that thrust "pussy" literally into his face and Altisidora's final revelation that she never loved him helped cure him of the madness of his self-induced infatuation for his imagined beloved Dulcinea.[15]

---

15 Henry W. Sullivan, *Grotesque Purgatory: A Study of Cervantes's Don Quixote, Part II,* University Park, 1996, pp. 146–9.

Zayas's baptism of Isidora, however, is unquestionably ironic. She is quite the opposite of the fourth-century Christian nun and Saint Isidora, an early "fool for Christ"; nor does she display any of the healing attributes of the ancient Egyptian goddess Isis. From the outset of their marriage, when Marcos finds her false teeth in his mustache and the wedding finery and his gold chain gone, it is clear that Marcos's -dora is a gift that takes and keeps on taking. Álvaro, the male narrator of her tale, does not leave this deceitful female fortune hunter unpunished, however. After she absconds with miserly Marcos's money, she loses it in turn to her young lover Agustín and his lover Inés, who becomes a courtesan in Naples to support him while Isidora is reduced to begging in Madrid.[16]

The table-turning tale that follows Isidora's, ETL 4, "Forewarned but Fooled," is fatal only to the honor and the self-respect of its protagonist, Fadrique, and to one scarcely mentioned husband. The narrator, don Alonso, introduces it by saying,

> Illustrious audience, it usually happens that the most anxious, the most compulsive person falls exactly into the trap he fears most, as you shall see in my enchantment. A man shouldn't rely solely on his own judgment, let alone dare to test a woman. He should watch out for himself and take each woman for herself and accept her as she is. In the final analysis, an intelligent woman is no dish for a foolish man, nor is a foolish woman right for an intelligent man, and as proof of this, I shall tell my tale.
>
> [Ya suele suceder, auditorio ilustre, a los más avisados ... caer en lo misi̵mo que temen, ... y para certificación de esto digo así:][17]

Fadrique is a wealthy young nobleman from Granada, whose parents have died. He is schooled by a succession of women, the first being Serafina, whom he courts with little success because she loves another, less-wealthy suitor, Vicente. She falls into melancholy as Vicente's attentions cease and Fadrique presses his suit, regaling her maids and singing a sonnet to her one night when she appears on her balcony. Although the listeners praise his grace and skill, the sonnet that repeats "eyes" twelve times in as many lines strikes me as intended for comic effect, or an ironic reflection

---

16 See Anne J. Cruz, "María de Zayas and Miguel de Cervantes: A Deceitful Marriage," *Tradition and Innovation in Early Modern Spanish Studies: Essays in Memory of Carroll B. Johnson*, ed. Sherry Velasco, Newark, 2008, pp. 89–106. Cruz considers Inés and Marcela the heroines of Zayas's version.

17 Zayas, *Enchantments*, p. 114; *Novelas*, p. 293.

on his blindness to her pregnancy. Fadrique asks her parents' permission to marry her, to which they agree happily, and Serafina agrees as well, once she recovers from her melancholy. Late one night several months later, Fadrique sees her emerge from her house and go to an outbuilding where she gives birth to a baby and leaves it on the ground. Fadrique rescues the baby girl, names her Gracia and gives her into a relative's care, with instructions to place her in a convent after three years, so she will be raised without corrupting contact with the world. He sends Serafina a mysterious sonnet saying he has been undeceived and leaves for Seville. Unable to discover what happened to her baby, Serafina enters a convent where her penitence earns her the reputation of a saint.

Fadrique arrives in Seville insulting all women without exception, declaring that he would not trust them, and especially a clever one, because being clever they were given to being mischievous and licentious and deceived men with their shrewdness.

> For a woman should not know more than how to do her needlework and pray, govern her household and raise her children; and everything else was prattling and subtleties that served for nothing but to get them lost more quickly.
>
> [El decía que no había de fiar de ellas, ... una mujer no había de saber más de hacer su labor y rezar, gobernar su casa y criar sus hijos; y lo demás eran bachillerías y sutilezas que no servían sino de perderse más presto.][18]

He repeats that creed with variations after each lesson but the last. But the sight of a lovely young, rich widow, Beatriz, undermines his resolve. A colleague arranges an introduction to talk of marriage with her. She is interested but tells him she promised not to remarry for three years after her husband's death, but if he waits the remaining year, she will not accept another of her suitors in the meantime. He spends six months waiting patiently, seeing her some evenings on her balcony and serenading her when she appears. Then one night he finds the door of the house open and enters cautiously. She is melancholy, but one of her maids coaxes her into playing the harp and singing, as Fadrique watches and listens, unobserved. When she retires to her bedroom, he cannot leave because the coachman has closed the house, so he sits down to wait until morning. Two hours later, he is amazed to see her emerge beautifully attired and carrying a candle, and food and drink on a silver tray. Following her into

---

18 ETL, pp. 107, slightly modified; *Novelas*, pp. 300–301.

the stable, he sees her go to serve it to an ugly black man who is clearly on his deathbed. He pushes away her caresses, saying,

> What do you want of me, madam? Leave me now, for God's sake! What is this, that even as my life is ending you pursue me? Is it not enough that your dissolute nature has me as I am, but that you want me, when I am at the end of my life, to come to carry out your depraved appetites? Get married, madam, get married, and leave me now, for I neither want to see you nor eat what you give me; I want to die, for now I am in no condition for anything else.
>
> [¿Qué me quieres, señora? ¡Déjame ya, por Dios! ¿Qué es esto, que aun estando yo acabando la vida me persigues? ... no estoy para otra cosa.][19]

Fadrique flees the house in the morning and in the afternoon, sees the black man brought out to be buried. A few days later, a maid brings him a note from Beatriz offering to marry him with no further delay, which he answers suggesting that she mourn her "ill-fated black man" [su negro mal logrado] at least another year.[20] Beatriz then marries another suitor.

Fadrique goes to Madrid, where he and his cousin Juan will court Ana and her cousin Violante. Both Juan and Ana are fettered by engagement to cousins: Juan to a ten-year-old girl whom he is to marry when she is of age, and Ana to a cousin in the Indies. (The significance of these cousin relationships is discussed in chapter 6.) These ties do not seriously inhibit their appetite for romance and sexual adventures. In one small gesture to propriety, Juan says that his and Ana's "honest love" has not gone beyond "chaste conversation, reserving the prize of it for when her betrothed returns," when they will be able to enjoy more "amorous mischief" [honesta conversación, reservando el premio de él para cuando venga su esposo].[21] Juan shows Fadrique a long poem Ana has written him, praising her intelligence as well as her beauty. When Fadrique repeats his rejection of clever women, Juan disagrees vehemently:

> "You can't really mean that!" don Juan exclaimed. "I can't imagine any man wanting a foolish woman to talk with for fifteen minutes let alone to love! Why, the most famous philosophers in the world say that knowledge is food for the soul; then, so long as eyes feed on white skin, graceful hands, lovely eyes, a striking figure, in short, on beauty that's worthy of being loved in a woman, it's not right that the soul's desire

---

19 ETL, p. 117; Novelas, p. 310.
20 ETL, p. 118; Novelas, p. 312.
21 ETL, p. 119; Novelas, p. 313.

should be denied or should have to feed itself only on nonsensical boring dullness! Since the soul is pure, we should not nourish it with unrefined food."

"¿Lo decís de veras? – dijo don Juan –, porque no sé qué hombre apetece una mujer necia, ... siendo alma tan pura criatura, no la hemos de dar manjares groseros."]²²

Juan is speaking of Ana, but also of Ana's cousin Violante, referring to the two cousins as the "sibyls of Madrid." Despite Juan's warning that Violante is not dumb either, Fadrique goes to visit the cousins and finds the elegantly attired Violante, who was having her portrait painted, even more beautiful than Serafina or Beatriz, whom he has quickly forgotten. In short order, he was so enamoured that he wanted to marry Violante, but she never mentioned marriage because she didn't want to lose her freedom. Doña Ana's fiancé returns from the Indies and they are married. He keeps the house tightly closed, which puts a halt to visits with the cousins and strains Juan and Fadrique's patience. They stroll the cousins' street repeatedly but catch no sight of them, although they do see Ana's husband accompanied by his brother, a handsome young student. Juan then manages early one Sunday morning to give a note to a servant during Mass. The servant brings back an answer saying the husband is very jealous, but that he will travel to Valladolid the following week; some days later, Juan sees Ana enter a chapel and manages to whisper to her. She says the only chance to see her would be that night, if Fadrique comes with him to take her place in bed next to her husband. Fadrique argues long against such a risky scheme but finally agrees.

Zayas, through her male narrator, relates with abundant comic detail the hair-raising night Fadrique passes in darkness fending off the "husband," only to learn the next morning that he had been in bed with Violante, as she and Ana laugh at his terror. After this mortifying start, Fadrique carries on an affair with Violante for several months until her interest in him wanes. One night when she had thought he was ill, he arrives to find the young student brother about to get in bed with Violante. Unarmed, the student grabs a shoe and pretends it is a pistol with which to shoot Fadrique. Violante laughs at the trick of the shoe, and an offended Fadrique turns his fury on her, beats her badly, and leaves.

Fadrique's reaction to Violante's laughter illustrates just what Zayas aims at with this table-turning story: that is, to criticize male emotional

---

22 *Enchantments*, p. 124; *Novelas*, p. 318.

fragility and its consequences for women. Understanding that men despise being laughed at, she exposes Fadrique's emotional fragility through his violent overreaction to Violante's laughter at the "trick of the shoe." We can also understand why she gives these stories to male narrators. She exposes these men's foibles with humor but does so through the voices of male narrators. This way she relates them as stories one man tells on another foolish man, to lessen the sting for male hearers and readers.

Narrator don Alonso then summarizes Fadrique's experiences in Naples: where various things happened that confirmed his opinion that intelligent women destroyed men's reputations with their cunning. At his next stop, Rome, Fadrique's love life causes one husband's death. Just who killed the man, however, is hidden by the imprecision of the third-person singular Spanish possessive pronoun "su," which is used to mean "his," "her" or "your (formal)." Boyer reads the passage as "He had an affair with a woman who one night, for his sake, murdered her own husband, stuffed him in a sack, carried him on her back down to the river, and dumped him in." Greer and Rhodes make Fadrique both killer and porter: "He had a friendship with another [woman], for whose cause he killed her husband one night and carried him, in a sack on his back, to throw him in the river" [donde tuvo amistad con otra, que por su causa mató a su marido una noche y le llevó a cuestas en un costal a echarles en el río].[23] Either translation is possible, depending on how one imagines the size of the ill-fated husband and his wife's strength. In either case, don Alonso tells us that after sixteen years of travel, and finding himself short of cash, Fadrique returns to Spain, disembarking in Barcelona where he buys a mule to take him to Granada.

Fadrique has a penultimate adventure on the way home, however. A lovely Valencian duchess sees him and admires his gallant figure; her husband is out for a day of hunting. She invites him in, hears him recount all his adventures and his bad view of discerning women. She refutes it and invites him into her bedroom where they dine and "play a bit" until nightfall, when the maid tells them the duke is coming up the stairs. The duchess hides him in a wardrobe, has a leisurely supper with her husband and, to play a trick on Fadrique, asks her husband to write down everything made of iron, betting him 100 gold *escudos* he will forget something. When he has made his list, she notes his omission and then tells him about her day with the man from Granada, whom she now has in the wardrobe. The alarmed duke goes to fetch the wardrobe keys and she

---

23 *Enchantments*, p. 143; ETL, p. 134; *Novelas*, p. 329.

laughs and tells him that these are precisely the item made of iron he forgot. The duke admires her clever reminder and leaves the bedroom. She lets a terrified Fadrique out, gives him the money she won and more, then sends him on his way, yet more persuaded of the danger of clever women.

Back in Granada, he takes the lovely, perfectly simple Gracia out of the convent, hires equally dim maids, decks Gracia in jewels and finery and marries her, then tells her that as his wife she must don armor and guard his honor while he sleeps at night. After a week, he has to leave Granada on business. A gentleman from Córdoba sees Gracia on the balcony. With the help of a savvy neighbor woman, he persuades Gracia to give him entry and shows her a more pleasurable kind of married life. When Fadrique returns, she tells him she prefers the married life her other husband taught her. Fadrique realizes that something the duchess told him was right, "that discerning women know how to keep the laws of honor, and if sometimes they break them, they keep their error quiet" [que las mujeres discretas saben guardar las leyes del honor, y si alguna vez las rompen, callan su yerro].[24]

Concluding his tale, the narrator don Alonso repeats his initial warning: the most compulsive man falls into the very trap he feared. In this case, Fadrique has learned his lesson from a dim-witted woman. After living with Gracia for years, a resigned Fadrique dies and leaves his fortune to her on the condition that she become a nun in Serafina's convent. For Serafina, he leaves a letter telling her that Gracia is her daughter and so mother and daughter end their years happily, having spent Gracia's inheritance to build a larger convent.

When don Miguel occupies the narrator's seat for N. 7, he relates a more complicated tale of tables turned, in which blame and rewards are more evenly distributed between men and the desired and desiring woman at its center. Brief, discretely veiled remarks also extend part of the blame to the highest level of the patriarchal sociopolitical order that anchored Zayas's own identity. N. 7, "Al fin se paga todo," which Boyer translates as "Just Desserts," involves more bloodshed, and a feminine protagonist and internal narrator, Hipólita, who has a hand in it, literally and figuratively speaking. In the opening paragraph, narrator Miguel inserts an observation with political overtones cast in terms of familial ties. The story is set in Valladolid in the brief period, 1601–6, when Philip III's favorite, Francisco Gómez de Sandoval y Rojas, the Duke of Lerma, persuaded the king to move the capital to that city. Miguel introduces us

---

24 ETL, p. 143; Novelas, p. 340.

to Hipólita's rescuer, García, "a gentleman, one of the noblest sons of the city of Madrid, that widowed then by her beloved master's disdain and neglect, decided to send the king her dearest and noblest remaining sons to serve him and oblige him to love her as she loved him" [Madrid, que viuda entonces de su amado dueño, ... le había de obligar a que le pagase en amor el amor que le tenía].²⁵ We could read this as only a minor note of local pride voiced by Madrid-born Zayas against Lerma's moving the capital to his hometown. But she reinforces it later in the tale, as Hipólita begins her account to her rescuer, telling García,

> Then, as you know, the court moved to this city. Would that God had heeded all the cries, tears and complaints of those who rued this change but clamored out in vain. If the court hadn't come here, I would have been spared these misfortunes, for that was the cause of all my woes. Among the many parasites who follow the court, there was one whose name was don Gaspar, Portuguese in nationality, a soldier by profession, he hoped to receive his reward for the many services he had done the Spanish king in Flanders and elsewhere. For that reason, he followed all the people who followed all the chancellors or, more accurately, all the chaotic confusion that the court and all its sycophants really are.
>
> [En este tiempo se vino, como veis, la Corte a esta ciudad... . este caos de confusión, que tal es la Corte y los que la siguen.]²⁶

The move was one of many Lerma policies that served to enrich the royal favorite's coffers. Zayas does anticipate, in reverse, the feminist slogan "The personal is political," making the political personal by characterizing Madrid as a bereft widow and making her own misfortunes stem from the parasites who followed the court to Valladolid. As we will see in the following chapter, the analogy between the political and personal is clearer in the *Desengaños*, in which the last story is again set in the reign of Philip III and in which she baptizes one of the characters "Gaspar," the name she gives Hipólita's faithless Portuguese seducer in "Just Desserts."

Crossing the street late one icy December night, García sees Hipólita thrown out of a house in just her undergarments. When he goes to help and sees that the *bulto* (package) violently hurled out is a woman, beaten

---

25 My translation, modifying *Enchantments*, p. 215; *Novelas*, p. 413.
26 *Enchantments*, p. 219; *Novelas*, p. 418. On the move of the court to Valladolid, see Elliott, pp. 301–4, and for an opposing view, Antonio Feros, *El duque de Lerma: Realeza y privanza en la España de Felipe III*, Madrid, 2002, pp. 168–73, 459–63.

so badly she can barely stand with his help, she begs him to hide her until she can take refuge in a convent. She tells him that when she reached a marriageable age, her beauty and wealth drew many suitors. Her parents married her to Pedro, the elder of two brothers. His younger brother, Luis, continued to pursue her despite her efforts to discourage him. But after eight years of happy marriage to Pedro and after the court moves to Valladolid, the Portuguese soldier and court follower Gaspar saw her in church and began to pursue her. She responded in kind, having her maid carry messages to him. Hipólita tells García a string of sensual and comic mishaps that marked her attempts to meet Gaspar. One night when her husband has gone hunting, she takes her bed out into the garden to meet Gaspar, but her husband returns and joins her in the garden bed, so that Gaspar's only satisfaction is a kiss while her husband sleeps. Then she smuggles her would-be lover into the house, but it catches on fire; another time, Gaspar gets stuck trying to climb through a small window and has to flee, frame and all. In their final misadventure, her husband returns home quickly to "do his necessities" and she hides Gaspar in a trunk. Thinking he has suffocated she enlists her husband's brother, Luis, to remove him and the trunk. Gaspar revives, Luis threatens him, and he is cured of further interest in Hipólita.

But Luis, who lives in a house adjoining that of Pedro and Hipólita, has not given up his own pursuit of her, and after removing Gaspar, he becomes more insistent and daring. One night he lets out the horses so that Pedro has to get up to retrieve them. Then he sneaks through the attic into Hipólita's house and bed. She thinks Luis is her husband and they make love; then her husband returns with the same in mind and the next day at Mass Luis lets her know he has slept with her. Finding the passageway between the houses, she sneaks over the next night and kills Luis. She leaves the bloody knife in her house and flees to Gaspar's inn, taking her jewels and two thousand ducats with her. Gaspar beats her and calls her a whore, then throws her out on the street where García finds her.

Going to Hipólita's house the day after hearing her tale, García learns that Pedro has been arrested and charged with Luis's murder. García sees her safely installed in a convent, from which she writes the authorities to tell them that Pedro is innocent. He is released and begs her to return to live with him, but she refuses because she doesn't think he would trust her. The saddened Pedro dies a year later, leaving all his wealth to Hipólita. Sometime later, a highwayman confesses to having killed Gaspar on the route from Valladolid to Lisbon, while he was robbing him of the jewels and money Hipólita had brought him. García visits Hipólita frequently in the convent and they eventually marry and have children.

Concluding his narrative, Miguel tells his listeners that the events happened in "our times," that he learned of them from those to whom they happened. He adds that he wrote it to show that everyone should take care what he does, since "Al fin todo se paga," which Boyer renders as "just desserts," Miguel's conclusion and the story title. The justice delivered to all participants strikes me as less than perfect, particularly to Pedro, Hipólita's husband. Literally, that phrase means "Everything is paid for in the end," or perhaps "Things come home to roost," or "As you give, you receive." How might Zayas's phrase extend to her view of the familial politics of the time? Although Lerma would eventually see much of his property and wealth returned to the monarchy early in the reign of Philip IV and Olivares, I do not see a particularly anti-Lerma import in her story, which never mentions Lerma by name. I suggest rather that it reflects Zayas's loyalty to Madrid and its nobility, since the primary beneficiary along with Hipólita is the faithful Madrid noble, García. She writes of Hipólita's marriage to him that he thereby became "master of her beauty and her rich estate, which was all he lacked to be perfect, since although he had a moderate income, it was not enough to all that his nobility required" [haciéndole señor de su belleza y de su gruesa hacienda, ... que siendo tan noble era fuerza tuviese].[27]

Although Zayas tells us that the fictional audience gathered to hear Miguel's tale applauded it loudly and thanked him heartily, she may have been less than confident that her reading public would find the payback fairly distributed. Whether for that reason or a more general desire to please her masculine-dominant public, the following male-narrated tale, N. 8, "Triumph over the Impossible," is not a story of tables turned on a foolish or faithless man but one of a man whose devotion to his beloved Leonor and his prayer to a figure of Christ by her burial vault resurrect her from death to be his bride.

---

27 My translation; *Novelas*, p. 444.

Chapter Five

Bodies in Pain: *Tales of Disillusion*

ZAYAS'S SECOND VOLUME was published ten years after the first, in 1647, in a decade of disasters for Spain and its empire.[1] We see reflections of two of those disasters – the 1640 rebellions of Catalonia and Portugal – in the first and last stories of *Tales of Disillusion*. The Catalonian revolt ended in 1652, but that of Portugal only concluded with Spain's recognition of Portuguese independence in 1668. The mounting national mood of *desengaño* (disillusion) of the era surely fed the darkness and violence of the *Tales of Disillusion* as a whole. Calling the stories "disillusions," as they are labeled, is a decided understatement; not only are women disabused of hopes and illusions, but their bodies are tortured and broken by their husbands, brothers and fathers. Another difference is the absence of a "To the Reader" introduction in Zayas's explicitly authorial voice. Zayas does refer to "my entertaining soiree" in the first framing paragraph and announces that Lisis would not wed Diego on New Year's Day, as promised at the end of *Exemplary Tales of Love*. In the rest of this volume, however, she projects her intentions through Lisis, her alter ego.

The majority of the Disillusions seem to me a kind of authorial rewriting of the stories in her first volume, either in terms of narrative voice, tone and structure, or in significant motifs. Furthermore, they intertwine, as their heroines try different methods to defend their lives and

---

1   For a concise summary of the period, see Barton, pp. 137–9. On Zayas's approach and objective in this second volume, see Elizabeth Rhodes, *Dressed to Kill: Death and Meaning in Zayas's Desengaños*, Toronto, 2011. Although a literal translation of *desengaño* is "undeceiving," Greer and Rhodes preferred "disillusion" for reasons set forth in ETL, "Notes on the Translations," p. 42.

reputations, to no avail, making evident the box with no escape other than – for some survivors – retreat to a convent, in the fundamentally misogynist society in which Zayas depicts them.[2] I center my discussion here on D. 1, D. 5 and D. 10, the most clear rewritings of N. 1, N. 5 and N. 10, with brief comments on other stories in this volume.

Lisis, we are told, has suffered a relapse of the illness of the quartan fever (see chapter 3), a melancholy lovesickness she attributes to having agreed to the engagement with Diego to avenge herself on don Juan for preferring Lisarda. Recognizing that she does not desire Diego, she sinks into despair and renewed illness with serious relapses lasting over a year. She recovers when a beautiful, talented slave enters her household, the "Zelima" who entertains Lisis and will narrate D. 1, "Her Lover's Slave."

Lisis presides over the rescheduled soirée, declaring that she aspires to restore the reputation of women. She says that "since men are the ones who preside over everything, they never recount the bad deeds they do, but rather the ones done to them and ... there would be no bad women were there no bad men" [como son los hombre los que presiden ... lo cierto es que no hubiera malas mujeres si no hubiera malos hombres].[3] Switching to the first-person singular, Zayas has Lisis proclaim,

> I speak not to those [men] who are not this way, for just as the false, inconstant, fickle, and ill-reputed woman is not to be called a woman but rather a wild beast, so I reprehend not the sane, well-intentioned man who knows, in the midst of vice itself, how to take recourse in the virtue and nobility to which he is obliged, but rather I speak to those who, having forgotten their obligations, do otherwise than that which is just; such men will not be called men but monsters, ... the women of whom I will speak in this book are not of the common sort.... . – but rather of those undeserving of misfortunes.
>
> [Y como son los hombres los que presiden en todo, jamás cuentan los malos pagos que dan, sino los que les dan; ... las no merecedoras de desdichados sucesos.][4]

Lisis sets the rules for the second soirée: only women are to tell tales, all of which must be true cases, to be called tales of disillusion. While opting for exclusively female explicit narrators, however, as the declaration cited above illustrates, Zayas does continue to balance her presentation

---

2   Rhodes, *Dressed to Kill*, pp. 76–7, 90–1.
3   ETL, p. 200; *Desengaños*, p. 197.
4   ETL, p. 200; *Desengaños*, p. 197.

by including a few positive masculine characters. The ten tales are told over three nights, four stories each on the first two nights and two on the last night, which is planned to end with the new announcement of Lisis's engagement to don Diego. Zayas adds more discussion in the frame narrative than in the previous volume, and more disagreement between men and women follows half the tales, although Lisis always has the last word. In addition to the first and last tales, at least three others have political valences: D. 2, D. 4 and D. 7.

Disillusionment 1

Zayas gives Zelima/Isabel's story in D. 1, "Her Lover's Slave," the same autobiographical structure as Jacinta's in N. 1. Zelima reveals as she starts her story that her true name is Isabel Fajardo. She tears off the brand of slavery affixed to her face, saying that it is "but a shadow of the one that a man's ungratefulness put on my character" [estos hierros que veis en mi rostro no son sino sombras de los que ha puesto en mi calidad y fama la ingratitud de un hombre].[5] The brand was presumably made of papier-mâché, although Isabel had made it all but literal, having herself sold into slavery – twice. She relates her adventures and losses in multiple episodes to the frame-tale audience. She was born the only child to wealthy and loving parents in Murcia; her beauty and talents drew many suitors by the time she was fourteen, including one particularly devoted young noble, Felipe, whom she scarcely noted because he was too poor to ask for her hand. Then the political fortunes of the Spanish monarchy shape her story. As Isabel puts it, "the rebellion of Catalonia took place at this time, as a punishment for our sins, or for mine alone, for although those losses have been great, mine is the greater: those who died in this event earned eternal fame, and I, who remain alive, won disgraceful infamy." [Sucedió en este tiempo el levantamiento de Cataluña, para castigo de nuestros pecados, … que quedé viva, ignominiosa infamia].[6] That rebellion was the historical context of Zayas's participation in the poetic competition in Barcelona in 1643, and the publication of the *Desengaños*.

5   ETL, p. 207; *Desengaños*, p. 207. On the branding, see ETL, pp. 198–9, n. 4, and p. 207, n. 1.
6   ETL, p. 209; *Desengaños*, pp. 209–10. On the rebellion, see John H. Elliott, *The Count-Duke of Olivares: The Statesman in an Age of Decline*, New Haven, 1986, pp. 565–639; and Don W. Cruickshank, *Don Pedro Calderón*, Cambridge, 2009, pp. 237–70.

The rebellion, an attempt to annex Catalonia to France, was the result of conflicts between Catalonian natives and Spanish troops that the Duke of Olivares dispatched there during Spain's war with France; it was not resolved until 1652, with surrender to the Spanish king. Isabel's father answers the monarch's call for noblemen to serve in "those civil wars" [estas civiles guerras], taking his wife and daughter with him to Zaragoza, in Aragon. Thus, while repeating the autobiographical narrative of N. 1, Zayas rewrites the protagonist's family structure, giving her a living mother and a father who tries to balance pleasing his wife and daughter with the military service expected of the nobility.

The political nature of the "civil war" in the Spanish monarchy turns disastrously personal for Isabel. Lodged in rooms in the house of a moderately wealthy Zaragoza widow, Isabel says, "the fire was inside my house, since my misfortune had seen me without my even going out" [Dentro en mi casa estaba el incendio, pues sin salir me había ya visto mi desventura].[7] The widow's son Manuel takes advantage of Isabel's friendship with the widow's daughter, Eufrasia. Manuel courts Isabel with song, a pleading love letter, and illness brought on by her resistance, but he does not ask her father for her hand. Isabel intersperses her tale of woe with frequent warnings to weak, naïve or desiring women who might believe men's deceits, and passionate condemnations of masculine wiles, such as:

> Oh, deceitful lover, oh, false gentleman, oh, executioner of my innocence! and oh, weak and ill-advised ladies, who let yourselves be won over by well-dressed lies, whose gilding endures no longer than appetite! .... Now, now do I see this, at my own expense, this fact that you carry no other banner than to pursue our innocence, affront our understanding, knock down our fortress, and, rendering us vile and common, exalt yourselves with the empire of immortal fame. Let ladies open the eyes of their understanding and not let themselves be won over by the one from whom they can fear the payback that I got.
>
> [¡Ay, engañoso amante, ay, falso caballero, ay, verdugo de mi Inocencia! ¡Ay, mujeres fáciles y mal aconsejadas ... no se dejen vencer de quien pueden temer el mal pago que a mi se me dio.][8]

One afternoon when Isabel is going to Eufrasia's room, Manuel stops her, pulls her inside his room and rapes her. Isabel does not explicitly call it rape, but it is clear in the double meaning of the Spanish phrase

---

7   ETL, pp. 209–10; *Desengaños*, p. 210.
8   ETL, pp. 215–16; *Desengaños*, p. 218.

she uses, "me entró dentro," which can mean both "he drew me into his room" and "he entered me." She says she does not know what happened because she fainted. Early Modern literary heroines conventionally faint as they are about to be raped because consciousness might imply participation in the act and therefore guilt.[9] When she recovers consciousness, Isabel tries to kill Manuel with his sword, but he calms her down with a promise to marry her, as he was required to do under Spanish civil and canon law. But he continues to postpone it, instead renewing a previous relationship with the married Alejandra.

Isabel's history then takes on characteristics of a Greek romance, minus the happy ending of lovers reunited. Manuel secures a position as chamberlain with the Lord Admiral of Castile, who is to be viceroy of Sicily, and departs secretly. But Felipe, who has followed Isabel to Zaragoza and is serving in her household under the name of Luis, finds out Manuel's plans and tells her where he has gone. Like Jacinta in N. 1, Isabel takes jewels and money and leaves home to follow Manuel and persuade him to marry her. On the road, she learns from a former servant, Octavio, whose help she has sought, that her father has died from the shock of her disappearance. Dressing herself as a Moorish slave, she has Octavio sell her to the Lord Admiral's chief steward. On an outing to a nearby island, Manuel, Isabel and Felipe are kidnapped and taken to Algeria, where their captor gives them to his daughter, Zaida. Zaida loves Isabel, falls passionately in love with Manuel, and arranges to take all of them back to Spain, where she intends to be baptized as a Christian. They arrive in Zaragoza six years after Isabel left. She presses Manuel to keep his promise to marry her, but he treats it almost as a joke. He never meant to keep that promise, he tells her, and she has demeaned herself chasing after him; he will marry Zaida instead. Isabel considers her branding as a slave a sign of her damaged reputation, worked by Manuel's rape and refusal to marry her, but Manuel scorns the brand and her Muslim dress as a self-administered lowering of her noble status.[10]

---

9   On the presentation and implications of rape in Zayas and Early Modern Spanish literature, see Stacey L. Parker Aronson, "Monstrous Metamorphoses and Rape in María de Zayas," *Revista Canadiense de Estudios Hispánicos* 29.3, 2005, pp. 525–47, and Marcia Welles, *Persephone's Girdle. Narratives of Rape in Seventeenth-Century Spanish Literature*, Nashville, 2000.
10 Rhodes, *Dressed to Kill*, pp. 28–9. See also Renato Barahona, *Sex Crimes, Honour, and the Law in Early Modern Spain: Vizcaya, 1528–1735*, Toronto, 2003; Scott K. Taylor, *Honor and Violence in Golden Age Spain*, New Haven, 2008.

Neither Isabel nor Manuel initiates the final episode of D. 1, however; faithful Felipe does that, stabbing Manuel to death as he proclaims that he has avenged Manuel's offense, exclaiming "Oh, false and evil gentleman! And this is the fashion in which you repay the commitment and goodness you owe an angel?" [¡Oh falso y mal caballero! ¿Y de esta suyerte pagas las obligaciones y finezas que debes a un ángel?][11] Felipe flees, vowing to look for her if he escapes, but Zayas never brings him back. In a rough parallel to the role of Fabio in N. 1, we see him at the outset of the tale and near its inconclusive ending, balancing the negative role of Manuel with his devotion. Isabel finds Octavio and persuades him to accompany her to Valencia, where she has Octavio sell her as a slave again, this time to Lisis's uncle. When the uncle pursues her, his wife sends her to Lisis in Madrid – and this is how "Zelima" comes to tell the first of the Disillusionments. Concluding her story, Isabel tells Lisis that she wishes to join a convent as did Jacinta in N. 1. There she will again be a slave, but only to God. She offers herself to him with the same title as her tale, "Her Lover's Slave."

Zayas extends her narrative of rape, revenge, rebellion and convent refuge through D. 2, "Most Infamous Revenge," adding new valences to their depiction, while also rewriting elements of N. 2. Whereas Aminta kills her seducer in N. 2, the innocent wife Camila raped in D. 2 trusts instead to her own virtue and seclusion to protect her. And no other abused protagonist of a tale of disillusion takes her own violent revenge.

Zayas assigns narration of D. 2 to Lisarda, Lisis's rival for don Juan's love. She sets the tale in Milan, where Octavia and Juan were raised as children of a Spaniard, a soldier posted there who had gambled away most of his fortune and married a noblewoman of limited wealth. Carlos, son of a rich senator of Milan, falls in love with the beautiful Octavia and courts her assiduously, even as he knows that his father would never agree to his marrying such a relatively poor woman. Carlos seduces Octavia under promise of marriage before being persuaded by his father to break off with her, obliging her to go to a convent, and marrying the wealthy Camila. Octavia's brother, Juan, then rapes Camila.

Camila's rape is a masculine instrument of revenge. Zayas shows Juan using Camila's body to avenge the offense to *his* honor in Carlos's refusal to marry Octavia. However contrary this seems today, Elizabeth Rhodes thinks it accords with the social valence of rape in Zayas's day:

> Historical and literary evidence suggests that rape in the early modern world was not interpreted as an aggression against a woman's personal

---

[11] ETL, p. 244; *Desengaños*, p. 253.

identity as much as an attack against social order, an entire web of relationships. Like most authors of her day, Zayas represents the physical violation of an unwed noblewoman less as unconditional dishonor than as an imperative that the rapist marry the noblewoman he rapes, which is precisely what the law dictated.[12]

However valid that may be in general and of Camila's rape, it is not true of how Zayas represents Isabel's reaction to hers. She says she feels like a viper that had been trod upon. Zayas effectively dramatizes the perverse rivalry that is at the heart of the honor code. In effect, the honor code is not about a woman as much as it is about control of a female body that can serve as a site of contention between men, a place where men flex their power. Juan does not restore his sister's honor but seeks to ruin the honor of Carlos's wife, Camila.

Zayas has Lisarda contextualize her tale in the years of Spain's campaign to secure the Marquisite of Montferrat, first in the war waged between 1613 and 1617 by its former ally, the Duke of Savoy, Charles Emmanuel, to secure Montferrat for his granddaughter when the young duke Francisco IV died, and its continuation in the war of Mantuan Succession of 1528–1631. Yllera notes, however, that the observation Lisarda adds is a reminder of the Catalonian Rebellion rather than the War of the Montferrat Succession:

> The long and dangerous wars broke out in those realms then, that we mourn as well as do they, because that was the cause of the invasion of Spain and costing us all that it costs; and in one of the battles, Octavia's father died, as an elderly man continuing in the exercise of his youth, which was bearing arms. And his mother died a few months later as well, from the pain of having lost her beloved husband.
>
> [Ocasionáronse en este tiempo las largas y peligrosas guerras de aquellos reinos, ... Y su madre a pocos meses murió también de pena de haber perdido su amado esposo.][13]

Although the Montferrat and Mantuan war was part of the long-standing conflict between Spain and France over territory in northern Italy on either side of Spanish-controlled Milan, no troops invaded Spain, as did the French during the Catalan Rebellion.

---

12 Rhodes, *Dressed to Kill*, pp. 40–1.
13 Yllera, *Desengaños*, p. 271, and n. 5. *Desengaños*; my translation. On the war over Montferrat, see Antonio Feros, *El Duque de Lerma*, pp. 266–7, 303, 382, 415–19, 430; Parker, *Europe in Crisis*, pp. 113–18, 147–8; and Elliot, *Olivares*, pp. 337–46.

D. 3 ("His Wife's Executioner") is a radical rewriting of Cervantes's novella inserted in *Don Quixote*, "The Man Who Was Recklessly Curious." It occupies the same position in this volume as Zayas's table-turning rewriting of the Cervantine novella "The Deceitful Marriage" does in N. 3 in the first volume. N. 3 was mainly comic despite ending in the death of the foolishly deceived miser don Marcos. By contrast, although Cervantes's novella concludes with the death of the recklessly curious husband, this rewriting of it ends with the death of the honest heroine Roseleta.

Narrator Nise explains that the objective of telling true cases as Lisis ordered is "to counsel women to be responsible for their honor and, with all the freedoms [they profess] in this day and age, to fear that what has happened to others they've heard about may happen to them" [de aconsejar a las mujeres que miren por su opinión y teman … no les suceda lo que a las que han oído y oirán les ha sucedido].[14] Rhodes points out that most presentations of the honor code treat it as if only men have honor, honor that women threaten. Zayas, however, depicts women as well aware that they too have honor to protect, and she crafts her second volume to motivate her noble readers, female as well as male, to reform their relations accordingly. Nise criticizes both genders but says that since men pretend to be nature's perfection, their fault is greater. Her tale, she concludes, will shed light on the preceding one, specifically on Camila's fate:

> Now you shall see that if Camila was ruined because she didn't tell her husband about don Juan's courtship, in the disenchantment I'm about to tell it did another lady no good to inform her husband about the pretensions of a different don Juan in an effort to keep her faith with him and despite the fact that heaven supported her cause.
>
> [Y por que se vea que, si Camila perdió con su esposo por callar las pretensiones de don Juan … aunque el Cielo abonó su causa.][15]

Rhodes proposes that Zayas attempts to train readers to use their wits, to read against the grain to resolve contradictions in her presentation of the *Desengaños*. One particularly clear contradiction lies in how the narrators in the frame sections declare that their goal is to defend women, while the narrated tales often involve the brutal sacrifice of innocent wives, a contradiction made abundantly clear in D. 4, "Too Late Undeceived" and its frame.[16] In her introduction, the designated narrator Filis

---

14 *Disenchantments*, pp. 113–14; *Desengaños*, p. 298.
15 *Disenchantments*, p. 115; *Desengaños*, p. 300.
16 Rhodes, *Dressed to Kill*, pp. 6, 9–10, 75–6, 98–9. For my reading of D. 4 informed by psychoanalytic theory, see Greer, *María de Zayas*, pp. 176–96.

skips from topic to topic: she excuses men, then blames women's misfortunes on the stars; she lists the accomplishments of contemporary women (see chapter 8), then gives an impassioned condemnation of the fear and envy that drive men's repression of woman. She exhorts women to defend themselves with the very skills men seek to keep from them:

> I don't think I'm off track to say that out of fear and envy men deprive women of both letters and arms, the same way that Moors do to Christians who serve among their women, turning them into eunuchs to be sure of them. Oh, beautiful ladies, what things I could tell you if I could be sure that those who listen to me wouldn't criticize me! Come, let's give up our finery, our curls, and our flowers; let's defend ourselves, some with wit, others with weapons! That would be the best kind of disenchantments for women living today and for all days to come.
>
> [De manera que no voy fuera de camino en que los hombres de temor y envidia las privan de las letras y las armas ... el mejor desengaño para las que hoy son y las que han de venir.][17]

But then, after asking men's pardon for the tale she is about to tell, Filis does not relate it herself; rather, she has two male internal narrators tell the two-episode story. This creates a suggestive link to the corresponding story, N. 4, "Forewarned but Fooled," narrated by don Alonso. In D. 4, the concluding suicidal madness of the innermost male narrator, Jaime, seems to me a heightened punishment for misjudgment and abuse of women visited on them by don Fadrique in N. 4.

Disillusionment 5

The thematic link between N. 5, "The Power of Love," and D. 5, "Innocence Punished," is Zayas's rewriting of the recourse to magic to secure the beloved object. Another could be the conversion of the straying husband of N. 5 into an obsessed would-be lover in D. 5 – both named Diego. In D. 5, Diego falls in love with Inés, a married woman. A predatory neighbor

---

See also Frederick A. de Armas, *The Invisible Mistress: Aspects of Feminism and Fantasy in the Golden Age*, Charlottesville, 1976, and "Psyche's Fall and Magdalene's Cross: Myth and Hagiography in María de Zayas's Tarde llega el desengaño," *Estudios en honor de Janet Pérez: El sujeto femenino en escritoras hispánicas*, ed. S. Cavallo et al, Potomac, 1998, pp. 3–15. Matteo Bandello's version of the second episode is in the novella 12, second part; that of Marguerite de Navarre is *Heptameron* story 32.

17 *Disenchantments*, p. 141; *Desengaños*, p. 231.

facilitates sex between Diego and a woman he thinks is Inés but is really a prostitute of similar appearance attired in one of her dresses. Inés enlists a corregidor, a royal magistrate, to defend herself and deter Diego, but he persists, employing a Moorish sorcerer to make a magic statue of a nude Inés that brings her unconscious body to his bed when lit. The spell is only broken when she is seen and woken by her brother, the royal magistrate, and his officers. Like the feminine protagonist of N. 5, Inés eventually takes refuge in a convent; she has gone blind, however, from years of torment inflicted on her by her family. Inés is Zayas's "most tested perfect wife," Rhodes points out, and she proves her worth independently, without the intervention of her husband or brother, by making Diego confess to the corregidor. She also documents the unconscious state worked by the magic candle by telling her confessor of her "disturbing dreams." Rhodes demonstrates how Zayas reworked in this story the legends of two popular saints, Theodora of Alexandria and Thäis, both of whom suffered penitently in forms similar to the punishment inflicted on the innocent Inés; the saints, however, did commit their sins. Another critical difference between the saints' tales and Zayas's story is in the objective: this is not a tale meant to inspire women to admire and imitate a martyr's suffering penitence and saintly death, but a tale to transmit a message that might effect changes in behavior of the nobility to avoid their fates.

The beauty of socially martyred wives like Elena of D. 4 and Inés, which persists despite their suffering, is a mark of their innocence. But what of Inés's continuing blindness? This detail troubles many readers, who question its poetic justice and narrative logic. Eyes code the operation of desire in Zayas's stories, in several modes, beyond the traditional poetic topos of the eyes as the pathway to the soul. They can express awakening female desire, as in Jacinta's case in the first novella, who loved Félix in a dream even before seeing him in the flesh. Or women can be caught by men's desiring gaze, reciprocated or not, as are Inés in this tale and Beatriz in D. 9 ("Triumph over Persecution"). Both genders live continually aware of the eyes with which others judge their guilt or innocence. Awareness of that social gaze is what drives Jaime in D. 4 to move to his rural castle, and Inés's family to move to the outskirts of Seville: "Her crafty husband amiably told her how he and her brother had made up their minds to move their families and households into Seville. First, to get away from the eyes of all the people who knew about her misfortune and pointed their fingers at them" [Un día, … le dijo el cauteloso marido cómo su hermano y él … por quitarse de los ojos de los …

que los señalaban con el dedo].[18] Inés's blindness, however, is a misplaced punishment, since she never expressed any illicit desire. It is inflicted on a woman whose beauty aroused desire in the eyes of others, envy in those who do not possess her, and in Inés's case, her cruel sister-in-law's thirst to punish her in the flesh.

A wronged, innocent wife also features in D. 8, and parallels can likewise be seen with N. 8. In both N. 8 and D. 8, paternal thirst for wealth derails their daughters' choice of a partner, and both stories include miracles. In contrast to N. 8, however, the miracles in D. 8, "Traitor to His Blood," do not save either of the two women in the story. Francisca, the narrator of D. 8, introduces it by trying to balance the relative failings of men and women: men for deceiving women, for speaking badly of them after encounters with free women who only offend a man's purse, and women for letting themselves be deceived. Francisca acknowledges the mobility of desire that victimizes wives, directing her lecture on the subject to men:

> Every time I say I want something, once I get it, I'm disillusioned, for I can no longer desire what I already possess. Why does the married man, who has a wife, seek out another woman? ... You don't serve or love the one you have at home, so what makes you think you'll serve or love the other one.
>
> [Pues todas las veces que yo dijere que deseo una cosa ...No amas ni sirves a la que tienes en casa, ¿y lo harás a la que buscas fuera?][19]

Although that charge applies to two husbands in this story, the real culprit in it is the family patriarch, who sets all the events in motion. Because of his pride and greed, his son, Alonso, stabs his sister, Mencía, to death and beheads his wife, Ana.

Using what Rhodes calls "baroque poetics," Zayas in the *Desengaños* employs the beauty of female corpses as heaven's message to a corrupt society of their perfect innocence. They also show plainly what society has lost and the virtues it must recover if its dysfunctional nobility – Zayas's primary audience – is to survive.[20] Significantly, doña Ana's son is the only offspring of the protagonists in this second volume. No other children are born to these doomed marriages.

---

18 *Disenchantments*, p. 192; *Desengaños*, pp. 282–3.
19 *Disenchantments*, p. 273; *Desengaños*, pp. 510.
20 Rhodes, *Dressed to Kill*, pp. 35, 74, 113.

Disillusionment 10

The thematic link between N. 10 and D. 10, "The Ravages of Vice," is rivalry for love between siblings. No chivalrous devil gives up the soul promised to him as in N. 10, and the carnage wrecked by that rivalry is vastly expanded in D. 10. Lisis narrates this last tale, saying at its end that she learned it from Gaspar himself, a gentleman of the royal chambers who accompanied Philip III on a trip to Lisbon. In that city, he began visiting the youngest of four sisters, who lived in part of a distinguished residence. Entering one night by a side door to which they have given him a key, he hears moaning coming from a cellar and finds a freshly buried body of a young man, dead but still moaning. He has the unidentified man buried and takes it as a divine warning to stay away from such a house.

Then at Mass he sees two beautiful women, Magdalena and Florentina, who appear to be sisters. Magdalena is married to Dionís and Florentina lives with them, in such seclusion that Gaspar has no luck approaching her. But one night he finds Florentina in the street, nearly dead from sword wounds. He takes her to his inn and has her cared for. When she regains consciousness, she tells him to take ministers of justice to don Dionís's house, where they find a massacre. She tells him that although she and Magdalena were raised as sisters, they were born of previous marriages of their father and mothers. When Dionís courted and married doña Magdalena, Florentina also fell in love with him. Eventually she told him so, and they were lovers for four years and vowed to marry after doña Magdalena died. During Holy Week, Florentina confesses the affair to a priest, who puts the fear of hell in her. She also tells the truth to a maid who has been with her from childhood. The maid suggests that they arrange for Magdalena to die, since she in her innocence will earn a martyr's crown in heaven, and once married, Florentina will be able to make sacrifices and penitence like king David for his seduction of Bathsheba and secure forgiveness. The maid tells Dionís that Magdalena is betraying him with a handsome young servant and arranges a nighttime scene that supports her false testimony. Dionís kills the servant and Magdalena, as well as two of Magdalena's maids, two pages, and three kitchen slaves. Florentina's maid, repentant and horrified, tells Dionís that her testimony was false, that she arranged it so he would marry Florentina. Dionís kills her. Florentina appears, and he tries to kill her too, but a black kitchen slave puts herself between them, giving Florentina time to escape. Dionís then falls on his sword, and Florentina stumbles to the street – which is where Gaspar finds her and takes her to his inn to be cared for. Florentina becomes a nun, maintaining a friendly correspondence with Gaspar, who returns to Toledo and marries. Although Florentina confesses to Gaspar her own role in the massacre, the king pardons her, and she inherits Magdalena and Dionís's fortune.

Among Zayas's modern critics, this is the tale that has provoked the most puzzlement and disagreement. Some see Florentina's seduction of Dionís as undermining the author's professed defense of women. Edward Friedman points out the self-serving and manipulative nature of Florentina's partial confession, which he attributes to a feminist impasse, the necessity for women to define themselves in accord with the misogynistic ideology they wish to alter.[21] Paul Julian Smith argues that occasional female rebellions, such as that of Aminta in N. 2, do not provide an alternative model for women. While the woman displaces the man, she reproduces masculine actions and values, accepting a patriarchal code of honor and "the law of the dagger and the phallus." Critics of twenty-first-century films in which raped women seek violent revenge level the same charge, as if there were an easy remedy for women to heal from the psychic and physical damage men have done to them that the men are ignoring. I read the tale through the trope of the "enemy within" in three dimensions: first, the rebellious Portugal and the Portuguese within the Spanish monarchy, criticized by the narrator Lisis as having little sympathy for Castilians like Gaspar, "for even though they live among us, they are our enemies" [por la poca simpatía que esta nación tiene con la nuestra, que, con vivir entre nosostros, son nuestros enemigos].[22] Secondly, servants within noble households, who like Florentina's maid, wittingly or unwittingly cause their employers' downfall. And finally, desire within the body of women, since active sexual desire was considered legitimate only for men.[23] Nancy Lagreca interprets the tale as illustrative of Zayas's mastery of baroque literary techniques that oblige the reader to think, to

21 Edward H. Friedman, "María de Zayas's Estragos que causa el vicio and the Feminist Impasse," *Romance Languages Annual* 8, 1997, pp. 472–5; Paul Julian Smith, *The Body Hispanic: Gender and Sexuality in Spanish and Spanish American Literature*, Oxford, 1989, p. 33; see for example "Catharsis without the Healing," *New York Times* January 17, 2021.
22 ETL, 292–3; *Desengaños*, p. 645.
23 See Greer, *María de Zayas*, 309–15; ETL, p. 293; Nancy Lagreca, "Evil Women and Feminist Sentiment: Baroque Contradictions in María de Zayas's 'El prevenido engañado' and 'Estragos que causa el vicio,'" *Revista Canadiense de Estudios Hispánicos* 28, 2004, pp. 565–82; Greer, "María de Zayas and the Female Eunuch," *Journal of Spanish Cultural Studies* 2.1, 2001, 41–53.

read beyond surface meanings to uncover the truth beneath. In this case, Lagreca reads the story as a roman à clef in which Florentina is akin to the Spanish duchess Luisa de Guzmán, who, after marrying a Spanish nobleman, became an impassioned supporter of Portuguese independence. I suggest that given the contradictory pressures of Zayas's desire to defend women versus her loyalty to the aristocratic ideology that repressed them but grounded her identity, we might see this story as revealing her awareness on an unconscious level that only willful, actively desiring women like Florentina who refused the castrating knife of social codes could have the power to challenge patriarchy's rules and survive to inherit its wealth.

Chapter Six

Identifying the Subject

"I Am Who I Am."

THAT STATEMENT MAY strike readers unfamiliar with the Spanish equivalent, "Soy quien soy," as a mindless tautology. But in Early Modern Spanish literature, characters regularly voiced it in moments of conflict, when their security in their hierarchical society came under pressure. The repeated outbreaks of violent racial, ethnic, religious and political conflicts in the twentieth and twenty-first centuries illustrate the impulses and the passions behind "I am" statements – "I am ... white / black / Asian / Christian / Jewish / Muslim / a man / a woman / other." In this chapter I explain their import in Zayas's writings and in her time.

We read multiple versions of "ser quien soy" (to be who I am) in Zayas's novellas. In N. 1, "Taking a Chance on Losing," when Félix leaves Jacinta with his aunt during the year the pope has ordered the lovers to be separated, Félix leaves her there "with the charge to be who you are and who I am" [con la deuda de ser quien eres, y quien soy].[1] Three years after Félix's death, when Jacinta first responds to Celio's attentions to her, she says, "In so doing I understood I was doing him no little favor, given who I am" [en ello, entendí hacerle harto favor, siendo quien soy], and "being who I am, it was not right to love anyone but that one who would be my legitimate husband" [siendo quien soy, no era justo querer si no era al que había de ser mi legítimo marido]. Fabio repeats the "being who you are" phrase after hearing Jacinta's story in the wilds of Montserrat. He insists

---

1 ETL, p. 86; *Novelas*, p. 199; ETL, p. 91; *Novelas*, p. 204; ETL, p. 91; *Novelas*, p. 205.

on taking her back to a Madrid convent, telling her that there "you will live more in conformity with who you are" [estarás más conforme a quien eres]. Moreover, he attributes his own insistence to "the obligation I have to be who I am and the obligation I owe to Celio, my friend, from which I plan to emerge with many thanks, if I have luck in leading you away from this intention, so contrary to your honor and reputation." [la obligación en que me has puesto con decirme tu historia ... tan contrario a tu honor y fama].[2] Note in this last citation how the "who I am" identity phrase is joined to honor and reputation. Men were as controlled as women by the often-conflicting demands of the honor system – to God, king, family, friend, and beloved. Fabio is saying in effect that his sense of his own identity as a noble gentleman requires him, in obligation to his friend Celio, to ensure Jacinta's safe return to a convent.

In N. 2, "Aminta Deceived and Honor's Revenge," despite having been deceived and seduced by Jacinto/Francisco, Aminta removes herself from Martín's arms, maintaining and asserting her sense of identity to Martín with the classic phrase, "Do not think, just because I'm in this compromising situation, I cease to be who I am" [Y no penséis que, aunque estoy en este lugar, dejo de ser lo que soy].[3] Laura in N. 5, Sancho in N. 6, and Gaspar in N. 7 make classic "ser quien soy" statements, as does Felipe to Isabel in D. 1, Blanca to María in D. 7, and Federico to Beatriz in D. 9. These statements were even more common in the popular drama of the period, which filled the theaters of cities and towns throughout Iberia. A search of the ProQuest Spanish Theater of the Golden Age database of plays performed and published between 1567 and 1744 yields over eight hundred citations of the phrase "Soy quien soy."[4]

What was the origin of these "I Am" declarations, and how can we explain their frequency in Early Modern Spain? There is a scriptural model. In Exodus, book 3, which narrates God's command to Moses to lead the Israelites out of Egypt, he speaks to Moses in the burning bush. Moses, fearing the Israelites will not believe him, asks his name, and God answers, in verse 14, "I AM; that is who I am. Tell them that I AM has sent you to them." As my edition explains in footnotes, the divine name, Yahweh (Jehovah) is derived from the verb "to be." The Israelites understood

---

2 ETL, 94; *Novelas*, pp. 208–9.
3 *Enchantments*, p. 65; *Novelas*, p. 235.
4 Teatro Español del Siglo de Oro, https://search-proquest-com.proxy.lib.duke.edu/teso/advanced?accountid=10598, consulted January 14, 2020, thanks to Duke University Library resources.

the very essence of the deity to be expressed by his name, over all time and verb tenses. God adds, "I am the God of your forefathers, the God of Abraham, the God of Isaac, the God of Jacob." In the following chapter, he gives Moses the power to turn a staff to a snake and back, and to turn his hand leprous and clean again, to persuade the Israelites of his power and authority. Obviously, Early Modern Spanish literary personae are not declaring themselves divine. But they are similarly declaring what they claim to be their essential nature. They are not invoking the concept of an innate, autonomous subjectivity, but one based on gender, social and political position and the privileges, respect and obligations they entail.

The Spanish historian José Antonio Maravall explains "Soy quien soy" in secular terms:

> To our way of seeing, from all the data we have gathered, it is clear that "I am who I am" is not a principle that obliges one to be faithful to oneself in the sense of realizing through one's actions that internal nucleus of personality in each person which defines it as a unique being. On the contrary, it is a principle that is always spoken in relation to social behavior, as an obligation to function in a certain way that is proper according to qualities of estate.
>
> [A nuestro modo de ver, de todos los datos que hemos reunido resulta claro que 'soy quien soy' no es un principio que obligue a ser fiel a sí mismo, ... la obligación de conducirse según el modo que a la figura social de uno le corresponde.] [5]

Aristocratic characters made their "I am who I am" declarations seriously, in accord with their position in the sociopolitical hierarchy, the earthly apex of which was the king. The occasional ironic "I am" statement by a plebeian character, such as the comic lackey Coquín in Calderón's play *El medico de su honra* (The surgeon of his honor), can reveal how much that position constrained as well as privileged the nobility. When Coquín stumbles inadvertently into the presence of the rigorous king known as Pedro the Cruel (or the Just), and the king asks him who he is, the frightened Coquín answers (in one English prose translation):

> (*Aside*: Heaven help me!) I'm whoever your Majesty would like, plain and simple, because a very discreet man gave me some advice yesterday. He said never to be anyone you didn't like, and I learned the lesson so well that it went backwards and forwards in time: even before then I

---

5 José Antonio Maravall, *Teatro y literatura en la Sociedad barroca*, Barcelona, 1990, p. 62.

made sure to be whoever you wanted; in the future I'll be whoever you could possibly want, and right now I'm exactly the one you like..."

[Yo / (¡válgame el cielo!) soy quién / vuestra Majestad quisiere, ... quién os place soy;]⁶

Coquín's answer defines the nature of being as an effect of power, an effect that results from one's relation to the king's absolute power. But other discourses and practices are in play as well. For Zayas, of course, the primary identity discourse is that of gender, in an era in which women were presumed always inferior and necessarily subject to men. But her work also factors in blood, status, family, race, religion and wealth – although it's worth saying that in some of these matters, her attitudes are more typical of her time, in contrast with her more creative and vocal approach to the role of women. In the long transitional Early Modern period, these factors sometimes overlapped and reinforced one another, and sometimes were contradictory and conflictive, as George Mariscal's analysis in *Contradictory Subjects* demonstrates.

Class and Identity

Zayas, as we saw in chapter 1, was a member of the low-middle aristocracy, and her books of tales were directed primarily to members of that class – or, to use the term applied to class strata in her era, that estate. Her declared objective of entertaining and instructing both men and women with cautionary tales of the dangers of sexual desire legitimized that class structure, Rhodes argues. The moral codes Zayas advances, and the ethical stances she urges them to adopt, are a "class-conditioned morality" for the nobility; when her tales relate a servant's power over a member of the nobility, as in Florentina's acquiescence with her maid's unethical counsel in D. 10, "that power signifies the nobility's failure to maintain proper control over that servant and the serving class's inherent unreliability which justifies that control."⁷ That is indeed the explicit lesson reiterated by Zayas's narrators, who repeatedly pile vituperation on servants, as "domestic enemies," even those with whom they have been raised since childhood, as was Florentina's maid, who confessed to don Dionís that

---

6   Pedro Calderón de la Barca, *The Physician of His Honour*, Dian Fox ed. and trans., 2nd ed., Oxford, 2007, p. 77; Calderón, *El medico de su honra*, ed. Don W. Cruickshank, Madrid, 1981, p. 108.
7   Rhodes, *Dressed to Kill*, pp. 20–1, 60–1; ETL, p. 323; *Desengaños*, p. 685.

she had set up the betrayal of Magdalena that led to the slaughter in that tale. The maid belatedly tries to stop the bloodshed by confessing that the guilt was hers, and Dionís runs her through with his sword. But in her closing frame Lisis condemns passionately both the maid and another self-sacrificing servant, the black slave who shields Florentina with her own body, also killed by Dionís. They are, Lisis says, "domestic animals and unavoidable enemies whom we regale and on whom we spend our patience and estate and in the end like the lion who turns against the lion keeper weary of raising and feeding it and kills him, so do they, in the end, kill their masters and mistresses" [los criados y criadas son animales caseros y enemigos no excusados, ... y al cabo, como el león, que harto el leonero de criarle y sustentarle, se vuelve contra él y le mata].

Although there was a certain amount of social mobility in Early Modern Spain, with economic changes and the effects of necessarily incorporating new peoples and groups in the social structure of the expanding Spanish empire, that mobility was considered suspect among the upper classes. Zayas's narrators sometimes register this satirically, as in D. 6, having the cross-dressed carpenter's son Esteban/Estefanía laugh at women who give their pets the noble titles "don" and "doña" and propose a tax on use of those titles. In the first volume, narrators paint the merchant class as suspect in N. 2, in the form of Aminta's neighbor, the wife or widow of a merchant who facilitated Aminta's seduction by Jacinto, and, in N. 6, Clara's merchant father, who had reportedly made a great fortune in Spain, Italy and the Indies, but was in fact going bankrupt. After seeing his daughter married, the man departs for the Indies, leaving her destitute and obliged to wear humble clothes, do her own housework, and make and sell embroidery to support her two daughters. Occasionally, however, Zayas's narrators recognize the contribution of merchants. In N. 2, the narrator says, "Segovia is a city as splendid in its architecture as in the greatness of its nobility, and rich in merchants who, through their business, spread its good name even to the most remote provinces of Italy" [Segovia (ilustre ciudad de Castilla, ... hasta las más remotas provincias de Italia].[8]

Zayas does not specifically invoke the alternative discourse advanced by moralists, of nobility earned by virtue of character and ethical behavior rather than noble birth, except in the negative: that is, she sometimes refers to aristocrats, male or female, who act unethically and immorally not as nobles but as beasts. Nevertheless, the plots of at least two of her

8   *Enchantments*, p. 47; *Novelas*, p. 213.

tales support that ethical discourse of nobility. The merchant's daughter Clara in N. 6, "Disillusionment in Love and Virtue Rewarded," despite the hardship of her impoverishment, refuses the courtship and offers of support of the marquis Sancho until her husband Fernando is dead and buried. Sancho then renews his vow of love and secures the king's permission for their marriage. Narrator Phyllis concludes, "Doña Clara lived many years with don Sancho. They had beautiful children who inherited their father's estates. Because of her virtue, doña Clara was loved and appreciated beyond all imagining, for this is how heaven 'rewards virtue'" [Doña Clara vivió muchos años con su don Sancho, de quien tuvo hermosos hijos ... premia el cielo la virtud].[9] In D. 8, "Traitor to His Own Blood," Mencía's greedy father, Pedro, refuses to give her a dowry yet spurns the wealthy Enrique, who wants to marry her even without one, because Enrique's grandparents were commoners. When Mencía and Enrique exchange marriage vows nevertheless, Pedro has his son Alonso stab her to death and lure Enrique to her window to kill him as well. Enrique survives to become a Franciscan monk and build a chapel in which to inter Mencía's miraculously still-bleeding body. Zayas thus writes heaven's approval of Mencía's marriage with the commoner Enrique, against her father's will.

Wealth and Identity

If noble birth is the primary qualifying factor in a subject's status for Zayas's narrators, wealth is a close second.[10] Several stories feature suitors who are disqualified from consideration as spouses by parents or by the potential bride or husband because they are poor, or less wealthy than another candidate. Leonor's parents in N. 8, "Triumph over the Impossible," reject her beloved Rodrigo, preferring a wealthy Italian count; in N. 6, "Disillusionment in Love and Virtue Rewarded," Fernando's widowed mother serves as his excuse for not marrying Octavia, and she then arranges his marriage to the supposedly wealthy merchant's daughter Clara. Another Octavia is similarly rejected in D. 2, "Most Infamous Revenge," because her lover Carlos would not disobey the will of his father, who thought no woman yet born was good enough and wealthy enough for his

---

9 *Enchantments*, p. 212; *Novelas*, p. 408.
10 Elvira Vilches, "The Character and Cultures of Credit in Early Modern Spanish Texts: Matters of Trust, Belief, and Uncertainty," Cacho Casal and Egan, *Routledge Hispanic Studies Companion*, p. 124.

son. Once Octavia becomes a nun, Carlos's father arranges his marriage to the exceedingly wealthy and virtuous Camila, whom Octavia's brother rapes in revenge. Isabel Fajardo herself overlooks the devoted and noble Felipe in D. 1, "Her Lover's Slave," because he is not wealthy. In D. 8, as we have seen, Mencía's father has her killed to keep her from marrying, so as to preserve his whole estate for his son Alonso, and then disinherits the son for marrying Ana de Añasco because he had "expected his son to give him as daughter-in-law a great lady from that country who would augment his house with her nobility and his estate with her wealth" [pues cuando entendió que le diera por nuera una gran señora de aquel reino, ... que antes servía de afrenta a su linaje que de honor].[11] Because primogeniture reserved the vast bulk of estates for the eldest son, younger sons are disqualified – with perilous consequences – in N. 7, "Just Desserts," in N. 8 and in N. 10, "The Deceitful Garden."

Family Identity

In Zayas's tales of the adventures of people of noble birth, family is by definition a fundamental ingredient in one's identity. Characters in Zayas's stories regularly initiate their tales with a vague assertion of having been born to a noble and wealthy family. If the narrator provides more detail, that self-identification expands to include the character's paternal genealogy; this applies to both male and female characters. In N. 5, Nise tells us that Laura's father was don Antonio, "of the Garrafa family, closely related to the duke and duchess of Nochera. He was lord of Piedrablanca, an estate located four miles from Naples" [Era don Antonio, que éste es el nombre de su padre, ... que tiene su asiento cuatro millas de Nápoles].[12] Aminta's tale in N. 2 opens with the genealogy of her paternal uncle, Captain don Pedro, in whose care she lived after her father's death. The narrator, Matilde, adds that she does not mention don Pedro's last name and lineage, out of respect for the family. Similarly, in D. 5, "Innocence Punished," the narrator tells us the name but not the surname of Francisco, Inés's brother whom she respects and obeys as a father. In D. 8, the narrator tells us that Mencía and Alonso's father was "one of the richest and noblest gentlemen of all Andalucía. He was a cruel, haughty man

---

11 *Disenchantments*, p. 293; *Desengaños*, p. 537.
12 *Enchantments*, p. 159; *Novelas*, p. 345; *Disenchantments*, p. 275; *Desengaños*, p. 512; *Enchantments*, p. 47; *Novelas*, p. 213.

whose name was don Pedro" [en una ciudad de las nobles y populosas del Andalucía, ... hombre soberbio y de condición cruel]. Narrators regularly omit the mother's name and her maternal genealogy; in N. 2, for instance, we learn only that "don Pedro married a lady his equal in birth and in wealth" [Caso en Segovia ... con una dama igual en nobleza y bienes de fortuna]. We may be told that the mother died giving birth to the heroine, as in the case of Laura's mother in N. 5, or that the mother died before her daughter's engagement was arranged, as was Jacinta's case in N. 1. In that tale, Lisarda tells us that Félix's family name was Ponce de León.

For Zayas's characters, however, the family that anchored identity could be as much an enemy as a haven in the pursuit of their desires. The last story in each volume hinges on the dangerous jealousy of siblings, who are rivals for parental love and inheritance. We also see this danger repeatedly in the greed of fathers (or uncles who serve in their stead), in their desire to privilege sons and preserve family wealth at all costs. Prime examples would be Jacinta in N. 1, whose father cares only for her brother, and D. 8, in which a father's avarice destroys both Mencía and Alonso.

In Zayas's tales, family identity can be an issue from a very young age. Whether in kinship solidarity or to solidify kinship identity or economic ties beyond the nuclear unit, parents in Zayas's tales often arrange for their young sons and daughters to wed their cousins, well in advance of their maturity. In N. 2, Aminta is engaged to marry Luis, her uncle Pedro's son, who is serving in Italy. After her seduction by Jacinto/Francisco and her marriage to Martín, and after she kills Jacinto and his lover, Aminta and Martín live under assumed names in Madrid, out of respect for her broken engagement to Luis. For the same reason, she does not collect the inheritance due her after her uncle's death. Cousin love also complicates Jacinta's story in N. 1; Félix's cousin Adriana is in love with him, and her fury over his preference for Jacinta leads her to suicide. Nor should readers forget that the frame narrator heroine Lisis, Zayas's alter ego, suffers jealousy and illness because don Juan, the object of her affections, prefers her cousin Lisarda. In the last pages of the *Desengaños* frame tale, Lisis/Zayas punishes Juan by having Lisarda marry a wealthy foreign gentleman, whereupon Juan suffers an attack of madness that ends his life. Sweet authorial revenge. In N. 4, Violante and Fadrique limit their sexual play to preserve her technical virginity because she is engaged to a cousin in the Indies, whom she marries on his return.

In the *Desengaños*, Manuel's sister Eufrasia is also engaged to a cousin in the Indies; she then marries him and is his widow with a small son when Isabel returns to Zaragoza six years later (D. 1). D. 4's internal narrator, Martín, is returning to Toledo from Flanders to marry the cousin to whom he was engaged, and whom he eventually marries, when his ship is wrecked in the Canary Islands and he takes refuge in don Jaime's castle; Jaime reveals that he had killed Elena's cousin who lived with them, believing the false tale that Elena and her cousin were lovers. And in D. 7, "Marriage Abroad: Portent of Doom," Marieta, Blanca's young sister-in-law, is married to a cousin but still living with her family. After a manservant of Marieta's is mysteriously killed, her cousin-husband and father strangle her as well. For all these cousin marriages and romances, however, only two clearly involve first cousins: the narrator specifies that Adriana is the daughter of Félix's aunt in N. 1, and Luis is the son of don Pedro's sister in N. 2. Elsewhere, the word "primo" is used, but in Spanish it does not necessarily signify the close connection that "cousin" usually does in English; that would be translated "primo hermano," literally "cousin brother." "Cousin," therefore, could equally indicate a third or fourth cousin, or a more distant relationship that one still considers part of a family connection.

What should we make of these cousin engagements, marriages and deaths? What anthropologist Joseph Henrich calls "kinship-heavy" societies used to be the norm, but what we now identify as wealthy Western democracies generally don't maintain the tradition of cousin marriage, and people identify not by their roles in their families but by personal achievements. Henrich attributes the shift to the Catholic Church's family policies, which increasingly banned close cousin marriage. Another path to viewing Zayas's treatment of cousin alliances is through the work of historian James Casey. Studying marriage patterns in *The History of the Family*, Casey finds that the nature of the dowry system and inheritance laws in Spain – particularly regarding sizeable female inheritance, which was not the norm elsewhere – functioned in combination with an aristocratic preference for endogamy (marriage within the social group) to hold family property together.[13] Casey's subsequent study, which centers on the kingdom of Granada from the late sixteenth to early eighteenth century, considers the issue of cousin marriage in some detail. Although the evidence he cites varies, he says that marriage to first cousins was relatively rare because of the lengthy and expensive process of acquiring a dispensation. In fact, in N. 1, Félix pacifies his aunt by agreeing to marry Adriana,

---

13 James Casey, *The History of the Family*, Oxford, 1989, pp. 75–85; Casey, *Family and Community in Early Modern Spain: The Citizens of Granada, 1570–1739*, Cambridge, 2007, pp. 113–18.

while counting on the lengthy process of securing a dispensation to afford him time to secure permission to marry Jacinta. Casey suggests that the prevailing pattern for patricians was to marry within a small circle of families, just outside the church-banned degrees of relationship. This pattern of relying on family and trusted friends helped their class sustain their position while also allowing enough flexibility to incorporate newcomers in the relatively fluid frontier society of Granada, which was in the process of repopulating itself with Christian settlers after the surrender of the last Moorish king to the Catholic monarchs Fernando and Isabel in 1492.

Honor and Identity

It is not necessarily enough to come from a good family, however. Characters' sense of honor is an important ingredient in their identity too, if we are to judge by how often it is named in connection with their "I am" statements, as I pointed out above. Lope de Vega defines honor succinctly in his play *Los comendadores de Córdoba* (The Knights-commander of Cordova), in dialogues between the Alderman of Toledo and his black slave Rodrigo. Honor, the Alderman (Veinticuatro) says, is "that which resides in another," since "no man is honored by himself, / but he receives honor from others; / being a virtuous man, and having merit, / isn't being honored, but just giving cause / for others you deal with to give you honor" [aquélla que consiste en otro; …para que los que tratan les den honra]. Rodrigo agrees, adding that "if your wife didn't have it, / she couldn't take it away from you; which means / that you don't have it." [porque si tu mujer no la tuviera, / no pudiera quitártela, de suerte / que no la tienes tú].[14] Most discussions of honor in the past consistently used masculine pronouns, as if honor were a masculine preserve in which women only mattered as the fragile vessel whose uncontained sexuality could threaten or destroy a man's honor.[15] Both male and female characters in Zayas's tales voice this concept of masculine honor, as does Adriana in N. 1, sending a note to Jacinta's father that someone was offending his honor. In D. 2, Juan does indeed devise a "Most Infamous Revenge," as the title

14 Lope de Vega, "Los comendadores de Córdoba," *Comedias de Lope de Vega*, Parte II, vol. 2, ed. José Enrique Laplana Gil, Lleida, 1997, p. 1120. My translation. See also Geraint Evans, "Masculinities and Honour in Los comendadores de Córdoba," *A Companion to Lope de Vega*, ed. Alexander Samson and Jonathan Thacker, Woodbridge, 2018, pp. 199–213.
15 See Rhodes, *Dressed to Kill*, pp. 161–7.

of that story has it. The tale's narrator, Lisarda, accords him the right to avenge his honor, but condemns his method:

> If don Juan had taken vengeance on the man who wronged him, as was proper, no one could have blamed him. But he took his revenge against Carlos on an innocent person, and in that way satisfied his perverse inclinations in avenging his sister's honor […] Don Juan decided to ruin Carlos's honor through his wife, Camila, the way Carlos had ruined his honor through Octavia. Imagine! Just how could the poor innocent Camila be guilty of any of this! Except for the fact that revenge against her husband could be taken through her.
>
> [y don Juan, su venganza, que si la tomara, como era razón, en quien le había hecho el agravio, … ¡Será para vengarse en ella de su marido!]¹⁶

In D. 4, "Too Late Undeceived," Jaime says after hearing the black servant's accusation, "While it may not have been true, it's enough for a married man to have suspicion where his honor is concerned, particularly when there's an eyewitness" [Aunque pudiera ser que no fuera [cierto]: que al honor de un marido sólo que él lo sospeche basta, cuanto y más habiendo testigo de vista].¹⁷ Although Dionís in the final tale was a fully willing participant in his four-year affair with Florentina, in his violent rage over the false story of Magdalena sleeping with her page, he blames the rest of the household for his lost honor. He stabs his sleeping wife "as many times as his blind rage required," saying, "'You traitor, and how comfortably you sleep in my dishonor'" [¡Ah, traidora, y cómo descansas en mi ofensa!] When he kills two maids asleep in her dressing room, he declares, "'That's how you pay, sleeping sentinels of my honor, for your carelessness and for letting your treacherous mistress spend her nights ruining my honor'" [Así pagaréis, dormidas centinelas de mi honor … para que velase a quitarme el honor].¹⁸

But Zayas also gives us women whose concept of honor is rooted in their own virtues and is not exclusively tied to sexual purity. Aminta in N. 2, "Aminta Deceived and Honor's Revenge," is one clear example. She insists on her honor despite her seduction by Jacinto, as well as on her personal right to avenge Jacinto/Francisco's abuse of it. Clara in N. 6 is another defender of her own honor, keeping the marquis Sancho at a distance despite her poverty. Isabel in D. 1, "Her Lover's Slave," tells Claudia

---

16 *Disenchantments*, pp. 103–4; *Desengaños*, p. 285.
17 *Disenchantments*, p. 158; *Desengaños*, p. 359.
18 *Disenchantments*, p. 392; *Desengaños*, pp. 670, 671.

that Manuel's first love note is an offense. "He's impugning my honor, [...] and this letter must die to prevent there being accomplices" [Con todo mi honor le está cometiendo ... será bien que éste muera].[19] In D. 9, Beatriz goes to great lengths to defend herself from vicious assaults against her honor and her life made by her brother-in-law, the prince Federico, many with the counsel and assistance of the demonic "doctor." Finally, the Virgin who has been her defender reveals that she is the Mother of God, awakening the embattled queen from her meditative rapture:

> Come to your senses, friend Beatriz; the time has come for you to leave this place and defend your honor. While you suffer without guilt and your long-suffering is sufficient reward for your trials, my son wants His brides to be in good repute. For that reason, He permits many who have lost their reputations to have them restored even after they've left this world, through investigations like those required for canonization. He wants to restore your good name to you.
>
> [Vuelve en ti, amiga Beatriz, que es ya tiempo que salgas de aquí y vayas a volver por tu honor, ... se la vuelva el mismo que se la ha quitado.][20]

Without such divine protection, however, even women who claim their own sense of honor express full awareness of the importance of maintaining their reputation in the eyes of society. Clara in N. 6 worries about what neighbors would say, that seeing the gallant and wealthy Sancho strolling by her doors, they will think he has bought her honor. Inés in D. 5 has the mayor witness Diego's account of his attempted seduction and tells him "that it was important to her honor for him to act as witness and judge of a very serious case" [Doña Inés envió a llamar al Corregidor... que fuese testigo y juez de un caso de mucha gravedad].[21] But the mayor only punished and exiled the female go-between who had helped Diego, not don Diego himself, and he did not stop his pursuit of Inés. When don Diego uses the magic candle prepared by the Moorish magician, he is jailed, turned over to the Inquisition, and never seen again. Yet this does not spare Inés from her family's torment, walled up in a tiny cell for six years. Only when the widow hears her, and the widow and the neighbor tell the archbishop, are Inés's husband, brother and sister-in-law sentenced to death.

---

19 *Disenchantments*, p. 49; *Desengaños*, p. 215.
20 *Disenchantments*, p. 358; *Desengaños*, p. 460.
21 *Disenchantments*, p. 183; *Desengaños*, p. 390.

Political and Ecclesiastical Authorities

Zayas's narrators generally turn a blind eye to the fact that political authorities, from mayors to viceroys, as well as the ecclesiastical hierarchy, were fully embedded in and committed to the patriarchal social order that repressed and regularly victimized women. Her tale-tellers almost always focus on abuses by patriarchal figures within the family, or extended family. Political and ecclesiastical figures often function as women's helpers in her stories, except in cases in which they are portrayed as enemies of the Spanish, such as the Portuguese in D. 10, or certain Flemish characters. In N. 1, Jacinta's father at first ignores her, then he and her brother turn their fury on her lover, Félix (later intercepting his letters to Jacinta and sending a false letter that he has died). The vicar and the abbess of the convent where Jacinta and Félix take refuge help him escape through a back door and board a galley for military service in Flanders. When Félix reaches Barcelona, however, he boards one of a fleet of ships that Philip III had called home to expel Moriscos, a process that lasted from 1609 to 1614.[22] The ships were awaiting "His Excellency Pedro Fernández de Castro, the count of Lemos" (who also happened to be Zayas's father's employer), "to take him to the kingdom of Naples to become viceroy and captain general." When Félix reappears years later, he and Jacinta travel to Rome, where they secure a papal dispensation to marry, after paying four thousand ducats. They are also helped by the Spanish ambassador in Rome and some cardinals and a donation of two thousand ducats to the Royal Hospital of Spain in Rome. Thus, Zayas had political and ecclesiastical authorities put Félix and Jacinta on a path to live happily ever after; but she then reverses that path by having Félix drown at sea.

In N. 5, "The Power of Love," Laura's family, feeling powerless to stop her husband Diego's abuse of her, finally intervenes after Carlos rescues her from the chapel with its charnel pit. They take her to the palace of the viceroy, who in a second, more lavish tribute, is named as don Pedro Fernández, Count of Lemos, and is praised by narrator Nise as "a very noble, wise, and devout prince whose rare virtues and outstanding qualities should be written on bronze plaques and on the tongue of fame rather than just on paper" [don Pedro Fernández de Castro, Conde de Lemos, ... en las lenguas de la fama].[23] Diego, who on finding Laura gone had been raging like a lion, "thinking that his noble wife has deserted him or run

---

22 See footnote 33 in ETL, p. 80; Novelas, p. 193.
23 Enchantments, p. 178; Novelas, p. 368.

away intending to destroy his honor" [creyendo que la noble dama era ida, o huyendo de él o a quitarle la honra],[24] is now chastened by hearing Laura's story in the viceroy's presence and offers to put his lover Nise in the viceroy's hands, so that she may be placed in a convent. Laura refuses, enters a convent herself, and Diego, we are told, is blown up by a mine in Philip III's war with the Duke of Savoy. Zayas has her narrator Francisca pay yet a third tribute to the Count of Lemos and his successor, the Duke of Osuna, in D. 8. Antonio and his friend Marco Antonio, planning to kill Antonio's wife, Ana, in hopes of recovering his father's favor and support, delay the slaughter until after the departure of the Count of Lemos, who at that point is arranging his 1616 return to Spain. Narrator Francisca tells us, "His brother don Francisco de Castro, count of Castro and duke of Taurisano, was to govern in his place until the new viceroy, the duke of Osuna, should arrive from Sicily" [lo dilataron hasta la partida del excelentísimo señor conde de Lemos, … conde de Castro y duque de Taurisano].[25] The very night that Lemos embarks, as if only his presence preserved her life, they behead Ana, throw her body in a well, and board a galley that would follow the viceroy's fleet. When her body is recovered from the well, her mother goes to beg for justice from the new viceroy, who responds:

> Deeply affected by her tears, he sent a long-boat carrying a squad of soldiers under the command of sergeant don Antonio de Lerma in pursuit of the galleys. He bore letters addressed to the marquis of Santa Cruz requesting that he, as general-in-command of the galleys, hand over the criminals.
>
> [lastimado de sus lágrimas, … pidiendo al marqués de Santa Cruz, como general de las galeras, los reos.][26]

When the long-boat catches up with the fleet in Genoa, they find Alonso and Marco Antonio have already been jailed for stealing silk stockings, and they are sent back to Naples to be tried and executed. Zayas thus has these two murderers face justice by human hands, but for the cruel patriarch who was the cause of the family tragedies that cost the deaths of two women, she leaves justice to a higher force. Her narrator comments, "But God, who is ill served by the haughty, sent him punishment for his

---

24 *Enchantments*, p. 179; *Novelas*, p. 368.
25 *Disenchantments*, p. 294; *Desengaños*, pp. 538–9.
26 *Disenchantments*, p. 297; *Desengaños*, p. 543. *Disenchantments*, p. 300; *Desengaños*, p. 546.

cruelty" [Mas Dios, que no se sirve de soberbios, le envió el castigo de su crueldad]. Servants find him dead in bed within a month, and he leaves a vast estate that his orphaned grandson inherits.

In the final frame summary of the *Exemplary Tales of Love*, Zayas's alter ego, Lisis, delivers a long, impassioned sermon that connects the misogyny of Spain's male nobility with the nation's political decline. Lisis opens her sermon with the loaded question, "What human or divine law do you find, noble gentlemen, to set you so staunchly against women?" [¿Pues qué ley humana ni divina halláis, nobles caballeros, para precipitaros tanto contra las mujeres?] She charges noblemen with wearing the insignias of nobility as mere showy decorations, like silk stockings and long hair. She asks how they can be idling along the Paseo del Prado while the king is on campaign against enemy invaders of Spain. She blames their lack of valor on the low estimation they have of women. Lisis harks back to the golden era of the later fifteenth century under King don Fernando the Catholic, when men were real men. Then, she says, men "offered up their estates and persons: the father to defend his daughter, the brother his sister, the husband his wife, and the gallant his lady" [ofrecían sus haciendas y personas ... y el galán su dama]. They did so, she says, in order not to see them made captives or dishonored.[27] She adds that if noblemen demonstrated such valor, commoners would follow their example. Instead, men invent malicious tales about women, a habit she blames on idleness, which offends God and their nobility. "The man who speaks badly of women," Lisis says, "is neither a gentleman, nor noble, nor honorable" [Y digo que ni es caballero, ni noble, ni honrado el que dice mal de las mujeres]. She winds up with a final zinger: "The clever man spoke well who said that the French have stolen your valor from you, and you their way of dressing" [Bien dice un héroe bien entendido que los franceses os han hurtado el valor, y vosotros a ellos, los trajes].[28]

Toward the end of her harangue, Lisis/Zayas dates its composition to 1646, during the Catalan uprising. The king's campaign to which she refers was Philip IV's 1642 venture in Aragon, for which the Count-Duke of Olivares endeavored with limited success to raise a force of noblemen to accompany the king. Despite Zayas's deep critique, by the 1640s, the muted enthusiasm of the nobility for that campaign was likely not due to a loss of Fernando-era valor, but rather because an urbanizing nobility had realized that its fortunes were better advanced by cultivating their economic,

---

27 ETL, pp. 320; *Desengaños*, pp. 680–1.
28 ETL, p. 321; *Desengaños*, p. 682.

social and political connections in Madrid than by military service. One of the spaces in Madrid where they could cultivate those connections was the tree-lined avenue, the venue of noble recreation that Lisis names, the Paseo del Prado and adjacent gardens, one of the first such public spaces in Europe, recently named a UNESCO world heritage site.[29]

Dress and Identity

Zayas's critique of noblemen for wearing noble insignia only for show is doubly meaningful, given the role that dress plays in her characters' identity. This is not unique to Zayas or Spain; in Early Modern Europe, clothing marked class and gender distinctions, often reinforced with sumptuary laws that dictated who could and could not wear gold and silver, silk and other rich fabrics.[30] To modify a contemporary phrase, clothing customs of the time made it clear that "you are what you wear" – or at least you should be. In Zayas's tales, therefore, attire often stands in for characterization. Zayas's descriptions of her heroines and heroes are generic, not detailed; in N. 2, we are told only that don Pedro's brother "had a beautiful daughter, the most beautiful in the whole province" [Tenía don Pedro un hermano que [tenía] la mas bella hija que en toda aquella provincial se hallaba];[31] we are not even told whether Aminta is fair or dark. In the first novella, Jacinta, the one exception who proves this rule, tells us that in her dream she met "the most handsome man I had ever in my life seen" [hallé un hombre tan galán que me pareció ... No haberle visto en mi vida tal]. Uncharacteristically, she does tell us he is dark: "If the god Narcissus was dark, then surely he was Narcissus" [si fue Narciso moreno, Narciso era el que vi]. She also evokes the erotic literary tradition of discovering a hidden or disguised woman by the sight of a white hand or foot: she says that Fabio was tipped off that the young shepherd he finds in Montserrat

---

29 See pp. 1–40 in the UNESCO nomination text at file:///Users/override/Downloads/1618-2331-Nomination%20Text-en.pdf; and the *Grandezas de España*, 1595 edition, p. 205, column A, which calls it the Prado de San Jerónimo. My thanks to Laura Bass for these references.
30 See Marjory Garber, *Vested Interests: Cross-Dressing and Cultural Anxiety*, New York, 1992, pp. 25–36; Amy Kaminsky, "Dress and Redress: Clothing in the *Desengaños amorosos* of María de Zayas y Sotomayor," *Romantic Review* 79.2, 1988, pp. 377–91, and Greer, *María de Zayas*, pp. 111–12, 220, 223–4.
31 *Enchantments*, p. 48; *Novelas*, p. 180. *Enchantments*, p. 18; *Novelas*, p. 180; *Enchantments*, p. 15; *Novelas*, p. 177.

was female by her hands, "so white that they could have made the snow envious" [sus blancas manos, tales que pudieran dar envidia a la nieve]. But far more attention is lavished on clothing. We learn that the dream man wore a fawn-colored cape, with silver hooks and catches, the attire of an aristocratic man.

Other than these hints in the first story, the only sketches of characters' physical appearances in the *Novelas* are in N. 4, of Beatrice and the black stable hand (on whom, see the following section on race). She is set in dramatic contrast to the man, in both her coloring and attire.

> Over her nightgown she was wearing a petticoat of red silk embroidered with silver trimming that sparkled like stars. The only other garment she had on was a mantilla of the same silk lined in blue plush, thrown on with such negligence that you could see the whiteness of her nightgown and its silvery handwork – an art for which Seville was famous. Her golden hair was caught in a blue and silver silk net, although a few loose strands curled down to frame the beauty of her face. Around her throat, she wore two heavy strings of pearls, matched by the pearls she wore on both slender wrists.
>
> [Traía la dama sobre la camisa un faldellín de vuelta de tabí encarnado, ... otras muchas vueltas que llevaba en sus hermosas muñecas.]³²

The narrator of N. 4, Alonso, describes Fadrique's next love object, Violante, only as most beautiful and lets her dress paint her aristocracy as she has her portrait painted: "It seemed, however, as if she'd dressed with such extravagance and elegance especially to conquer Fadrique. She was wearing a full black skirt covered with sequins and gold buttons, a belt and a necklace glittering with diamonds and circling her brow a band of rubies" [parece que de propósito para rendir a don Fadrique ... y un apretador de rubíes].

We do find other sketches of women's physical appearance in the ballads that lovers sing in the second and fourth novellas. In those ballads, Zayas follows the traditional courtly descriptions of feminine beauty of Renaissance poetry, cast in standard metaphors: teeth as white as pearls, hair that is pure gold, snowy white hands, a brow like white lilies, cheeks like roses, and a ruby-red mouth. Male narrators tell both these stories, so it is logical that they adhere to the masculine discourse of feminine beauty. A similar circumstance explains the cross-dressed wit of the ballad that begins "Your mad behavior, Lisardo" that Fadrique sends to Ana,

---

32 *Enchantments*, p. 126; *Novelas*, p. 308; *Enchantments*, p. 134; *Novelas*, p. 318.

who is jealous of his attention to another woman while their own affair is constrained in order to preserve her virginity until they are married. The feminine poetic voice in this ballad pretends to understand Lisardo's attraction to her rival's coal-black hair and black eyes, color coding that is meant to be read as negative attributes.

Cross-dressed characters present an anomaly in Zayas's treatment of dress and identity: most other characters are entirely fooled by cross-dressing disguises; they do not see the discrepancy between dress and gender identity. Fabio is a rare character who does see through Jacinta's male attire in N. 1, as we have seen. Aminta in N. 2 is a more typical case. She puts on male dress, cuts her hair, and secures employment with Jacinto/Francisco, who does remark on a certain resemblance, but only Flora suspects that this young man is indeed Aminta in male attire, and she keeps quiet rather than remind her lover of his erstwhile passion for her. In N. 9, "Judge of Her Own Case," Claudia-as-Claudio goes unrecognized by Carlos when she takes the position of his page; Amete, a Moorish captive in his household, overhears her story and has her dress as a woman again to accompany Estela, kidnapped and transported to Fez. When the Moorish prince Jacimin rescues her from Amete and Claudia, Estela cuts her hair, puts on masculine dress, and begins the soldierly career that will elevate her to the post of viceroy of Valencia, all without being recognized as a woman, even by her beloved Carlos, until she reveals it herself. These long-term cross-dressed disguises may seem implausible to modern readers, but this was a convention dramatized in the plays of the period as well.

The *Desengaños* stories follow the same pattern of nonspecific descriptions of beauteous heroines, and these tales lack even the poetic staples of blond, ruby-cheeked objects of love. Two exceptions, however, are the portrayals of the exotically Moorish-dressed Zelima of D. 1, and the immured Inés of D. 5, "Innocence Punished." Zayas tells us in the frame narrative that Lisis's cure was worked by Zelima, the beautiful Moorish slave given her by her aunt. Zelima's lovely face, she tells us, was not marred but enhanced by the brand of slavery on her cheek, the letter S and a nail (a Spanish rhebus: s + clavo = esclavo, slave). We also learn that her hair was chestnut blond. Zelima asks to tell the first disenchantment, and as the musicians play the last strains of a ballad, she astounds the audience by appearing exquisitely attired:

> she was wearing a blouse of transparent cambric, with wide bobbin-and-needle lace, sleeves that were very wide at the hand, a skirt of lamé in blue and silver flowers with three or four shiny adornments that blinded

in their brilliance, so short that it scarcely reached her ankles, and on her feet she wore sandals with many showy ties and silk ribbons; over this a tunic or vest of another light, colorful fabric of blue and silver, and tied at her shoulder a haik of the same fabric. She wore a tunic with sleeves so wide that they were the same as those of her blouse, showing her white and shapely arms with costly bangles or bracelets; her long, wavy, and lovely locks, which were neither gold nor ebony but rather a chestnut blonde color, fell over her shoulders, passing her waist by a yard, and gathered at her forehead with a ribbon or small clasp of diamonds, and then pinned to the middle of her head she wore a blue and silver veil that completely covered her; the beauty, poise, majesty of her graceful and even steps seemed like those of a princess of Algiers, a queen of Fez or Morocco, or a sultana of Constantinople.

[Traía sobre una camisa de transparente cambray, ... una reina de Fez o Marruecos, o una sultana de Constantinopla.]³³

Of Inés, in D. 5, we first read simply that she was not yet eighteen and one of the most beautiful women in Andalucía. Many years later, when she is rescued after she has spent six years walled in a tiny, totally dark space, the narrator adds abundant details: "Her splendid hair which when she entered was like threads of spun gold was now white as snow and tangled and seething with lice…. Her color was the color of death. Her body was so consumed and emaciated that you could count her bones as if the skin that covered them were a silken shroud" [sus hermosos cabellos, que cuando entró eran como hebras de oro, blancos ... el pellejo que estaba encima fuera un delgado cendal].³⁴ And other, yet more stomach-turning details.

In D. 9, "Triumph Over Persecution," the repeated miraculous reappearance of Beatriz's queenly dress – after its removal by her impassioned enemy, the prince Federico, and his helpers – serves to mark both her royal status and divine protection, as Amy Kaminsky points out in her good analysis of dress in the *Desengaños*. For horrific, practical reasons, in D. 8, "Traitor to His Own Blood," Alonso's wife, Ana, is identified by her clothing after her headless corpse is retrieved from the well in which her assassins stuffed it: "It was wearing a French-style overskirt with a green brocade bodice adorned with silver braid. As it was summer, doña Ana had worn no other garment except for a short black mantilla to draw across her face and iridescent silk stockings and black slippers scarcely six

---

33 ETL, pp. 204–5; *Desengaños*, pp. 203–4. See footnotes to these passages in both ETL and Yllera's edition for explanation of these dress details.
34 *Disenchantments*, p. 196; *Desengaños*, p. 407.

inches long" [Tenía vestido un faldellín francés con su justillo de damasco verde, ... con el zapatillo negro que apenas era de seis puntos].[35] Finally, the elegant, gleaming white attire that the frame-tale characters Lisis and Isabel don at the climax of the storytelling informs their suitors and their readers of their planned change of identity: when the story is done, they will withdraw to a convent.

"Race," Caste and Identity

Although in the first section of this chapter, I wrote of "class" and identity, the hierarchy of groups in question was termed "estate" in medieval and Early Modern Spain, and today might be named "caste."[36] Whatever terms we apply, those hierarchies were human constructions, both relatively fixed and yet shifting over time, circumstances, and the perspective of different populations. In the preface of her article "Unfixing Race," Kathryn Burns foregrounds the admixture of genealogy and religion appended to the concept of "race" (*raza*) in entries to early Spanish dictionaries. Sebastián de Covarrubias Horozco's *Tesoro de la lengua castellana* of 1611 defines *raza* as "the caste of purebred horses, which are marked with brands to distinguish them ... Race in cloth, the coarse thread that is distinct from the other threads in the weave. Race in lineage is understood to be bad [...], as to have some Moorish or Jewish race" [La casta de cavallos castizos, ... Raza, en los linages se toma en mala parte, como tener alguna raza de moro o judio].[37] A century later, the definition of *raza* in the *Diccionario de autoridades* (1726–1739) of the Spanish Royal Academy reflects the increasingly racialized discrimination that grew out of late medieval and Early Modern religious conflicts and competition for empire.

> Caste [*casta*] or quality of one's origin or lineage. Speaking of men, generally understood to be bad.... . [By the knightly rule] of [the military order of] Calatrava: "We order and command that no one, of whatsoever quality and condition, be received into the said Order ... unless he be a Gentleman ... born of legitimate matrimony, and not of Jewish, Moorish, Heretic, nor Plebian race."

35 Kaminsky, "Dress and Redress"; *Disenchantments*, p. 297; *Desengaños*, p. 542.
36 See, for example, Isabel Wilkerson, *Caste: The Origins of Our Discontents*, New York, 2020; also, the articles of Leslie Pierce and Kathryn Burns, in particular, in Greer, Mignolo, and Quilligan, *Rereading the Black Legend*.
37 *Tesoro*, pp. 896–7; translation by Kathryn Burns, "Unfixing Race," *Rereading*, p. 188; *Diccionario*, p. 500.

[Casta o calidad del origen o linage. Hablando de los hombres, se toma mui regularmente en mala parte... y que no toque raza de Judio, Moro, Herege, ni Villano.]

Leaving the question of religious affiliation to the following chapter, I focus here on how Zayas treats the skin color that would come to define "race" from the eighteenth century forward.

Notice that in these Spanish dictionary definitions of race in the seventeenth and early eighteenth centuries, skin color is not mentioned. Yet it is central in two dramatic images that Zayas sets before readers. The references to people of Moorish race could, but did not necessarily, imply dark-skinned individuals.[38] The Iberian Peninsula was from the late medieval era part of a trade network that included trade in slaves, often taken captive in wars between Christian and Muslim realms, some of whom were held for ransom.[39] These Muslim war prisoners were referred to as *moros* (Moors). A bit later, in the fifteenth century, Portuguese navigators sailed south along the African coast in search of gold, precious woods and a route to the spices of the east not under Muslim control; they also seized captives and brought them back to be sold at the slave market in Lagos, Portugal. (Elizabeth Wright relates how this distressed the people of the city, according to Gomes Eanes de Zurara's *Chronicle*, which describes their grief at seeing parents separated from children during the

---

38 See Trevor J. Dadson, "'Todos son uno': Moriscos and the Question of Identity in Early Modern Spain," Cacho Casal and Egan, *Routledge Hispanic Studies Companion*, pp. 521–36.
39 See Elizabeth R. Wright, *The Epic of Juan Latino: Dilemmas of Race and Religion in Renaissance Spain*, Toronto, 2016, pp. 21–38, 58–60; Erin Kathleen Rowe, "Enslaved and Free Black Africans in Early Modern Spain," Cacho Casal and Egan, *Routledge Hispanic Studies Companion*, pp. 539–48; "Introduction," Elizabeth R. Wright, *Iberia's Atlantic Households: How Slavery and Diaspora Powered a "Golden Age" of Empire (1444–1640)*, forthcoming; James Casey, *Family and Community in Early Modern Spain*, pp. 248–54; Simon Barton, *A History of Spain*, 2nd ed., Croydon, 2009, pp. 42, 44, 65, 78, 96; Chloe Ireton, "'Black Africans' Freedom Litigated Suits to Define Just War and Just Slavery in the Early Spanish Empire, *Renaissance Quarterly* 73, 2020, pp. 1277–80, 1283–90; Mary Elizabeth Perry, *The Handless Maiden, Moriscos and the Politics of Religion in Early Modern Spain*, Princeton, 2005; "Gurumbe: Canciones de tu memoria negra," created by Miguel Angel Rosales, Canal Sur TV with the collaboration of the Consejería de Cultura, Junta de Andalusia, 2016; José Ramos Tinhorão, *Os negros em Portugal: Uma presença silenciosa*, Lisbon, 2019, pp. 239, 261–3.

sale.) According to chroniclers, these later captives were also referred to as Moors, whether or not they were from regions adhering to Islam. Some black African slaves' suits for freedom argued that they had been enslaved illegally because they were Christian, and Christians had no right to enslave other Christians. At the other end of the spectrum, afterced Moriscos (former Muslims) were sold into slavery that the purchase price of slaves went down; some of these Moriscos were likely quite light-skinned, as were Berber slaves who came from the mountains of northern Morocco. Given the broad population of slaves and the broad use of the word Moor, it is unsurprising that in Zayas's stories, not all black people are slaves, nor are all slaves black. In D. 4, for example, four white maids with branded faces like that of Zelima are called to prepare beds for Martín and his friend.

Zayas also chooses accurate settings for the stories that involve black characters. Seville, (N. 4) together with Lisbon and later Cadiz, was a major slave market in Iberia, and a large number of Moriscos were transported there in 1570. Grand Canary Island (D. 4), due to its proximity to the West coast of Africa and cultivation of sugar, supported the presence of black servants and slaves. And Lisbon (D. 10), a port city enriched by Portugal's wide-flung trade, had a mix of black and white people performing manual labor, as portrayed in the story. James Casey notes that most slaves at the time were employed in domestic labor, not in manufacturing or agriculture, as they would later be in the Indies. He also writes that there was often little distinction between slaves and those bound to service by their families' poverty. In stories set in other locales, Zayas also inserts passing references to black people without specifying if they are free or enslaved and to slaves without indicating their skin color. Miguel, the narrator of N. 7, for instance, tells us that one of the incidents that prevented an encounter between Hipólita and Gaspar in Valladolid was a fire accidentally started by a black woman in charge of the kitchen; and a slave acted as a liaison between Leonor and Rodrigo in Salamanca in N. 8.

These story locations and the overlapping of color and religion with the status of domestic laborers and slaves show us that Zayas was aware of the multiracial nature of society in parts of Iberia. It is equally clear from her depiction of black-skinned characters, however, that she viewed that mixture negatively. She used blackness as a narrative foil to her main white characters, in images that are painful to read today.

The first of the arrestingly dramatic images of black characters is in Seville in N. 4, as Fadrique, patiently courting the beautiful widow

Beatriz, sees her descend late at night from her bedroom to the stable, in the elegant attire described earlier in this chapter. There, in a tiny room, lying in bed, he sees:

> a negro so black that his face seemed made of black silk. Although he looked to be about twenty-eight or thirty, his aspect was hideous, abominable. Don Fadrique thought the devil himself couldn't have looked more awful, though it's hard to tell whether this was true or simply the result of don Fadrique's sense of outrage. The negro's arched chest gave him a grotesque appearance, and his emaciated face indicated he would die before long.

> [un negro tan atezado que parecía hecho de un bocací su rostro.... porque tenía el pecho medio levantado, con lo que parecía más abominable.][40]

Alonso repeatedly inserts in his description contrasts between Beatriz's beauty and the "devilish black face" of Antonio, her emaciated lover, while narrating his rejection of her caresses.

> "What do you want of me, madam? Leave me alone, for the love of God! How can you pursue me even as I lie dying? Isn't it enough that your lasciviousness has brought me to this end? Even now you want me to satisfy your vicious appetites when I am breathing my last? Get yourself a husband, madam, marry, and leave me in peace."

> ["¿Qué me quieres, señora? ... pues ya no estoy para otra cosa".]

Thus, Zayas's male narrator gives us a double contrast, between the "devilishly ugly" black stable hand and the beautiful white widow, and between Antonio's ethical rejection of her advances and her illicit sexual pursuit of him, even while she holds Fadrique at bay, saying she is honoring her dead husband. Fadrique gives no indication of this black man's religious faith when he sees Antonio's body brought out for burial the following day.

In the other dramatic image of a black character, in D. 4, it is the white woman with whom she is contrasted, Jaime's wife Elena, who appears close to death in her emaciated pallor. Both women enter the dining hall simultaneously, and Elena is described as beautiful even though she is dressed in a coarse burlap sack tied at the waist with rope. The internal male narrator, Martín, describes the black woman's face as so fierce that "if

---

40 *Enchantments*, pp. 127–8; *Novelas*, pp. 309–10; Ramos Tinhorão, in *Os negros em Portugal*, pp. 239, 261–3, indicates that blacks were often employed as stable hands.

she wasn't the devil, she was his very likeness" [si no era el demonio, que debía ser retrato suyo], with a nose as broad as that of a bloodhound and a mouth like a lion's maw. [41] He gives her luxurious attire a typically long description: a dress of queenly scarlet brocade, along with a necklace and belt of diamonds, large pearls earrings and bracelets and hair ornaments of flowers and gems. The black woman wakes up that night in mortal agony, pleading for confession, proclaiming herself a Christian, albeit a bad one. But after she confesses that her accusation of Elena and her cousin was a lie, Jaime stabs her to death without allowing her that sacrament.

As I noted in chapter 5, these two relevant passages of N. 4 and D. 4 are both related by men. Don Alonso narrates N. 4, he says, to teach men not to rely on their own judgment nor to dare test a woman, lest he fall into the trap he fears most. Alonso tells us that it might have been Fadrique's sense of outrage that made him see Antonio as a fierce devil, the devil himself. Though Fadrique writes a pompous farewell note to Beatriz, citing conscience and scruples, it is clear that his quick departure from Seville stems from the double blow to his ego: not only did she reject him, but she rejected him for an "ill-fated negro." At the end of D. 4, the suicidal madness in which the internal narrator Martín describes Jaime is, I suggest, an amplified warning of the consequences of men's misjudgment and consequent abuse of women, turned from the generally humorous mode of N. 4 to the violence of Zayas's second collection. Once these two "devilish" black characters have served as didactic foils to her protagonists, Zayas has them both removed by death.

In sum, we can define the subjects about whom and to whom María de Zayas writes both by their "I am" statements – what her protagonists say they *are*, and by what her descriptions and plots say they are *not*. They are aristocrats, the men handsome and the women supremely beautiful and exquisitely dressed. They are wealthy and protective of their honor. They are *not* lower class, servants or slaves, merchants or black, or enemies of Spain, figures who often function in Zayas's novellas as foils for her heroines, whether they act as accomplices or adversaries. Her class bias and racial prejudice are distasteful and unsettling for modern readers who appreciate her audacity as a woman writer and her proto-feminism. We will see in the next chapter, however, that her attitude toward religious difference is, if not tolerant, somewhat more complex and unusual for her day.

---

41 *Disenchantments*, p. 146; *Desengaños*, p. 343.

Chapter Seven

I Believe:
Religion, Magic, the Supernatural

I DESCRIBED MARÍA DE Zayas in chapter 1 as "a successful published woman author of page-turning tales of love and death." That description, however, leaves out an important adjective: secular. She was a successful secular woman author. By "secular," I do not mean that her stories are godless or irreligious, but that they deal with normal human life, not the life of a saint, a mystic, or another pillar of religion. She was a secular writer in an age in which one's religious faith was of paramount importance, an age of fierce conflicts between the major religions and between different segments of the major denominations. She was far from the only secular woman author, of course; Baranda and Cruz's volume makes clear the volume and diverse kinds of texts penned by Early Modern Spanish women writers, as well as guiding readers to those that now have been published or that remain in manuscript. Zayas was, however, one of the very few published in her lifetime, whose success served as a model for other writers and whose legacy endures and draws new attention today. In this chapter, I consider Zayas's religious belief and practice, her depiction of convent life, how she portrays Jews and Muslims in her novellas, and her treatment of magic and the supernatural.

Religions and Religious Life

Categorizing Zayas as a secular writer is important because of the debate over the function of religion in her own life and whether she entered a convent. Her twentieth-century editors and biographers reached different conclusions based on their reading of her texts and other documents, perhaps influenced by their own religious beliefs. Her first biographer, Lena Sylvania, while not placing Zayas herself in a convent declared her "an ardent Christian." Sylvania wrote in her 1922 dissertation published by Columbia University that

> Doña María reveals herself as an ardent Christian, to whom a religious life represents the perfect state. In her novels, after passing through the trials and tribulations of this world, it is not unusual to find the heroine entering a convent in order to escape the persecution and ill-treatment of man. There, at last, she finds true happiness and peace, and is content to remain in the shelter of the church for the remainder of her natural life.[1]

The suggestion that Zayas might have entered a convent apparently originated with Agustín G. de Amezúa y Mayo, who published the first complete modern editions of Zayas's two volumes in 1948 and 1950, with an imaginative biography in his introduction to them. Amezúa speculated in his prologue to the 1950 edition that she might have entered a convent, to explain the absence of any later word from her after 1647. That speculation was followed by María Martínez de Portal in her 1973 edition, Isabel Barbeito Carnero in her 1992 biography of Zayas, and Montesa Peydro in his analysis of her novellas and their context. Alicia Yllera, however, says that Zayas might possibly have entered a convent after 1647, but that such a speculation is not demonstrable, nor is it indicated in the editions of her novellas.[2]

None of Zayas's heroines declares an initial religious vocation; those who retreat to the convent do so after mistreatment by a lover or husband, disillusioned with the possibility of finding another safe space and reliable life partner among men. Even Beatriz of D. 9, whose story is Zayas's version of a saint's tale, was happy to marry Ladislao initially and lived contentedly as his wife until he left to defend the realm from an aggressor. The nun Estefanía, who narrates D. 9, is Lisis's cousin, on leave from

---

[1] Lena Sylvania, *Doña María de Zayas y Sotomayor: A Contribution to the Study of Her Works*, New York, 1922, p. 15.
[2] See Agustín Amezúa y Mayo: "Prólogo," *Desengaños amorosos: Parte segunda del sarao y entretenimiento honesto de doña María de Zayas y Sotomayor*, ed. Agustín G. de Amezúa y Mayo, Madrid, 1950, p. xxii; María Martínez de Portal, "Estudio preliminar," *Novelas completas de María de Zayas*, ed. María Martínez de Portal, Barcelona, 1973, p. 29; Barbeito Carnero, *Mujeres*, p. 181; Montesa, *Texto y contexto*, p. 31, and Yllera, "Introducción," 2021, pp. 25–6, n. 59.

her convent to recover from quartan fever. Her comments to the other frame-tale characters at the conclusion of D. 5 "Innocence Punished," do bless her own religious vocation. Reflecting on the cruel tortures Inés has suffered, Estefanía says:

> Alas, my heavenly Bridegroom! If every time we offend against you, you punished us like that, what would become of us? But I'm foolish to compare you, merciful Lord, with earthly husbands. I've never been sorry for a moment that I consecrated myself to be your bride and even less so today. I shall never regret it and if I should ever offend against you, I know that with my first tear you'll forgive me and take me back with open arms.
>
> [¡Ay, divino Esposo mío! Y si vos, todas las veces que os ofendemos, nos castigarais así, ¿qué fuera de nosotros?... me habéis de perdonar y recibirme con los brazos abiertos.] [3]

Significantly, however, we meet this nun outside her convent, and she is realistic about the nuns and young women raised in their care. Of the convent-raised Gracia of N. 4, "she seemed a lovely figure, but without a soul [which], having been raised among nuns who are not ignorant of anything [was] a new miracle" [parecía figura hermosa, mas sin alma, milagro nuevo para haberse criado entre monjas, que no ignoran nada]. Then, in commenting on D. 9 before narrating it, Estefanía says,

> it's earthly matters that teach us to deceive. This you can see in the many ignorant men who cling to the bars of convents, unable to tear themselves away. They drink in Circe's deceptions like Ulysses, and they live and die in their bewitchment without ever realizing that we nuns deceive them with honeyed words, that they'll never get what they're after.
>
> [la hacienda que primero aprendemos [es] el engañar, ... y que no han de llegar a conseguir las obras.] [4]

Zayas gives us brief glimpses into convents but shows them more often as practical spaces of refuge or havens for the repentant than as initial choices for the truly devout. For example, Jacinta and Félix of N. 1 take temporary refuge there from Jacinta's father and brother's fury. Their first

---

3 *Disenchantments*, p. 198; *Desengaños*, p. 410.
4 ETL, p. 138; *Novelas*, p. 134; *Disenchantments*, p. 310; *Desengaños*, p. 558. See Elizabeth A. Lehfeldt, *Religious Women in Golden Age Spain: The Permeable Cloister*, Aldershot, 2005, and Rhodes, *Dresssed to Kill*, pp. 125–30.

devotion is to their very human love, not to God, while Félix lives. The enraged Juan of D. 2, "Most Infamous Revenge," flees to a monastery to escape punishment or reprisals for having raped Camila, just as he had earlier taken refuge in one after killing a man. Zayas sends both repentant male and female characters to them: for example, Serafina in N. 4 after she abandons her newborn baby, and don Pedro in D. 3, "His Wife's Executioner," saved by the enlivened hanged man. "He then went to the monastery of the Barefoot Carmelites and became a monk, donning the habit of the immaculate lady who had saved him from such terrible danger" [se fue a un convento de religiosos carmelitas descalzos, y se entró de fraile, tomando el hábito de aquella purísima Señora que le había librado de tan manifiesto peligro].[5] Zayas has the misogynistic, greedy don Pedro pressure his daughter Mencía to become a nun in D. 8, "Traitor to His Own Blood," in order to save all his wealth for his son, before resorting to her assassination. Although Zayas's don Pedro clearly did not lack resources for Mencía's dowry, in Early Modern Spain, convents did in fact serve as parking places for young women whose families lacked sufficient resources to provide dowries and good marriages for all their progeny.

Nor does Zayas paint for us descriptions of the experience of religious ecstasy such as those written by St. Teresa of Ávila in her *Life* (1611) and *The Interior Castle* (1588). Zayas undoubtedly knew Teresa's detailed portrayals of the rapture of the union of the soul with God and of the difficulties of communicating the experience in ordinary human language. In a famous passage in her *Life* that might have inspired Bernini's statue "Ecstasy of Saint Teresa," she wrote of the cherubim who inflicted it:

> In his hands I saw a great golden spear, and at the iron tip there appeared to be a point of fire. This he plunged into my heart several times so that it penetrated to my entrails. When he pulled it out, I felt that he took them with it, and left me utterly consumed by the great love of God. The pain was so severe that it made me utter several moans. The sweetness caused by this intense pain is so extreme that one cannot possibly wish it to cease, nor is one's soul then content with anything but God. This is not a physical, but a spiritual pain, though the body has some share in it – even a considerable share.[6]

The early publication of Teresa's works and her canonization in 1622 made her the model for the writings of other religious women. Nevertheless,

---

5 *Disenchantments*, p. 132; *Desengaños*, p. 322.
6 Teresa of Avila, *The Life of Saint Teresa of Avila by Herself*, trans J. M. Cohen, London, 1957, p. 210.

when, in D. 9, Beatriz's mysterious protectress finally reveals herself as the Mother of God and Beatriz recognizes her, Zayas's narrator Estefanía describes her attire and appearance externally, as the Virgin of the Immaculate Conception regularly appears in religious imagery such as *The Immaculate Conception of Los Venerables* painted by Murillo, now in the collection of the Museo del Prado:

> She was revealed in her diaphanous blue mantle. While it was blue, it was more radiant light than mantle. In her slipper of silvery moon, in her crown of stars, in the brilliant radiance of her holy and divine countenance, in the angelic cherubin that surrounded her, Beatriz recognized Our Lady the sovereign Queen of the Angels and Mother of God.
>
> [Como ya era la voluntad de Dios y suya que la conocieran, ... conoció Beatriz aquella soberana Reina de los Ángeles, Madre de Dios y Señora nuestra.]

Estefanía then adds, "Kneeling before her, she remained motionless and enraptured for a long time, gazing in absorption at such a glorious vision" [Conoció Beatriz aquella soberana Reina de los Ángeles, ... en tan gloriosa vista]. Estefanía adds no further details of what Beatriz felt. Instead, she continues her lecture to women not to trust men for a page and a half before saying, "Let Beatriz enjoy this longed-for favor while I ponder the mystery of the event." Which is, she tells us, that only the power of the Mother of God could free Beatriz from a man. After this lecture, Estefanía gives readers another external glimpse of Beatriz's rapture – "Let us now go back to Beatriz, whom we left rapt and enthralled by that divine vision" [Ahora volvamos a Beatriz, que la dejamos elevada y absorta en aquella divina vista] – and then resumes her sermon to women for another half page before returning to Beatriz:

> Well, as I was saying, Beatriz was kneeling, enraptured, beholding that Divine Lady who had come to her aid. She would have stayed like that until the end of the world if the Blessed Virgin had not said to her:
>
> "Come to your sense, friend Beatriz, the time has come for you to leave this place and defend your honor."
>
> [Pues, como digo, estaba Beatriz arrodillada, y tan fuera de sí, ... volver por tu honor.][7]

---

7 *Disenchantments*, p. 356, 357–8; *Desengaños*, pp. 620, 621, 623, 624.

Zayas's objective, as Rhodes points out, is not to inspire noblewomen to become saints, mystics or visionaries like Teresa, but to protect their honor and that of their estate in this world.

Zayas does demonstrate her religious faith and her adherence to the Catholic Church so closely linked with Spain and its monarchy throughout her novellas, as early as her opening image in N. 1 of Fabio climbing up Montserrat to worship at the shrine to the Black Virgin, patroness of Catalonia in its Benedictine monastery (see figure 2). Her winding sentence, one of the longest she wrote, challenges translators as much as the pilgrims' path.

> Midst the harsh crags of Montserrat, pinnacle and splendor of God's power and miraculous wonder of His divine Mother's excellencies, where the effects of her mercies are seen in divine mysteries, [...] among which is not the least the miraculous and sacred temple, as adorned with riches as with marvels. So many are the miracles therein, and the greatest of all that true portrait of the Most Serene Queen of the Angels and Our Lady. After having adored her, offering her a soul full of devout affection, and having beheld attentively those grandiose walls covered with shrouds and crutches, with other infinite number of insignias of her power, Fabio, an illustrious son of the noble town of Madrid, luster and adornment of her greatness, was ascending.
>
> [Por entre las ásperas peñas de Monserrat, ... subía Fabio, ilustre hijo de la noble villa de Madrid, lustre y adorno de su grandeza.]⁸

Zayas made this image the second paragraph of her first story, marking at the outset her Catholic faith and her devotion to images of the Virgin Mary.

Two signatures and a series of documents give possible if inconclusive evidence of María de Zayas's personal adherence to the doctrine of the Immaculate Conception of the Virgin and of when and where Zayas might have died. A 1617 petition for papal recognition of that doctrine signed by a group of male and female, secular and religious associates of the Brotherhood of the Defenders of the Immaculate Conception includes a signature by María de Zayas (written "çayas") along with that of that María's husband, Juan de Valdés.⁹ Was this our author? Barbeito Carneiro asserts it is, but Rodríguez de Ramos and Treviño give arguments both for and against that identity. The name María de Zayas was quite

---

8   ETL, pp. 61–2, slightly modified as well as abbreviated. Boyer rewrites this passage more completely. *Novelas*, pp. 173–4.
9   Barbeito Carneiro, pp. 166–7; Serrano y Sanz, *Apuntes*, vol. 2, pp. 583–7.

Figure 2 The Virgin of Montserrat and pilgrims on the road to the monastery. Engraving. © Monasterio de Santa María de Montserrat.

common in the seventeenth century; Serrano y Sanz and other researchers have found several death certificates from mid-seventeenth-century Madrid for women with that name.

In her novellas, Zayas displays an affection for the convent of the Immaculate Conception. Laura in N. 5 chooses to enter "the rich, noble, and holy convent of the Immaculate Conception" [se entró en la Concephción, convento noble, rico y santo]. Juana in N. 6 joins the same convent, and Clara's daughters become nuns.[10] In the frame of the third night, Isabel and Lisis appear wearing the habit of the Immaculate Conception, thus signaling Isabel's final choice to be a nun in that convent, where Lisis becomes a secular resident. Their mothers join them, with Isabel's mother becoming a nun along with her daughter. In addition, the narrator Filis of D. 4, in the preface to her story praising outstanding contemporary women, includes María Barahona, a nun in the same convent, as an example of a learned woman and poet.

Jews and Muslims, Conversos and Moriscos

Can we take these demonstrations of Zayas's faith as evidence of her family heritage as "old Christian?" Probably, but perhaps not incontrovertibly. (The term "New Christian" served to designate families of Jewish, or possibly Muslim origin.) Yolanda Gamboa asserts that Zayas's paternal family may have been of *converso* (converted Jewish) origin, and that her publisher, Esquer, was Jewish. Other critics reject those assertions. Since Jews were expelled from Spain in 1492, the assertion about her publisher, Esquer, is illogical; he might have had *converso* ancestry but not open affiliation and practice of Judaism in seventeenth-century Spain. The claim about the Zayas family is based on the family name "Zayas," or "çayas," as it appears in signatures, said to mean silversmith in Judeo-Spanish, which might indicate a *converso* genealogy. To counter this claim, others point to Zayas's father's membership in the military-religious Order of Santiago, which investigated the genealogy of proposed members to eliminate any candidates of "unclean" blood or illegitimate birth.[11] We should defi-

---

10 *Enchantments*, pp. 179; *Novelas*, pp. 369, 389.
11 Sander Berg, *The Marvellous and the Miraculous in María de Zayas*, Cambridge, 2019, pp. 13 and 36, n. 8; Julian Olivares, "Introducción," *María de Zayas y Sotomayor, Honesto y entretenido sarao (Primera y segunda parte)*, ed. J. Olivares, Zaragoza, 2017, vol. 1, p. lxxx, n. 121. On the expulsion and subsequent converso and morisco histories, see María Rosa Menocal, *Ornament*

nitely not read that possible trace as an indication that María de Zayas's Christian faith was less than sincere. There were distinguished figures in Spanish Catholicism of *converso* origin, including Saint Teresa of Ávila and San Juan de la Cruz, as well as notable writers like Cervantes and renowned political figures such as Phillip IV's *privado*, the Count-Duke of Olivares.[12] Yet it is worth noting that María de Zayas never mentions a Jew or a *converso* in any story. I suggest, speculatively, that she might have avoided mentioning Jews or *conversos* with much the same care as she avoided association with Sappho and the question of lesbian love. In an era beset by antisemitism and genealogical and inquisitorial investigations to root out Spaniards charged with having "impure blood" or divided religious loyalties, it would have been wise to draw no attention to the subject.

On the other hand, Zayas might have considered Jews and *conversos* more dangerous enemies of Christianity than Islam and *moriscos* (converted Muslims), particularly if Zayas knew of and appreciated Islamic respect for the Virgin Mary. She could well have been familiar with the thirteenth-century *Cantigas de Santa María*, in which the Virgin performs miracles for Muslims and expresses her preference for them over Jews.

In contrast to her omission of Jews and conversos, Zayas neither ignores nor erases Muslims and *moriscos* from her stories. She does not, of course, address the history of Muslims in Iberia, which began in 711 when Arabs and Berbers invaded from North Africa. The Visigothic state collapsed, and by 720 all but the most mountainous parts of the western and central Pyrenees were under Islamic control. The long, sporadic campaign of Christian forces to regain control ended in 1491–2 with the surrender of the last Islamic kingdom of Granada to the Catholic King Ferdinand and Queen Isabella. They promised religious and cultural tolerance for their Islamic subjects who remained in Iberia rather than emigrating, but it lasted only a decade. Instead, forced conversions turned those who

---

of the World: How Muslims, Jews, and Christians Created a Culture of Tolerance in Medieval Spain, Boston, 2002, pp. 244–52; David Nirenberg, *Communities of Violence: Persecution of Minorities in the Middle Ages*, Princeton, 1996, pp. 166–99, especially pp. 190–9; and Margaret R. Greer, "The Politics of Memory in El Tuzaní de la Alpujarra," *Rhetoric and Reality in Early Modern Spain*, ed. Richard J. Pym, London, 2006, pp. 113–30.

12 On their converso ancestry, see J. M. Cohen, "Introduction," *The Life of Saint Teresa of Ávila by Herself*, London, 1957, p. 17; Anthony J. Cascardi, "Introduction," *The Cambridge Companion to Cervantes*, ed. A. Cascardi, Cambridge, 2002, p. 4; Elliott, *The Count-Duke of Olivares*, pp. 10–11.

remained into nominal Christians, known as *moriscos*. Subsequent edicts banning the use of Arabic language and cultural practices over the course of the sixteenth century led to serious *morisco* rebellions, the most serious in 1568–70 in the Alpujarra mountains of Granada.[13]

Writing in the mid-1600s, Zayas would almost certainly have been aware of the controversy earlier in the century over relics unearthed in the destruction of the principal mosque in Granada and, a few decades before that, in caves on the hills outside Granada. The relics included the Torre Turpiana parchment, a tablet with a painted image of the Virgin and a box containing the "lead books" written in a form of Arabic and also a cloth the Virgin supposedly used to dry Christ's tears. They were transferred in 1623 to Madrid, where they remained for a decade, displayed prominently by the altar in the San Jeronimo church, generating much popular interest. The books' message upheld the thesis of the Immaculate Conception of the Virgin, as did their ardent defender, archbishop Pedro de Castro, Vaca y Quiñones. The books were then sent to Rome, and another forty years passed before they were finally declared falsifications in 1682. They are now thought to have been the work of two assimilated *moriscos*, Miguel de Luna and Alonso del Castillo, who served as translators for the Crown, and probably were an attempt to halt expulsion of the *moriscos* and the extinction of their culture.

Zayas introduces the *moriscos* in her storytelling fleetingly in N. 1, when Félix leaves the convent where he and Jacinta had taken refuge from her father's wrath and, attacked by her father and brother, kills her brother in a sword fight. In response to the mayor's threat to forcibly remove him from his convent haven, Félix goes to Barcelona, where, as Zayas tells us, "the galleys were that the companies sent by His Majesty Felipe III had brought for the expulsion of the *moriscos*, and that were awaiting His Excellency don Pedro Fernández de Castro, conde de Lemos" [las galeras que habían traído las compañías para la expulsion de los moriscos ... conde de Lemos].[14] Zayas presumably sets Félix's departure in these ships as a first opportunity to associate him with Lemos, not to pair his exile with that of the *moriscos*. She makes no comment on the expulsion order itself, either favorable or unfavorable. Supporters of Philip III and the Lerma regime led a concerted propaganda campaign in favor of expulsion, but this did

---

13 Greer, "The Politics of Memory"; A. Katie Harris, "The Sacromonte and the Geography of the Sacred in Early Modern Granada," *Al-Qantara: Revista de estudios árabes* 23.2, 2002, p. 518.

14 ETL, p. 80; *Novelas*, p. 193.

not extinguish variously motivated resistance. Within Spain, the archbishop of Granada and other church authorities there were against the decision, and the pope in Rome condemned exiling baptized Christians.

As for Félix, when he receives no letter from Jacinta (due to her father's meddling), he continues from Naples to Flanders. Intentionally or not, with the setting of Flanders, Zayas creates a suggestive link between the *morisco* expulsion and the truce with the Dutch rebels that Spain had fought for forty years. The *morisco* expulsion was decreed on April 9, 1609, the very day that Philip III and the Duke of Lerma signed a "humiliating twelve-year peace treaty with the Dutch rebels." As J. H. Elliott observes, "by the use of skillful timing, the humiliation of peace with the Dutch would be overshadowed by the glory of removing the last trace of Moorish dominance from Spain, and 1609 would be ever memorable as a year not of defeat but of victory."[15] Yet the truce would be allowed to expire in 1621, so the independence of the northern provinces effectively became permanent in 1609. Nor did the expulsion succeed in removing all *moriscos* temporarily or permanently.

In N. 9, "The Judge of Her Own Case," Zayas paints a distinction between good and bad Moors based on their actions and class. She first describes Amete as "a genteel and gallant Moor who had belonged to Carlos's father and, having been ransomed, was just about to go to Fez, where he had been born," and where "his father was a very wealthy pasha" [un gentil y gallardo moro, ... irse a Fez, donde era natural] [Era el moro discreto, y en su tierra noble, que su padre era bajá muy rico].[16] This reflects the practice of both Christian and Muslim captives in the Mediterranean, who served as slaves unless or until they could raise sufficient ransom to arrange their repatriation. Spanish literature usually shows Spanish Catholics captured by Arabs, not the reverse, understandably. Zayas does this as well in D. 1, when both Zelima/Isabel and Manuel are captured by Moorish corsairs and taken to Algiers. In N. 9, Amete freely admits to the cross-dressed Claudia that he is enamored of Estela. Claudia, thinking only of her own desire to keep Estela from eloping with

---

15 Trevor Dadson, "Official Rhetoric versus Local Reality: Propaganda and the Expulsion of the Moriscos," *Rhetoric and Reality in Early Modern Spain*, ed. Richard J. Pym, London, 2006, p. 1; Elliott, *Imperial Spain*, p. 305. See also Geoffrey Parker, *The Dutch Revolt*, rev. ed., London, 1985, especially pp. 260-6.

16 ETL, p. 156, n. 8; *Novelas*, p. 492.

Carlos, helps Amete and winds up "kidnapped" and on the way to Fez as well. She condemns Amete, who rejoins,

> The best arrangement in the world, Claudia, [...] is to repay the traitor with the means by which he or she offends; aside from which it is not right to trust someone who is disloyal to self, nation, and homeland. You want don Carlos and he wants Estela, to obtain your love you take away your lover's life, removing his lady from his presence. Well, how do you expect me to trust that a person who commits such a betrayal, such as giving Estela over to me on a mere whim, would not alert people in the city of my intention and they would seek me out and kill me?

> ["Al traidor, Claudia," respondió Amete, "pagarle en lo mismo que ofende, es el mejor acuerdo del mundo; ... y me darán la muerte?"][17]

Zayas intertwines the treachery of Claudia and Amete initially and in Fez; when Estela continues to refuse Amete, Claudia marries his brother Zayde and again betrays Estela with a false plan to escape and return to Spain, in order to leave Estela in a deserted spot where Amete beats her and tries to rape her. Her screams are heard, however, by Prince Jacimín, son of the king of Fez. Jacimín rescues Estela and condemns Claudia and Amete to death. When he frees Estela, he gives her jewelry and help to go wherever she chooses. His generosity is not a surprise. Both in the historical record and in other literary works, the highest-ranking Moors were often depicted as possessing a nobility of character. This portrayal did not extend to lower-status Moors, nor to *moriscos*, even those who had converted to Christianity before they were obliged either to convert or emigrate in 1492.

Zayas also associates Moors with the use of magic. She first gives this association a humorous touch in N. 3, "The Miser's Reward," when the maid Marcela's "magician" boyfriend promises to conjure a demon who will reveal where Isidora has gone with Marcos's wealth. This enchanter summons up the demon with the name Calquimorro, literally "Any Moor." The "demon" that appears is a tortured cat, and observers of the scene laugh at Marcos's gullibility. Later, in the darker world of the *Desengaños*, Zayas paints a more sinister image of Moorish sorcery. Diego, depressed and despairing over his frustrated passion for Inés in D. 5, "Innocence Punished," suddenly remembers hearing of a "great Moorish necromancer and magician" [habiendo oído decir que en la ciudad había un moro, gran hechicero y nigromántico, le hizo buscar] who lives

---

[17] ETL, p. 158; *Novelas*, p. 494.

in the city. "The Muslim necromancer promised him that within three days he would bring that lady into don Diego's power, which, in fact, he did. These things aren't hard for people who aren't Catholic and who, in difficult cases, don't hesitate to press the devil into service" [El nigrománstico agareno le prometió que, ... con apremios que hacen al demonio].[18] A necromancer is someone who consults the spirits of the dead, which is the way *nigromancia* is defined in the 1611 Covarrubias dictionary, and as Cervantes dramatizes it in his tragedy *La destruición de Numancia*, written in the 1580s. But in Early Modern Europe, it came to denote demonic magic, as Zayas employs it, and as it is defined in the early eighteenth-century *Diccionario de autoridades*: "The abominable art of executing strange and abnormal things by means of the invocation of the devil and a pact with him." The Moor escapes punishment by disappearing. Diego confessed to the corregidor, was jailed, taken before the Supreme Tribunal of the Inquisition, and thence also "disappeared," the implication being that he was killed in secret by the Inquisition for using the Moor's magic to gain sexual access to Inés. Zayas adds, "It was no small mercy that he met his punishment in secret, for otherwise he would have died at the hands of doña Inés's husband and her brother, given that the crime he'd committed deserved no lesser punishment" [Y no fue pequeña piedad castigarle en secreto, ... el delito cometido no merecía menor castigo].[19]

Free Will and the Stars

A question hotly debated between religious sects in Zayas's era was whether human beings have free will, or whether God, or fortune or the stars determine one's fate.[20] Zayas often refers to the influence of one's star, or the stars. She proclaims its importance in the first sentence of her first story, which she says will show "how neither the models of good behavior nor the models of bad behavior suffice to alter the doom of a woman when her stars incline her to it" [cómo para ser una mujer desdichada, cuando su estrella la inclina a serlo, no bastan ejemplos ni escarmientos]. In that same tale, she says that the determinative influence of one's star applies to Celio as well as Jacinta: "I believe his star inclines him to love where

---

18 *Disenchantments*, pp. 185, 186; *Desengaños*, pp. 392–3. See Berg, *Marvellous and the Miraculous*, pp. 70–91 for detailed descriptions of Zayas's use of sorcery.
19 *Desenchantments*, p. 191; *Desengaños*, p. 401.
20 See Berg, *Marvellous and the Miraculous*, pp. 134–8, and Sullivan, *Tirso de Molina and the Drama of the Counter Reformation*, Amsterdam, 1981, pp. 28–40.

he is abhorred and abhor where he is loved" [su estrella le inclina a querer donde es aborrecido, y aborrecer donde le quieren].[21] She blames the stars again for Laura's suffering in N. 5, and in N. 8, in the introduction to the story of Rodrigo and Leonor, she adds a threatening reference to the star of Pyramus and Thisbe. In D. 7, she mentions the star that foretold the deaths of the four sisters married to foreigners.

Zayas twice spells out the question of fate more fully. The first instance is in the introduction to D. 4, when the narrator Filis says, "While it's said that free will is not bound by the stars, since we can prevail over them by using reason, I'm still convinced that if you're born to be unfortunate, then it's impossible to avert misfortune" [Y cierto, que aunque se dice que el libre albedrío no está sujeto a las estrellas, … es imposible apartarnos de ellas].[22] This principle, according to Filis, was demonstrated by the tragic fate of both Camila and Roseleta, both killed by husbands although Camila prudently kept silent about her pursuer and Roseleta bravely told the truth. Zayas inserts the same concept in a paragraph describing Mencía's thought process as she falls in love with Enrique in D. 8, "Traitor to His Own Blood":

> She decided that the error of marrying against her father's wishes could be overcome with time. Her decision most likely was fated, despite the fact that it's said the wise man is master of his stars, may God free us from the stars that lead us to misfortune! No matter how much one fears them and tries to escape their influence, one has to be extremely careful to keep them from exercising their power. Because of her own inclination, certainly, and because of her servant's urging and, if you think about it, because her father's will was so contrary to her own, doña Mencía surrendered to her suitor's love.
>
> [Pareciéndole a doña Mencía que el yerro de casarse sin gusto de su padre con el tiempo se doraría, … al gusto de su padre por ser tan contrario al suyo.][23]

Although Zayas phrases it in terms of "stars," she is trying to reconcile the two fundamental yet contradictory tenets of Christian faith: the doctrine of free will and that of divine omnipotence and omniscience. Either one has free will and is therefore at least partly responsible for his or her salvation or condemnation, or everything depends on a preexisting

---

21 ETL, p. 93; *Novelas*, p. 207.
22 *Disenchantments*, p. 139; *Desengaños*, p. 228.
23 *Disenchantments*, p. 278; *Desengaños*, p. 374.

divine plan. While the problem dated much further back in Christian history, it was given new urgency by Luther and the Protestant Reformation, which made predestination a fundamental tenet, a position rejected by the Vatican and rebutted at the lengthy Council of Trent by its conclusion in 1563. That rejection did not erase the problem within Catholicism of defining just how divine grace preserved for human beings the freedom to choose, or reject, or to cooperate with, the divine will to achieve salvation. Spanish playwrights Calderón and Tirso de Molina dramatized the theological debate and their staunch defense of free will in famous plays such as Calderón's *Life Is a Dream*. While the dramas express "a profoundly optimistic faith in free will and God's boundless compassion," in Zayas's novellas, as Berg notes, "this optimism is replaced by a deep pessimism" about the position of women in society and their power of self-determination.[24] That is undoubtedly an accurate assessment of her second volume.

Magic and the Supernatural

Zayas includes scenes and episodes that can be classed as marvelous, miraculous, magical or fantastic in more than half of her twenty novellas. Although she wrote during the ferment of the Renaissance and Reformation that gave rise to a shift toward science and the Scientific Revolution in learned circles, I see no direct evidence of that epistemological shift in her novellas, except perhaps in the care she takes to distinguish apparently marvelous happenings worked by the devil from true miracles worked by God or the Virgin Mary, while leaving a few other marvels that fall in neither category.[25] Berg advances a clever and accurate image for Zayas's treatment of magic and sorcery: "she sits on the epistemological fence" as she counterposes contradictory presentations of magic as fraudulent or true, sometimes treated humorously, sometimes as life-threatening.

24 Berg, *Marvellous and the Miraculous*, pp. 136–7.
25 See Berg's survey of this shift and his separation of the preternatural order – marvels and wonders and the devil's theater of operations – from the strictly supernatural, "the exclusive domain of God, who alone can contravene the laws of Creation" (p. 42); and Zayas on the fence, p. 70. See also Eva Lara Alberola's thorough survey of seventeenth-century belief in magic and witchcraft, particularly as it involved attribution of belief in it related to the Count-Duke of Olivares: "El conde-duque de Olivares: Magia y política en la corte de Felipe IV," *Studia Aurea* 9, 2015, pp. 565–94.

I believe it is important, however, to consider her two volumes separately. She clearly focuses on the motivations behind the use of magic both in the *Novelas* (1637) and in the *Desengaños* (1647), but in the first volume, she presents magic with lighter touches. Alvaro, the narrator of N. 3, "The Miser's Reward," tells us that Marcela's plan was to deceive Marcos and "bilk him as much as she could" [a engañarle y estafarle lo que pudiese], as well as playing "an outlandish trick on the miser" [una solemne burla al miserable],[26] with the incantation worked with an old copy of *Amadis of Gaul* in Gothic script and a tortured cat. By having Marcelas's lover stage the spell, Zayas adheres to an established gender division in the realm of magic. Finding lost or buried treasure was almost exclusively a masculine purview, according to María Helena Sánchez Ortega.[27] Marcela's lover's performance is a demonstration of "magical thinking," the belief that humans can impose their will on the world with the correct ritual, which, according to James George Frazer, preceded religion.[28] When the truth of the procedure was revealed in court, everyone in the court – except Marcos, of course – laughed long and hard, and the judges dismissed the case and told Marcos not to be so easily fooled.

In the original version of the story, Zayas wrote a convoluted and dramatic climax that brought the devil into play as the ultimate motivator of dirty tricks. The marriage broker Gamarra – who had talked Marcos into the "noose" of a fraudulent marriage, reappears saying that he himself was in dire straits with his master, the Duke of Osuna – and supplies the two real nooses with which both he and Marcos can hang themselves. But the second noose is found dangling empty beside Marcos's. As we saw in chapter 4, investigators conclude that the second man must have been the shape-shifting devil disguised as Gamarra, whose lies drove Marcos to despair. In the second, corrected version of the story published shortly after the first, in 1637, Marcos receives Isidora's insulting letter, which compounds his dejection, and he sickens and dies "miserablemente" (miserably). This is the only story Zayas revised so significantly. Why did she do so? Not for fear of censors, since the volume had already been approved, even with the first tale involving a suicide of despair. I believe she

---

26 *Enchantments*, p. 106; *Novelas*, pp. 284, 285.
27 María Helena Sánchez Ortega, "Sorcery and Eroticism in Love Magic," *Cultural Encounters: The Impact of the Inquisition in Spain and the New World*, ed. Mary Elizabeth Perry and Anne J. Cruz, Berkeley, 1991, pp. 58–9.
28 James George Frazer, *The Golden Bough*, cited in Berg, *Marvellous and the Miraculous*, p. 45.

made the change to shift the blame from the devil – which made Marcos a victim worthy of some pity – to Marcos himself and his miserly nature. His object of desire is not the love of a woman, but money; he tells Isidora that "to him money was his honor" [su honra era su dinero].[29] Indeed, the implied critique is in the adverb Zayas uses to describe his death in the second ending: "miserablemente," which means not just unhappily, in extreme poverty, and avariciously, but most literally, as a miser.

Maintaining the gender divide in magic, Zayas depicts a woman who resorts to love magic in N. 5, "The Power of Love." Love magic was the kind most often attributed to women; they were thought to use it to change men's behavior, recover a straying lover or husband, or manipulate men for financial gain. The protagonist, Laura, is a young wife in Naples whose husband, Diego, now pursues another woman and ignores or abuses Laura. Sánchez Ortega, who has studied Inquisition records on the practice of love magic in Early Modern Spain, observes that there was no lack of women who sought the help of sorceresses to recover husbands who were distracted by other women, as Laura does in N. 5.[30] Zayas attributes the possibility of finding a sorceress in Naples to the absence of the Inquisition there:

> In Naples, sorceresses enjoy such freedoms to exercise their superstitions and schemes that they work their spells publicly. They do strange and amazing things that appear so true you almost have to believe in their powers. The viceroy and the clergy are concerned about this problem, as there's no restriction by the Inquisition or other punishment sufficient to frighten them, for in Italy the usual penalty is a small fine.
>
> [Hay en Nápoles, en estos enredos y supersticiones, ... porque en Italia lo más ordinario es castigar la bolsa.][31]

The sorceress – or as Zayas labels her, "the false sorceress" – out to bleed Laura's purse tells Laura to bring the teeth and hair from the head and beard of a hanged man. This is consistent with Sánchez Ortega's research, in which a hanged man's rope appears in some conjurations, along with other body parts. Laura goes at night to a chapel outside Naples that housed a deep pit around which executed criminals were hung on hooks to decompose until their bones dropped into the pit. As she stands in dread on a narrow ledge among the bodies, her brother Carlos wakes with

---

29 *Enchantments*, p. 102; *Novelas*, p. 280.
30 Sánchez Ortega, pp. 61, 70–2, 83–4.
31 *Enchantments*, p. 173; *Novelas*, p. 362.

a cry that his sister is in danger, and he gallops on horseback toward the city. In Zayas's telling, this sympathetic mental telepathy extends to the horse, which stops at the chapel and refuses to move until Carlos rescues his sister. Zayas's attitude toward magic is not easy to classify neatly; she is right in crediting the skeptical attitude of the Inquisition in restraining witch hunts in Spain, as Berg points out, and the converse would be the lack of that attitude in Naples if the Inquisition did not operate there. But she also includes unclassified occurrences that fall outside natural causes, such as the mental telepathy experienced by Carlos – and his horse.

In the next story, N. 6, "Disillusionment in Love and Virtue Rewarded," Zayas gives another sorceress the role of antagonist and rival to both Juana and Clara for the love of Fernando. Lucrecia is a friend of Juana and neither Juana nor others know her to be a witch, since she is wealthy and uses her magic only for her own benefit. In this story, unlike in N. 5, the sorceress is not false: Zayas casts no doubt on Lucrecia's spells. Despite being forty-eight years old, Lucrecia succeeds in drawing Fernando away from Juana – although her wealth may be an added lure. Instead, Zayas takes the story to the preternatural theater of the devil, bringing in demons, which are somehow contained in two rings that Juana gets from a student from the University of Alcalá to learn whether Fernando will ever marry her. Again, this has a parallel in the historical record: Sánchez Ortega cites the case of one María de Padilla, of the circle of King Pedro I of Castilla, who bewitched men using a ring containing an enchanted demon.[32] Juana wears the magic rings when talking to Fernando, then tells a maid to put them away, but instead, the maid wears the rings to the river to show to other maids washing clothes there. In response to this disrespect and mistreatment, the demons knock the university student off his mule and beat him nearly to death. They also tell the student that Fernando will never marry Juana, as they are already burning in hell's fire. Juana nurses the student back to health, and he teaches her the words of a ritual she can use to summon back a former suitor, Octavio. The incantation works, and Octavio appears, dragging heavy chains, surrounded by flames and uttering frightful moans, to tell Juana that after she spurned him for Fernando, he died as he left a gambling house. All this successful necromancy would imply the power of the devil, but Zayas counters this with Octavio's frightful voice, which tells Juana to give up her sinful pleasures:

32 Sánchez Ortega, p. 73.

Rest assured that even though the devil is the father of all lies and deceits, God may allow him to utter truths for the benefit and usefulness of men, to warn them of their perdition, as He has done with you. Through the voice of the student, He has warned you of your danger. Be fearful, for He has told you that you are burning in hell's fire, and give Him thanks because, sorrowful for your perdition, He has given you warning.

[Cánsate ya de la mala vida en que estás, teme a Dios y … dale gracias porque te avisa enternecido de tu perdición.][33]

Juana heeds this warning and persuades Fernando to pay her dowry to enter the convent of the Immaculate Conception.

Lucrecia, however, continues to use love magic to bind Fernando to her after his marriage to Clara, so that he neglects and abuses his wife. He leaves Toledo with Lucrecia, and Clara tracks them down in Sevilla and takes employment as a servant in their house, without Fernando recognizing her. She eventually discovers the secret of Lucrecia's spell over Fernando: a chained and blinded rooster. Removing the blinders from the bird, she also frees her husband. Lucrecia commits suicide, and the court burns her body along with the rooster and all the other charms she had been using. Clara nurses Fernando, but he nonetheless weakens and dies; doctors conclude that he had been consumed and killed by Lucrecia's spells. Berg classifies this episode as magical thinking, according to which the rooster is an analogy of Lucrecia's power to blind Fernando and bind him to her.

Zayas regularly attributes the malefic use of magic to foreigners: both the false sorceress of N. 5 and the formidable Lucrecia are Italians, and the necromancer of D. 5 is a Moor. In N. 8, Rodrigo in Flanders first unmasks a local false phantom attempting to seduce a widow, then prays so fervently to a statue of Christ in his beloved Leonor's tomb that she miraculously stirs back to life. Berg finds the contrast fitting for "Zayas's overall xenophobic agenda," a valid observation.[34]

Equally salient is Zayas's distinction between Leonor's resurrection as a heaven-sent miracle, and the Rodrigo-Leonor marriage in Tridentine Catholic rites, a kind of terrestrial legalization, further validated by a famous professor from the University of Salamanca, and the student chorus of voices. The marriage writes a happy ending, an unexpected conclusion

---

33 *Enchantments*, p. 194; *Novelas*, p. 387; Berg, p. 46.
34 Berg, p. 119. See also Greer, *María de Zayas*, pp. 264–7, and Edwin Morby, "The Difunta pleiteada Theme in María de Zayas," *Hispanic Review* 16, 1948, pp. 238–42.

for a tale that began with the dark foreshadowing of two lovers born under the star of Pyramus and Thisbe, the doomed lovers in Ovid's *Metamorphoses*. (English speakers would know the story from Shakespeare's *Romeo and Juliet*, which Zayas would not have known.) Leonor insists that "she had indeed died a real death, as she proved by telling things that aren't important here and so aren't described" [Ella naturalmente había sido muerta, refiriendo algunas cosas que bastaron a hacer bastante esta verdad, que por no ser de importancia al suceso, se ocultan].³⁵ Zayas's addition of this detail and the consultation with a famous Salamanca professor are evidently a reaction to a play she would have known, *La difunta pleitada* (The deceased bride suit), probably by Lope de Vega.³⁶ The play concludes with legal arguments between two fathers, both said to be expert lawyers, citing Justinian, Papinian and other legal authorities, as well as theologians and the resurrection of Lazarus. After hearing their arguments regarding the dissolution of marriage by death, the Prince awards the bride to her first husband on the grounds that she had not really died, despite her long, deathlike swoon. Zayas has Leonor add that she had died a real death to assure her readers that Leonor's case was a true miracle of resurrection. She thus distinguishes it from the final "miracle of love" story in her first volume, N. 10, "The Deceitful Garden." In that tale, the devil creates an apparently miraculous garden, and then yet more marvelously, renounces his claim on Jorge's soul. Zayas has the narrator, her mother, undercut belief in that marvel in her introduction to it.

While the *Novelas* see a generally light use of magic, the *Desengaños* are, in keeping with the overall darker themes of Zayas's second volume, devoid of humor when it comes to the elements of the preternatural and supernatural. The lightest it gets is in her first use of the supernatural, in the broad sense, in D. 2, "Most Infamous Revenge." A mysterious voice announces to the protagonist, Camila, that she will die, and this is not a terror but a welcome relief from the suffering visited on her by her husband's poison. Such voices frequently appear in plays of Zayas's era, not only in saints' plays but as supernatural warnings to other characters as well, from Alonso in *El caballero de Olmedo* to don Juan and his lackey Catalinon in *El burlador de Sevilla*. In this case, Zayas uses it as heaven's validation of Camila's virtue. As the poison paralyzes Camila's swollen

---

35 *Enchantments*, p. 269; *Novelas*, p. 481.
36 Lope de Vega included a play of that title in the list of his plays that prefaced his *El peregrino en su patria*. See the digital copy in the Biblioteca Digital Hispánica of the Biblioteca Nacional de España.

body, Zayas writes that "God must have wanted this unfortunate and devout woman to suffer even greater martyrdom so that she could receive her reward in haven" [Debía de querer Dios que esta desdichada y santa señora padeciese más martirios para darle en el cielo el premio de ellos], and six months later, "she heard a voice that said, 'Camila, your time has come.' She gave thanks to God for removing her from such a painful life; she took the sacraments and the next night she died to this world to live in eternity" [Oyó una voz que decía: 'Camila, ya es llegada tu hora.' ... y otro día en la noche murió, para vivir eternamente].[37] In the *Desengaños*, Camila is the first in a string of brutally sacrificed innocent wives. As Rhodes argues, Zayas crafts the wives' images and those of their tormentors not to encourage other women to imitate them but to discourage their abusers. The sinful behaviors that lead to their wives' deaths also threaten the Spanish nobility, not only ethically, but biologically, as wives in these tales almost always die before they bear children. In the *Desengaños*, only one child is born to aristocratic parents: in D.8, a boy survives his mother Ana's murder, for which his repentant father is executed.

Roseleta, the murdered wife in D. 3, "His Wife's Executioner," is the next secular martyr, a perfect victim. As the narrator Nise says in the introduction, nothing can save a woman, neither keeping silent about assaults on her virtue – as Camila did in the preceding tale – nor telling her husband, as does Roseleta. Nise's preface also serves to distinguish the tale implicitly from its well-known Cervantine predecessor, as she defends the originality and veracity of her story (see chapter 5) and, with her emphasis on the truth of the case she presents, also tacitly supports the reality of the miracle Zayas adds: a hanged thief who is reanimated twice, to save the life of Juan, who loves Roseleta. Rhodes suggests that the resurrected thief was Zayas's variant of a miracle that appeared in Cantigo 13 of the thirteenth-century *Cantigas de Santa María*, a songbook in praise of the Virgin. Cantigo 13 relates the hanging of a thief who always commended himself to the Virgin in prayer, as does Juan on his way to his supposed assignation with Roseleta. The Virgin rewards his devotion by placing her hands under his feet so that he survives for three days. He is hanged again, and again survives to broadcast to all that credit for his survival is due to the Virgin. He is freed and enters a religious order, as does Juan.[38] In the Cervantes version of the tale, the emphasis is on what mystery of the

---

37 *Disenchantments*, p. 108; *Desengaños*, p. 291.
38 Rhodes, *Dressed to Kill*, on the *Cantigo*, p. 197, 21; on the beauty of dead wives, p. 113.

human psyche causes irresistible jealousy over a woman to arise between two devoted friends; Zayas concerns herself with the mystery of divine reasons for saving Juan, while giving Roseleta a martyr's death. This is reinforced by a debate among the listeners after Nise concludes her tale. Some of the women are amazed that God would save Juan's life and not that of the innocent Roseleta. To settle the matter, Lisis says that God's miracles and secret ways are incomprehensible.

The debate about the miracles continues among Zayas readers today, with other angles. Berg thinks that Zayas added the undead hanged thief to write "a shocking and thrilling story"; Rhodes sees Roseleta's collaboration with Pedro in attempting to assassinate Juan as evidence that Zayas does not condemn honor killings. That Pedro has Roseleta bled to death, as her father don Pedro has Mencía killed in D. 8, "Traitor to His Own Blood," seems surely to have been inspired by Calderón's magnificent drama *El médico de su honra* (The surgeon of his honor). The surgeon of the play's title, Gutierre, has his wife, Mencía, bled to death because he fears that she has been unfaithful to him with Prince Enrique, the half-brother of King Pedro I of Castile (1334–69). The play concludes with the king – who was known as both the Just and the Cruel – ordering Gutierre to marry Leonor, which implies a new cycle of violence, as the surgeon had earlier rejected Leonor because he considered her honor tainted as well. Critics have long debated whether Calderón supported or questioned honor killing. Ludovico, the surgeon who bleeds Mencía on Gutierre's orders, reports to the king that she exclaimed, "I die innocent; don't let heaven indict you for my death."[39] And Coquín, Gutierre's servant, risks his life to tell the king of her innocence, hoping to save her from the threat of Gutierre's mad jealousy. Traditional critics have argued that the audience at the time would have sided with Gutierre and discounted the judgment of lower-class characters such as Ludovico and Coquín. Yet that same audience would certainly have understood that when Enrique's dagger accidentally cuts King Pedro's hand, it is prefiguring the real events of 1369, when Enrique assassinated Pedro at Montiel, in the civil war that would bring Enrique to the throne and embroil Spain in the Hundred Years' War. I have argued that Calderón deliberately leaves the conclusion

---

39 Rhodes, *Dressed to Kill*, pp. 161–7; Berg, p. 123; Calderón, *The Physician of His Honor / El médico de su honra*, ed. D. Cruickshank, Madrid, 1981, trans. of Dian Fox, 2nd ed., Oxford, 2007, verses 2686–90 and 2728–64, pp. 190–5; Greer, "Spanish Golden Age Tragedy: From Cervantes to Calderón," *A Companion to Tragedy*, ed. Rebecca Bushnell, Malden, 2005, p. 363–4.

open, obliging the audience to decide the location of tragic guilt. As we have seen in chapters 1 and 6, however, Zayas identified with the aristocratic order and appears to have accepted the rectitude of its high officials without question. She directs her critique only at the immorality and unethical actions of individual nobles, not at the fundamental structure of patriarchy. In her version of the tale, she does introduce a future shadow over the married peace of her jealous and murderous pair of nobles, Pedro and Angeliana; Zayas leaves them "fearing only God's punishment which, if it didn't catch them in this life, surely would in the next" [se casó con Angeliana, con quien vivió en paz, aunque no seguros del castigo de Dios, que si no se les dio en esta vida, no les reservaría de él en la otra].[40] All Zayas's murdered wives are beautiful in death, however, an inscription of their innocence, as Rhodes explains, "In the fictional world of the *Desengaños*, bereft of heroes, heaven speaks to human beings through the dead."[41] The metamorphosis from abused body to paragon of beauty is clearly a justiciary moment when God intervenes to pronounce a divine verdict of innocence in the case of each perfect victim.

In D. 5, "Innocence Punished," the Moorish necromancer controls Inés with her candle-statue. When the candle is lit, Inés is "driven by some diabolic spirit that controlled her behavior" [forzada de algún espíritu diabólico que gobernaba aquello].[42] Later, the mayor and Inés's brother test the power of the candle repeatedly after finding her in the street at night. Berg, following Judith Whitenack, brings up the issue of human free will in relation to this tale, but Zayas does not; the truth of her enchantment is questioned only by her suspicious relatives, who suggest she feigned it to absolve herself from guilt.

D. 8, "Traitor to His Own Blood," has several preternatural or fantastic scenes, including shutters that open uncannily and the voice of the dead Mencía warning Enrique of imminent attack. Zayas attributes none of this directly to the devil or God, but she does say that the Blessed Mother interceded with God to plead for Enrique's life because he had promised to become a monk and would build a chapel to house Mencía's body.

In D. 10, "The Ravages of Vice," there is another marvelous element, a moaning dead body, "complaining as if it had a soul" [que se lamentaba como si tuviera alma], which Gaspar finds in the cellar of the house where his lover lived with her three sisters. The objects Gaspar finds in

---

40 *Disenchantments*, p. 135; *Desengaños*, p. 326.
41 Rhodes, *Dressed to Kill*, p. 113.
42 *Disenchantments*, p. 187; *Desengaños*, p. 394.

the corpse's pockets contain no name but do indicate a Catholic devotion and pursuit of some love affair. Gaspar believes the moaning corpse to be "God warning him to get away from the house in which such risks abided" [que era aviso de Dios para que se apartase de casa donde tales riesgos había], so he stops visiting the sisters.[43] (It doesn't spare Gaspar for long: he then falls in love with Florentina and pursues her fruitlessly until he finds her bleeding in the street, and she sends him to visit the "bedeviled mess" [endemoniado enredo] of a massacre that she left behind.) Again, Zayas provides no explanation for the fantastically moaning corpse, so it functions in the story largely as evidence of enduring human drives.

In the preceding story, D. 9, "Triumph over Persecution," however, Zayas stages a direct confrontation between the devil's preternatural operations and the divine powers of the Mother of God. Moreover, Zayas calibrates it shrewdly, reserving explicit recognition of their identities for the final pages. Readers in her own day would have been alert to the devil's capacity to disguise himself, and most would likely have realized that the fallen Queen Beatriz's kind helper was the Virgin Mary, but Zayas gives her readers the pleasure of decoding the mystery. At first, Beatriz cannot see the helper because her eyes have been pricked out; she can only hear a kind voice. The voice tells her, "God has granted you this martyrdom" [Dios ha permitido darte este martirio] and others to come. Then Beatriz's sight is restored, but she does not recognize the beautiful young woman who has helped her. The woman leads Beatriz to a pleasant meadow and tells her to wait: God will assist her in her trials.[44] Meanwhile, the devil uses a magic ring to allow Beatriz's tormentor, Federico, to become invisible and to make his lies believed; he employs other magic arts to travel swiftly and forge handwriting and signatures. The Virgin repeatedly restores Beatriz's queenly attire, and she removes Beatriz from Federico's arms, replacing her with a ferocious lion; later, she frees Beatriz from an execution scaffold. After Beatriz has lived for years in a hermit's cave, her helper reveals herself as the Mother of God and gives Beatriz herbs that make her a "miracle doctor": she can instantly cure any plague, so long as the patient confesses every one of his sins.

When the king summons Beatriz to cure Federico, who has fallen ill, the magician (as the devil has disguised himself) asks the miracle doctor how the cure works. Beatriz replies, "I cure by virtue of God, who is more powerful than your false magic" [En la de Dios, que puede más que no tu

---

43 ETL, pp. 289; 290, 310; *Desengaños*, pp. 641, 642, 669.
44 *Disenchantments*, p. 331; *Desengaños*, p. 431.

falsa mágica]. This doctrine of the limits of demonic versus divine knowledge was regularly repeated in *autos sacramentales*, the popular Spanish religious plays performed in public streets and plazas every Corpus Christi and often played in theaters as well. Zayas's narrator comments, "What a great mystery God had wrought for her to be speaking to the very ones who had persecuted her, without being recognized by any of them, least of all the magician!" [¡Gran misterio de Dios, que estaba hablando con los mismos que la perseguían, sin ser conocida de ninguno, ni el mágico menos!] When Beatriz tells Federico he must confess every one of his sins, the magician reminds him that he has promised never to do so. Federico asks him to leave so he can confess, but Beatriz, "inspired by heaven," speaks up: "Relax, hypocrite, and don't leave. It doesn't matter whether you're present, since you are ever present, but this time your cunning and knowledge will avail you naught, for there is one who knows more than you" ["Estáte quedo, engañador, no te vayas, que poco importa que estés presente, pues tu siempre lo estás a todo; mas por esta vez no te valdrán tus astucias ni saber, que hay quien sabe más que tu"]. Federico then confesses everything except how he had painted Beatriz as unfaithful to her husband, the king. She cautions him that if he has left any sin unconfessed, he will lose not only his life but his soul as well. He then recounts the whole story, and Beatriz appears in all her queenly attire and jewels:

> They all saw Our Lady, the Mother of God and Queen of the Angels, place her divine hand on the beautiful Queen Beatriz's right shoulder. At this heavenly and divine vision, the [demonic] doctor, who was sitting in a chair by Federico's bed, exploded as if an artillery shot had been fired. Shouting at the top of his voice, he screamed:
>
> "You win, Mary, you win! Now I recognize the shadow that protected Beatriz. How blind I have been until now!"
>
> He vanished, leaving the chair choked with thick smoke. The whole room was stunned by the shock, a chaos of confusion. Where Beatriz stood with her heavenly protectress, they beheld a perfect light and, where the false doctor and true demon had been, darkness and black shadow.
>
> [Viendo todos cuantos en la sala estaban […] cómo la Madre de Dios, … una tiniebla y oscuridad.][45]

---

45 *Disenchantments*, pp. 360, 361, 363; *Desengaños*, pp. 630, 631.

This, in my view, is how Zayas wants her readers to envision demonic and divine powers, with innocent, wise women bathed in divine light, whether in life or as beautifully lit corpses, while demonic darkness swallows their antagonists. The materials she chose to use, and her manipulation of those sources, reflect her focus on reforming the secular life of the nobility of her day, but she also grapples with significant religious questions of the time.

Chapter Eight

Zayas on Women

JUST BEFORE ZAYAS places Lisis in the narrator's chair to tell the last tale and close her collection, she comments, in Boyer's translation, "In this sad age, there is no real pleasure; we're coming closer and closer to the end, like the person who travels and journeys day after day and ends up back where he began his journey" [En esta penosa edad, no le hay [gusto] cumplido, porque nos vamos acercando más al fin, como el que camina, que andando un día una jornada, y otro día otra, viene a llegar al lugar adonde enderezó su viaje]. Much as I wish that were what Zayas wrote, it is not. In the Spanish original, her traveler walks the distance he can cover one day after another to reach his destination, not to go back to where he started.[1] I like Boyer's translation because it seems to me that all the stories in the *Desengaños* are essentially variations on the first one. Zayas gave a title only to the first *desengaño*, "Her Lover's Slave," as if all the others are also "Her Lover's Slave," stories of women enslaved or killed by their lovers. Moreover, looking at the two volumes together, many of the tales are variants of Jacinta's experience in N. 1, of the eventual failure of love and refuge in a convent, sheltered among other women from the dangerous love of men. As Boyer translates Zayas's comment, she would be directing us back to the start of her work, which could very well be her prologue to the *Novelas*, in which she defends the worth and rights of women.

Her opening salvo in that prologue is a challenge:

---

[1] *Disenchantments*, p. 365; *Desengaños*, p. 633. The mistranslated word is "enderezar," to straighten, or direct toward, not to come back to where he began. A "jornada" was used to mean the distance a man could walk in a day, or a day's work, or, by extension, one act of a play.

Who doubts, my reader, that you will be amazed that a woman has the audacity not only to write a book, but to send it for printing, which is the crucible in which the purity of genius is tested... . Who doubts ... that there will be many who attribute to madness this virtuous daring to bring my scribblings into light, being a woman, which, in the opinion of some fools, is the same as an incapable thing.

[Quién duda, lector mío, que te causará admiración que una mujer tenga despejo no sólo para escribir un libro ... es lo mismo que una cosa incapaz.] [2]

She directs that challenge to patriarchal culture, in particular against its concept of female inferiority – the prevailing ideology that a woman is by nature "an incapable thing." The philosophical principle of women's inferiority dates back at least as far as Aristotle, who claimed women were only passive contributors to the generation of offspring, while men, with their heat and movement, were the source of the seed for the embryo and thus contributors of the perceptual soul.[3]

Zayas rejects this traditional explanation of sexual difference and claims instead that women are the material and spiritual equals of men:

If this material of which we men and woman are made, whether a combination of fire and mud, or a mass of spirits and clods, is no more noble in them than in us, if our blood is the same thing, our senses, faculties and organs through which their effects are wrought are all the same, the soul the same as theirs – since souls are neither male nor female – what reason is there that they would be wise and presume we cannot be so?

[Porque si esta materia de que nos componemos los hombres y las mujeres, ya sea una trabazón de fuego y barro, ... presuman que nosotras no podemos serlo?][4]

Zayas's extension of women's material equality to the realm of intellectual capacity is probably not meant to argue specifically with Aristotle but is quite likely a response to a more recent scientific-philosophical account

---

2 ETL, p. 47; *Novelas*, p. 159.
3 Aristotle, *Generation of Animals and History of Animal I, Parts of Animals I*, ed. and trans. C. D. C. Reeve, Indianapolis, 2019, Generation, Book I, 1.19–1.22, 2.3. See also Sophia M. Connell, *Aristotle on Female Animals: A Study of the Generation of Animals*, Cambridge, 2019, pp. 1–34, 374–9 and Joan Cadden, *Meanings of Sex Difference in the Middle Ages: Medicine, Science, and Culture*, Cambridge, 1993, pp. 11, 13, 21–6, 31–4.
4 ETL, p. 47; *Novelas*, p. 159.

of human nature, the *Examen de ingenios para las ciencias*, published by Huarte de San Juan in 1575. Widely read and repeatedly published in Spain, as well as in France, Italy and the Netherlands, it was later put on the list of prohibited books in Portugal and Spain in 1581 and 1583, because examiners thought the thoroughgoing biological determinism of Huarte's organic explanation of the nature of intelligence cast doubts on the importance of free will and the immortality of the soul. A revised edition appeared in 1594, and its editorial popularity continued, including an English translation by Richard Carew, published that same year in London with the title and explanatory subtitle *The Examination of mens Wits. In which, by discovering the varietie of natures, is shewed for what profession each one is apt, and how far he shall profit therein*.[5]

We don't know if Zayas was aware of the Inquisition's objection to Huarte's original version, but regardless, her statement that souls are neither male nor female is significant as an extension of the Christian doctrine of the fundamental equality of all human beings, created by God and in his image. That doctrine coexisted with a belief in a divinely ordered hierarchy of earthly existence, however, in which certain material or spiritual elements were believed to give males superiority over females. Late medieval and Early Modern arguments in defense of women often relied in part on variant interpretations of the Biblical story of creation, such as reading a universalized or androgynous use of "man" in Genesis 1:27: "So God created man in his own image; in the image of God he created him in his own image; male and female he created them." The account of the creation of woman from Adam's rib was also sometimes interpreted as marking woman as a superior being because she was not created from the "dust of the ground," as was the man in Genesis 2:7, but from a more worthy matter, the flesh of man.[6] Such defenses of women were part of the vast and widely read network of medieval and Early Modern texts known as *La Querelle des femmes* – literally translated, the Dispute of Women, but commonly in English called the Woman Question – or, in Spanish,

---

5 See Guillermo Serés, "Introducción," in Huarte de San Juan, *Examen de ingenios para las ciencias*, Madrid, 1989, pp. 110–14, 120–1.

6 See Juan de Espinosa, *Diálogo en laude de las mujeres*, Granada, 1990, pp. 149–54; Teresa de Cartagena, *Grove of the Infirm* and *Wonder at the Works of God*, and Juan Rodríguez del Padrón, "El triunfo de las donas," in *Obras de Juan Rodríguez del Padrón*, ed. A. Paz y Meliá, Madrid, 1884, pp. 88–9. On the nature and participants of the Spanish *Querella*, see Emily C. Francomano, "The Early Modern Foundations of the *Querella de las mujeres*," Baranda and Cruz, *Routledge Research Companion*, pp. 41–59.

La querella de las mujeres. The works, written by both men and women, engage in political and rhetorical debates as they seek to define women's physical, moral and intellectual qualities, a practice that extended into works of fiction that preceded Zayas's novellas.

As for Huarte, he argues formidably against women's intellectual capacity. Starting with the foundation of Aristotelian natural philosophy, which emphasizes heat and cold, wetness and dryness, Huarte adds Hippocratic/Galenic humoral theory, which explained health and disease as a proper or improper balance of four bodily fluids, blood, yellow bile, black bile and phlegm. He was a strident spokesman for what has been labeled the "one sex" model of human sexuality. The theory, reasonably well-accepted in Huarte's time, saw females as imperfect males: women and men possessed the same sex organs, but her organs were located inside the body rather than outside.[7] There was no word for ovaries, which were called testicles in Huarte and in Covarrubias's *Tesoso de la Lengua* dictionary of 1611. In Huarte's formulation:

> A man, although his composition seems to us to be what we see, is no different from a woman, according to Galen, except in having his genitals outside his body. Because if we dissect a maiden, we will find that she has within herself two testicles, two seminal vessels, and the uterus with the same composition as the virile member, not lacking a single delineation.
>
> And this is true in such a way that if Nature, having finished making a perfect man, should want to convert him into a woman, it would require no other work than turning the generative instruments within; and if having made a woman, should wish to change her into a man, after pushing outside the uterus and testicles, [Nature] would have nothing more to do.
>
> [Y es que el hombre, aunque nos parece de la compostura que vemos, no difiere de la mujer, ... el frío las detiene y encoge.][8]

---

7 Thomas Laqueur, *Making Sex: Body and Gender from the Greeks to Freud*, Cambridge, 1990, pp. 1–6, 77–88. See also Joan Cadden, *Meanings of Sex Difference in the Middle Ages: Medicine, Science, and Culture*, Cambridge, 1993, who finds his description overly simplistic, pp. 3, 33–4.

8 Juan Huarte de San Juan, *Examen de ingenios*, ed. Guillermo Serés, Madrid, 1989, pp. 608, 609–10, 614, 615, my translation. For further details and an analysis in terms of essentialism and constructionism, see Greer, *María de Zayas*, pp. 64–72.

Huarte says that whether a creature is male or female depends on the quantity of heat it contains.

> The reason and cause why the genital organs are engendered within or without or coming out a female and not a male is very clear, knowing that heat dilates and enlarges everything and cold stops and shrinks them. And thus, the conclusion of all philosophers and doctors is that if the seed is cold and wet, it becomes a female and not a male, and in being hot and dry, it will engender a male and not a female. From which can be clearly inferred that there is no man who can be called cold in relation to woman, nor woman hot in relation to man.

Women need to have a cooler and wetter balance, Huarte says, in order to have "phlegmatic blood" to nourish a fetus and nurse a baby, but he maintains that those qualities inhibit intellectual development. He does admit variations and even concedes that women with the least coolness and wetness may have greater rational powers than the most imperfect male.

Zayas, for her part, strongly rejects Huarte's humoral analysis of intellectual capacity. First, she shifts from an essentialist focus on physiology to the socially constructed nature of gender roles, then she acknowledges women's apparent limitations, but places the blame on men, thanks to their

> impiety or tyranny in locking us up and not giving us teachers. And so the true reason why women are not learned is not a lack of ability but lack of practice. Because if in our upbringing, just as they set us to the cambric on our lace pillows and to stitching patterns in our embroidery hoops, they were to provide us with books and preceptors, we would prove as apt for posts and professorships as men.
>
> [su impiedad o tiranía en encerrarnos y no darnos maestros..... tan aptas para los puestos y para las cátedras como los hombres.]⁹

Continuing that sentence, she stands Huarte's evaluation on its head, saying that women might be "perhaps of sharper wit, since our disposition is colder, given that understanding is humid, as can be seen in quick wit and calculated deceit, for everything done with skill, although it be not virtue, is ingenuity [y quizás más agudas, por ser de natural más frío ...aunque no sea virtud, es ingenio]. Zayas thus appropriates Huarte's reluctant

---

9 ETL, pp. 47–8, 48–9; *Novelas*, pp. 159–60. Huarte, 616; on understanding, Huarte, p. 316. See also Teresa Soufas on other women writers' use of the inconsistencies of humoral theory in defending their creative intellectual powers.

admiration for exceedingly "cool" women who are astute, cunning and good at conversing, even with men. She could also have pointed to inconsistencies in his treatise, because at several points he links relative coolness with the highest mental faculty, *entendimiento* (understanding or judgment). Moreover, as José Rodríguez-Garrido proposes, Zayas shows that understanding and wit in action in the one play she wrote, *La traición en la amistad*, in which she associates women's coolness with their capacity for love.[10] (See the discussion below of the play.)

Zayas reinforces her argument for women's intellectual capacity with a list of foremothers, a time-honored practice of legitimating a praxis by citing accepted authorities – although of course, it is more often a list of forefathers. Male champions of women led the way in compiling lists of foremothers, from Bocaccio's *De claris mulieribus*, and King Juan II's favorite, Alvaro de Luna's *Libro de las virtuosas e claras mujeres* of 1466. In her "To the Reader" prologues, Zayas departs from the male models, however, both in the brevity of her list and in her choice of women. She focuses on those who were known as writers and teachers of men, from classical Greece and Rome to the early Christian era: Argentaria, wife of the poet Lucan; Themistoclea, Pythagoras's sister; as well as Diotima, who teaches the philosophy of love to Plato in his *Symposium*; Aspasia, the ancient Greek hostess of philosophical salons; Eudocia, Cenobia, and Cornelia.[11] In her second volume, in the introduction to the fourth *desengaño*, Zayas expands her list, citing a number of distinguished women from her own era: the intellectually gifted and politically empowered sisters of Charles V; princess Isabel Clara Eugenia of Austria, daughter of Philip II, who ruled the Netherlands with her husband the Archduke Alberto; queen Margarita of Austria, wife of Philip III and mother of Philip IV and Anne of Austria, wife of Louis XIII of France; learned nuns Eugenia de Contreras and María de Barahona; and two women poets, Isabel de Ribadeneira and Ana Caro de Mallén, of Seville, who was also a playwright.[12] The list ends with the equivalent of an "etc.": "and other infinite numbers of women of antiquity and of our times whom I pass over in silence

---

10 José A. Rodríguez-Garrido, "El ingenio en la mujer: *La traición en la amistad* de María de Zayas entre Lope de Vega y Huarte de San Juan," *Bulletin of the Comediantes* 49.2, 1997, pp. 357–73.
11 ETL, p. 50; *Novelas*, p. 160. See details of the list in ETL, 49–50, and in the *Desengaños*, pp. 333–6, footnotes 6–13.
12 *Disenchantments*, pp. 140-1; *Desengaños*, pp. 333–6; On Ana Caro, see Juana Escabias, "Ana María Caro Mallén de Torres: Una esclava en los corrales de comedias del siglo XVII," *EPOS: Revista de Filología* 28, 2012, pp. 177–93.

Figure 3. *Infanta Isabel Clara Eugenia and Magdalena Ruiz*. Portrait by Alonso Sánchez Coello, 1585–1588; © Madrid, Museo Nacional del Prado.

because you will surely know of it all, although you may be unlettered and might not have studied [y otras infinitas de la antigüedad y de nuestros tiempos que paso en silencio, porque ya tendrás noticias de todo, aunque seas lego y no hayas estudiado].

Even women who haven't studied can educate themselves, Zayas says, with the help of two resources: "polyantheas in Latin" – anthologies of wide-ranging information and snippets of wisdom that authors cited to appear widely read; and "summaries of moral dictates in the vulgar tongues" (that is, Spanish, French, English and other non-classical languages), with which, she says, "men who are not clerics and women can be educated" [Y que después que hay *Polianteas* en latín, y *Sumas morales* en romance, … ¿qué razón hay para que no tengamos prontitud para los [hombre] libros?].[13] She adds: "For if this is true, what reason exists why we would not have aptitude for books." In the first 1637 edition, however, that sentence read "aptitude for men." The second, "corrected" edition eliminated what I suggest was a classic Freudian slip, revealing a masculine judge and jury ever present in Zayas's mind, controlling access to the literary elite she sought to join.

Presumably, Zayas herself specified the correction, as her argument continues with a clear intention of "aptitude for books." Women can develop such an aptitude if they have Zayas's taste for reading:

> And more so if all women have my inclination, for when I see any book, new or old, I abandon my little lace pillow and do not rest until I skim it over. From this inclination was born knowledge, from knowledge good taste, and from it all the writing of poetry, even writing these novellas, either because it is an easier or more desirable business, for many books without erudition often seem good because of their subject matter, and others that are full of subtleties get sold but are not bought, because the material lacks importance or is insipid.

> [Y más si todas tienen mi inclinación, … porque la materia no es importante o es desabrida.][14]

As well as chronicling her own path to writing, this commentary highlights her awareness of the book market in her day, probably acquired through her relatives' involvement in publishing. Her observation about books that are sold but not bought means those that booksellers buy from the printers but which their customers don't purchase. After "insipid,"

---

13 *Disenchantements*, p. 141; *Desengaños*, pp. 334–5.
14 ETL, pp. 50–51; *Novelas*, p. 161.

Zayas – if she is the corrector – cut another sentence that appeared in the first edition, which also reflected her attention to market tastes:

> That is to say that the book to which I invite you can serve as fruit among other more substantial dishes, for human taste is so capricious and wary of seeing what goes on in the world that one must take recourse in farcical things to eliminate bitterness or make it possible to swallow life's surprises.
>
> [Esto es decir que el libro a que te convido puede servir por fruta entre otros platos de más substancias, ... o para tragar los sobresaltos.]¹⁵

Zayas then closes her prologue as she opened it, with a challenge to presumed male readers and a demand for their courtesy to women: "It is not necessary to warn you of the mercy you should have, for if it is good, praising it is nothing; and if it is bad, out of the courtesy owed any woman you will treat it with respect" [No es menester prevenirte de la piedad ... cualquiera mujer, le tendrás respeto].¹⁶ This is followed by two sentences, cut from that second edition, that tell men not to wield satire against women, as it only makes them look bad. She may have cut them to give more weight to what I see as her key sentence:

> There is no rivalry with women; the one who fails to esteem them is a fool, because he needs them, and the one who insults them is an ingrate, for he lacks the respect due the hospitality that women gave men in their first journey.
>
> [Con mujeres no hay competencias: ... ingrato, pues falta al reconocimiento del hospedaje que le hicieron en la primer jornada.]¹⁷

As Rhodes argues persuasively in her study of the *Desengaños*, the need that Zayas intends here is men's need for women to continue their lineage, and a man's "first journey" is the one in which a woman carried him to birth.¹⁸ Zayas then closes with the equivalent of a disarming curtsey: "I offer you this book ... confident that, should it displease you, you will be able to pardon me because I was born a woman, not with obligations

---

15 ETL, p. 51, nn. 17 & 18; *Novelas*, p. 161, nn. 8 & 9.
16 The cut sentences: "Satires and other works of fury were not made for those who have surrendered but rather for those exalted. The one who has honor gives what he has; each one behaves as the person he is" [Las sátiras y las furias ... con quien es]. ETL, p. 52, n. 18; *Novelas*, p. 161, n. 9.
17 ETL, p. 51; *Novelas*, p. 161.
18 See Rhodes, *Dressed to Kill*, pp. 36–40, 66–71, 151–3.

to write good novellas but with a great desire to succeed in serving you. Farewell" [Te ofrezco este libro muy segura ... acertar a servirte. Vale].[19]

Zayas in her prologue is, thus, a consistent defender of women, their dignity and right to respect from her implicit male addressee. Does this make her a champion of all women, and a feminist or proto-feminist? The answers to those questions are more mixed. Although the debates in the *Querelle des femmes* brought "the woman question" to light, it is nonetheless anachronistic to call a seventeenth-century writer a "feminist," because that word has such a distinct modern meaning. I believe it is valid, nevertheless, to call her a proto-feminist, with some qualifications. She was not philosophically consistent, presenting her case for women with rigorous, linear logic. Her two volumes of novellas are filled with passionate argumentation and shifting, sometimes contradictory tactics and rhetoric, mixing harangues against the abuse of women with the pathos of her fictional examples.

Do her novellas call for or depict an alliance of women? Eavan O'Brien's study *Women in the Prose of María de Zayas* provides the most complete examination of this question to date. Taking what O'Brien calls a "gynocentric" perspective, she proposes that Zayas demonstrates in the *Desengaños* that safety, peace and fulfillment for women depend on homosocial friendships between women, on "Gyn/affection" as she calls it, as it might be envisioned behind convent walls. But that is at best speculative, since Zayas gives us no view behind those walls. Rather, as Rhodes argues, the convent represents a symbolic dead end, a reaction to the problem women confront in the patriarchal society of their day, not its solution.[20] I describe Zayas as a qualified proto-feminist, because the alliance she would shape for women is sharply bounded by class. As pointed out in chapters 1 and 6, Zayas's identity was grounded in the low-to-middle nobility to which she belonged. The immediate audience for her fictional soiree is populated with women and men of the same class or estate (though servants may hover implicitly in the background), and she presumably wrote with a similarly composed group of readers in mind. Rhodes, arguing for the primacy of class over gender in the *Desengaños*, maintains that "when she writes 'woman' (*mujer*), she means 'noblewoman.' When she refers to a female of another class, she uses a different noun, such as '*vecina*'

---

19 ETL, p. 51; *Novelas*, p. 161.
20 Eavan O'Brien, *Women in the Prose of María de Zayas*, Woodbridge, England, 2010, pp. 6–7, 19–20, 48–55, 198–200, 203, 242–5; Rhodes, *Dressed to Kill*, pp. 123–5, and her chapter 4.

(neighbour woman), *'esclava'* (female slave), or *'criada'* (female servant). The *Desengaños* are not a defence of women; they are a defence of noblewomen."[21] This is generally true, particularly for Zayas's dark and violent second volume, and true of female servants and slaves in both volumes. Nor should it surprise us, given the tension between the dialectic of class and group identity that Fredric Jameson points out.

I do not find Zayas's defining lexicon of class quite as clear-cut as Rhodes argues, not in her analysis of the *Desengaños*, and less so in the *Novelas*. It can be blurred, for instance by Zayas's use of *dama*, most commonly translated as "lady," but it can refer to a ladies' maid or lady-in-waiting, or to a man's love-object, or mistress, or concubine. The latter use is found in D. 4, in which don Jaime calls his first beloved, the mysterious lover whom he visits, his "dama," and his "dama encantada," which Boyer translates as his "enchanted mistress." Judging by her residence and the lavish gifts she bestows on him, Jaime deduces that she must be a "mujer poderosa" (a powerful woman). He is right: she finally reveals that she is Madame Lucrecia, the Princess of Erne, sole heir to an elderly prince, and that although she receives many proposals of marriage, she will accept none until she can make Jaime her husband. In D. 7, "damas" appear in the form of ladies' maids, and Zayas leaves hazy the status of one of them, Doña María, Doña Blanca's surviving confidante. The two women had been raised together from childhood, Zayas says; presumably Doña María is a kind of lady-in-waiting. After Blanca is bled to death, María and her future husband don Gabriel accompanied the body back to Spain, "with all the other servants (*damas y criados*)" and their daughter would marry "one of Blanca's close relatives." Zayas's defense of noblewomen in the *Desengaños* is also qualified by her harsh rejection of "malas mujeres," bad women of any class, as she declares in the introduction: "I don't call the fickle, false, loose woman who has lost her reputation a woman but instead a wild beast" [a la mujer falsa, inconstante, liviana y sin reputación no se le ha de dar nombre de mujer, sino de bestia fiera]. Rather, she says, "the women I speak about in this book are not [common] women, women who make [their] profession [and earnings from being that] and are [like vermin], but rather the women who do not deserve the misfortunes that befall them" [las mujeres [de]

---

21 Rhodes, *Dressed to Kill*, p. 28; Fredric Jameson, "On 'Cultural Studies'," *Social Text* 34, 1993, p. 36; and Greer, *María de Zayas*, p. 494, n. 31.

que hablaré en este libro no son de las comunes, ... que ésas pasan por *sabandijas*, sino de las no merecedoras de desdichados sucesos].²²

In the *Novelas*, the boundaries of acceptable womanhood, as Zayas draws them, are less clear, both in terms of class and in terms of behavior. Her first heroine, Jacinta, is not the "chaste Diana" Fabio thought he might find in the meadow on the Montserrat mountaintop; she declares her nobility and that of her family repeatedly, but she laments that she is the dishonor of her father's house. Jealous over her beloved Félix's attentions to his cousin Adriana, Jacinta secures his promise to marry her, then lets him in the house and gives him "possession of [her] soul and body" [le di la posesión de mi alma y cuerpo].²³ Adriana takes revenge by sending Jacinta's father a letter denouncing the stain on his honor, while Jacinta and Félix take refuge in his aunt's convent. Félix steps out of the convent and is attacked by her father and brother; he kills the brother and flees to Naples. Thinking him dead, Jacinta professes as a nun. But when he reappears six years later, she welcomes him into the convent and sleeps with him almost every night while they wait for a papal dispensation to marry. Sex before marriage – on the grounds of a convent, no less – might strike us as scandalous, but as Rhodes points out, this was within the bounds of Zayas's code of noble behavior. Premarital sex was acceptable, as long as it was a prelude to matrimony. Marriage was an institution in crisis, in her depiction, in tandem with political crisis: the future of the Spanish nobility, "with honour and purity of blood," was at stake, and in turn, so too was the Spanish empire.

Throughout the *Novelas*, in fact, there is no shortage of sex outside marriage, as well as some outright crimes, and little of it is presented as dishonorable. In N. 2, Aminta is engaged to a cousin in Milan but seduced by Jacinto/Francisco. She kills her seducer (who had abandoned his wife), marries a better man, Martin, and the couple live in Madrid under assumed names. Serafina's lover in N. 4 fathers Gracia, whom Fadrique has raised in a convent and marries, but she in her complete innocence and ignorance accepts "another husband" before eventual reunion in a luxurious convent with Serafina. Fadrique's other lovers, Beatriz and Violante, both take other lovers themselves, and then marry, while the Duchess spends the afternoon enjoying Fadrique's (sexual) company and hides him in her wardrobe when the Duke returns. Hipólita of N. 7, married to

---

22 *Disenchantments*, p. 38, corrected; *Desengaños*, p. 197. "Sabandijas," Zayas's word, are "small vermin," such as fleas or lice, not leeches, which are "sanguijuelas."
23 ETL, p. 75; *Novelas*, p. 187. Rhodes, *Dressed to Kill*, pp. 39–40.

Pedro, after frustrating, comic attempts to meet her Portuguese gallant Gaspar, slays her persistent brother-in-law Luis. After Pedro's death, she marries Garcia and has children with him. Leonor's beloved Rodrigo engineers a bed switch to get out of marrying Flemish widow Blanca, then his prayers to Christ bring Leonor back to life to fulfill her first marriage vow to him.

As noted in chapter 4, two other novellas (N. 4 and N. 7), as well as N. 8, are narrated by men, a tactic that I think Zayas uses to strategically distance the narrative point of view from a feminine perspective and better engage a male reading audience. Notably, however, two of the tales, N. 6 and N. 10, portray how women can serve as allies of other women, and these are both narrated by women. In N. 10, Lisis's widowed mother, doña Laura, tells the story of another widow, Fabia, whose husband left her in charge of her noble daughters Constanza and Teodosia, who are courted by brothers Jorge and Federico, respectively. But Teodosia, jealous of Jorge's love for Constanza, provokes a duel in which her own suitor is killed. Jorge flees, and Constanza marries the ingenious Carlos, whose tricks and generosity outdo those of Teodosia's jealousy and the Devil himself. Despite Teodosia's repeated departures from a noble code of behavior, she is then united in marriage with Jorge. Before telling the story, doña Laura warns listeners against believing as proven facts the events she will relate as leading to the happy ending for both the daughters: "Discrete listeners, I do not wish to present to you as proven facts the events of this story, although well they might be" [No quiero, discrete auditorio, venderos por verdades averiguadas los sucesos de esta historia; si bien todos son de calidad que lo pudieran ser].[24] At its end, she says that no one ever found out that Jorge had murdered his brother Federico until after his death, when Teodosia revealed it, leaving a copy written in her hand that was found after her death.

I believe that the presence or absence of living mothers is key to the fate of daughters in Zayas's first volume.[25] Historians show that mothers did play a very significant role in Zayas's day; 80 percent of men named women as executors of their estates, or managers of it in their absence, as had doña Laura's and Fabia's husbands.[26] Mothers in Zayas's tales cannot, however, consistently counteract prevailing male dominance. In N. 6,

---

24 *Enchantments*, p. 295; *Novelas*, p. 512.
25 See further details in Greer, *María de Zayas*, pp. 14, 89–91, 93, 133, 135, 142–3, 147–57.
26 See Grace E. Coolidge, "Aristocracy and the Urban Elite," Baranda and Cruz, *Routledge Research Companion*, pp. 15–26.

another story of female alliance, narrated by Filis, Fernando is an unruly son whose widowed mother cannot control him, nor can she prevent him from taking advantage of the object of his affection, Juana (who herself is an orphan, with no mother to defend her). Later, Juana becomes a nun, and Fernando's mother persuades him to marry Clara, daughter of a supposedly wealthy merchant, and she protects Clara from his abuse until her death. As discussed in chapter 6, Clara is the rare non-noble woman who is also virtuous; after Fernando dies, her virtue is rewarded with a marriage to the marquis. As for Juana, she also helps Clara, by keeping Clara's young daughters with her in the convent while Clara spends a year trying to break the spell a sorceress has put on Fernando. Zayas's female narrators in the *Desengaños* also tell us of women's alliance in several tales, and women are key to Inés's rescue from her grotesque prison in D. 5.

Despite these female alliances, however, readers should not conclude they predominate in her stories; women also serve as rivals or dangerous enemies for her protagonists. In her very first tale, N. 1, Zayas gives us Adriana, Jacinta's rival for Félix's attention. Adriana initiates the chain of events that imperils Jacinta when she sends a letter to Jacinta's father alerting him to the "stain on his honor" from his daughter's secret trysts with Félix. Lisarda, the narrator of that novella, condemns Adriana to an ugly, scandalous death: she turns black after drinking a fatal poison. But throughout the frame tales of both volumes, Zayas makes Lisarda herself another hovering rival, as the object of don Juan's affection, whom her cousin Lisis also desires. (In the end, however, Zayas pulls back from blaming Lisarda for everything: for his disloyalty, Juan is sentenced to madness and death, while Lisarda is married to a wealthy foreign gentleman.) In the next story, N. 2, Zayas gives us Flora, the first of a well-populated class of female enemies, mistresses or former lovers of a suitor of the protagonist. Flora is a procuress as well, facilitating Aminta's seduction by "Jacinto" to tie him firmly to her until Aminta slays them both. Zayas doesn't specify Flora's class status, but she does describe Nise in N. 5 as an attractive noblewoman, if not of the highest rank, who is determined to win Diego's love back from his wife, Laura. In the next tale (N. 6), Juana's friend Lucrecia uses sorcery to draw Fernando away first from Juana and then from his wife, Clara, until the latter breaks the spell. Other formidable rivals are Claudia in N. 9, Alejandra and Zayda in D. 1, Angeliana and Roseleta in D. 3, and Clavela in D. 8. Tales in each volume also show women who operate for their own economic benefit, as Inés's neighbor helps Diego in D. 5, or Laura's friend persuades her to resort to sorcery in N. 5. And last but far from least, in each volume's last story, Teodosia (in N. 10) and Florentina (D. 10) are familial enemies of their own sisters. This lengthy list of female characters who are anything but allies of other women is what obliges me to describe Zayas as a proto-feminist, within limits. She does from the outset appoint herself as a champion of women's rights and an opponent of those who abuse women in words and in deeds. But she regularly adds that she does not defend all women.

Zayas did, however, demonstrate the power of an alliance between women in a three-act play, La traición en la amistad (Friendship Betrayed), which she may have written prior to the novellas. Since the revival of interest in Zayas in the late twentieth century, seven modern editions have been published, two digital and five in print; the print edition by Valerie Hegstrom includes a lively translation in English by Catherine Larson.[27] There have been at least four modern performances in the last two decades, including ones in the annual Spanish theater Festival de Almagro, one by the Compañía Nacional de Teatro Clásico in Madrid, one in Alcalá de Henares, and another in Cáceres. In the Juan Pérez de Montalbán tribute of 1632 that I cited in chapter 1, he declared that Zayas had finished a comedia, which is probably a reference to La traición. Montalbán admired the quality of the play's verse, which does work well in this comedy. Zayas generally follows the polymetric pattern set by Lope de Vega but gives its conventions her own individual stamp from a woman writer's perspective. The play existed only in manuscript form until it was published in 1903 by Serrano y Sanz in his Apuntes.[28] But judging by the comic asides directed to men and women in the audience, Zayas intended the play for performance, probably a private one in a home, to a mixed group of men and women rather like the audience that convenes to entertain Lisis in the frame sections of the novellas. On the other hand, in the third act, two women appear on an upper level – a balcony or a

---

27 María de Zayas y Sotomayor, La traición en la amistad/Friendship Betrayed, ed. Valerie Hegstrom, trans. Catherine Larson, London, 1999.
28 Serrano y Sanz, Apuntes, pp. 590–620; on modern performances, Yllera, "Introducción," p. 30, n. 69 and Alexander Samson, "Distinct Drama? Female Dramatists in Golden Age Spain," A Companion to Spanish Women's Studies, ed. Xon de Ros and Geraldine Hazbun, Woodbridge, Suffolk, 2011, pp. 165–8. On plays in the gardens and the gardens in plays of the period, see Stefano Arata, "Proyección escenográfica de la huerta del Duque de Lerma en Madrid," Siglos dorados: Homenaje a Augustin Redondo, Madrid, 2004, pp. 33–52 and Laura R. Bass, "Staging Madrid: Urban Comedy for a New Court Capital," Cacho Casal and Egan, Routledge Hispanic Studies Companion, pp. 323–42.

window – and this use of space suggests that Zayas envisioned a more typical theatrical structure, whether in a public theater or a private palace. We don't know when Zayas wrote this play, although if it is the one to which Montalbán referred, it was before 1632, and there is some evidence it was considerably earlier, before even her earliest published poetry. Zayas includes in the play two references to the "Huerta del conde Duque," the gardens of the Duke of Lerma, where he entertained Philip III during his tenure as the king's favorite. One of the references also says that the Duke built the garden for Philip III's beloved queen Margarita, who died in 1611. Those gardens, beside the Paseo del Prado at the point now occupied by the Palace Hotel, were frequently open to the public as well and were a point of reference in comedies of Lope de Vega and Tirso de Molina once the court returned to Madrid from Valladolid in 1606. This could date the play to as early as 1610.

La traición stages a comic, positive attitude towards women's clever capacity for alliance in the name of consolidating marriages.[29] Three women, Marcia, her cousin Belisa, and Laura manage this, despite the betrayal of their friendship by Fenisa, who pursues all their lovers, saying she has room in her heart for all the men she sees. In its positive spirit, the play is more similar to Zayas's first volume of stories, and far removed from her dark and violent *Desengaños*. One very specific link to the *Novelas* is the primary protagonist Marcia's description of her handsome suitor, Liseo, as Narciso, just as Jacinta describes Félix in the first novella. Liseo has slept with Laura under promise of marriage, but like so many suitors in the novellas, has then developed designs on someone else. Laura appeals to Marcia (Liseo's new interest) for help, and with Belisa, she takes up Laura's cause; together the three women operate almost as a collective protagonist. As they do so, and despite having been attracted to Liseo's good looks, they also agree to marriage with their long-term suitors. This leaves Fenisa – who had pursued all the men – alone at the end. The two servants, Fenisa's maid Lucía and Liseo's very bawdy and cynical servant León, add delightful comic notes. Lucía, for instance, in approving of Fenisa's taste for many men, quotes her grandmother: men are like garlic cloves, in that one should put a lot in the mortar so that if one flips out when crushed, there are plenty left. In the third act, León delivers

---

29 See Monica Leoni, "María de Zayas's *La traición en la amistad*: Female Friendship Politicized?" *South Atlantic Review* 68.4 (2003), pp. 62–84, and Juan Gil-Olse, "La tradición de la amistad femenina en *La traición en la amistad* de María de Zayas," *Bulletin of Hispanic Studies* 93.4, 2016, pp. 361–83.

a diatribe against deceptive appearances and dress; it's very similar to the speech on the contemporary Age of Iron that Matilde gives to her arch-deceiver, the cross-dressed Estefanía/Esteban in D. 6. Then, closing the play, León tells the men in the audience that he'd be glad to give them Fenisa's address if they'd like it.

La traición, however, is hardly set in reality. Women steer the plot and operate freely in an idealized social context, outside the limitations imposed on Early Modern women by their patriarchal society. Marcia tells Fenisa at the outset that with her father away in Lombardy, she is going to leap into the war of love by encouraging Liseo's interest in her. Fenisa, alleging concern for her friend, tries to dissuade her, using the same image that Lisarda does in narrating N. 1: don't, Fenisa advises, "throw your poorly governed little boat into the sea of love."[30] Laura's parents are dead; Fenisa's mother is only mentioned, and no brothers or other male authority figures are even named. In male-authored plays, in contrast, the almost invariable norm was that fathers or brothers controlled or tried to control women's contact with the opposite sex. In other aspects too, Zayas departs from the model of male-authored plays. She endows her five female characters with diverse, shifting personalities as she explores the nature of their friendship and relationships with the male characters. With the possible exception of Fenisa, Zayas's characters as written do not lend themselves to performance as trivial, empty-headed, bubbly voiced creatures, despite their portrayal as such in some stage performances.

Overall, then, I would say that Zayas does envision, and sometimes depict, an alliance of women, particularly in her first volume. As she aged and the political and economic climate in Spain darkened, so too did her view of the quality and quantity of women's support for other women. Like her proto-feminism, however, it is an alliance generally qualified by social class, rather than a solidarity with all women, everywhere. The dramatic alliance of women she staged in La traición was probably written early in her career, in tune with the varying moods of the Novelas, not the dark violence of the Desengaños. Already in 1637, she or an editor had eliminated from her prologue the invitation to her readers to "take recourse in farcical things to eliminate bitterness or make it possible to swallow life's surprises." By her second volume, along with the elimination of male storytellers, Zayas eliminates "farcical things," leaving most of her protagonists to meet death alone or, for the lucky few, to join hands with other women behind convent walls.

---

30 Zayas, La traición (Friendship Betrayed), p. 38; my translation.

Conclusion

Zayas's Afterlives

WHEN I STARTED working on my first book on María de Zayas in the 1990s, some colleagues warned me, "Everybody's working on María de Zayas." The subtext was that if there were already a couple of books on this supposedly little-known Spanish woman writer in the age of Cervantes, Lope de Vega, Calderón, Góngora and kindred much-studied male writers, no more were needed. What more of interest could be found in her work?

The skeptical colleagues were right about blossoming interest in Zayas, but they were wrong about what we found to engage us in her novellas of desire, death and disillusion. Years later, as I wrote conclusions to that book, I imagined a different comment from skeptics: "You're actually *finishing* this book on María de Zayas? Amazing!" Among fans and students of Zayas, I was not alone in finding so much to say and to puzzle over in her works that it was hard for us to write *finis* to our studies. With so much now written about her and more surely in process, however, I will here conclude by summarizing what has and has not been added to our knowledge of Zayas in the last few decades, as well as giving the highlights of her reception over the centuries since she first published.

Work on Zayas over the last quarter century has peeled away much of the earlier tendency to fill in the holes in her biography by reading the lives of her heroines as autobiography. Readers are no longer led to believe that a disappointment in love made her retreat to a convent, as did many of her protagonists, nor that she became a nun, as far as we know. Although convent life did afford women like Santa Teresa and Sor Juana Inés de la Cruz the space and even the obligation to write, Zayas's path to literary creativity was nourished by membership in an urban lower-middle aristocracy, as the daughter of María de Carasa, whose family was involved in the literary arts and publishing, and Fernando de Zayas, an infantry captain and member of the elite military-religious Order of Santiago. She lived primarily in Madrid from her birth in 1590 until at least 1647; recent research has shown that she had a younger sister, Isabel, and a third sister of unknown age. Given the settings of her stories in cities across the breadth of Iberia and its imperial extensions, scholars continue to propose that those settings could be based on her personal experience. She might have lived for a time in Valladolid, to which the court moved from 1601 to 1606; Zaragoza, where her two volumes of stories were published in 1637 and 1647; Naples, while the count of Lemos was its viceroy; and Barcelona. One possible death certificate for a María de Zayas could indicate residence in Valladolid (see chapters 1 and 7), and a satirical poem makes her a participant in a poetic competition in secessionist Barcelona in 1643. We do not know for certain where or when she died, nor whether she married, although one of the three Madrid death certificates for a María de Zayas raises that possibility.

We have known for some time Zayas's complete oeuvre: the eighty poems interspersed in her novellas and those written for poetic competitions or published as preliminaries to other writers' works – sonnets, *décimas*, songs and ballads, many of which subvert masculine poetic conventions to make them reflect a woman's perspective; at least one play, the three-act comedy *Friendship Betrayed* (*La traición en la amistad*); and the two volumes of novellas that made her an icon of Luso-Hispanic literature and culture. Although the play was apparently never performed in Zayas's lifetime and has only received much attention in the last two decades, the novellas did earn Zayas her fame in her own day,[1] not just in Spain but well beyond its boundaries, and their influence continues in our own time.

Zayas herself attested to the fame of her first volume in the frame section of the second collection of novellas: "If a few thought little of it, a hundred applauded it, and all sought it out and continue to seek it, and it has enjoyed three printings, two legitimate editions and one pirated" [Si unos le desestimaron, ciento le aplaudieron ... dos naturales y una hurtada].[2] In fact, as Yllera points out, there were five, or possibly six edi-

---

[1] Antonio Carreño, in editing Lope's praise of her in the *Laurel de Apolo*, n. to vv. 583–6, calls her "la más conocida escritora del siglo XVII" (the best-known woman author of the seventeenth century).

[2] *Desengaños*, p. 371, my translation; Yllera, pp. 94–107. She lists all the combined editions on pp. 99–105, the partial editions on pp. 107–23.

tions of the first part between 1637 and 1646, two editions of the second part, in 1647 and 1649, and from 1659 through 1814, the two parts were published together in multiple editions. Beginning with the 1659 edition, however, Zayas's "Al que leyere" prologue in her own voice was omitted, as well as the anonymous "Prologo de un desapasionado" (Prologue of an impartial person) and the preliminary verses, so readers lost contact with her important authorial statement.

Spanish historian Eustaquio Fernández de Navarrete declared in the nineteenth century, "There has hardly been a writer more liked by Spanish readers than María de Zayas, according to the numerous editions of her works that have been published" [Caso no ha habido novelista más simpático a los lectores españoles que doña María de Zayas, según las muchas reimpresiones que se han hecho de sus obras].[3] Agustín G. de Amezúa, in his prologue to the first new full edition of her *Novelas* in 1948, classed Zayas's works as best sellers, right on the heels of Cervantes, Mateo Alemán and Quevedo in her own century. Treviño's more recent research shows, however, that Zayas's novellas did not quite reach the position that Amezúa asserted (and which I along with other Zayas scholars repeated). Publications of the novellas of Pérez de Montalbán outnumbered hers. Compiling such ranking is complicated, however, and depends on how one defines comparable works of prose fiction. Publication of Zayas novellas reached the height of their Early Modern popularity in the eighteenth century, with the last republication of her two complete volumes appearing in 1814. Publication of her two complete volumes in Spanish would not resume until the mid-twentieth century. In the meantime, however, selected stories were published, with the same few stories regularly repeated, in partial editions that sometimes listed her as author, or in collected editions of novellas along with those of Cervantes and other authors, and frequently uncredited. The selection published by the novelist, critic and professor Emilia Pardo Bazán in her turn-of-the-twentieth-century series *Biblioteca de la Mujer* is an exception, in that it not only credits Zayas's authorship but also offers a larger selection of Zayas stories from the two volumes, as well as an interesting introduction.[4]

---

3 Eustaquio Fernández de Navarrete, *Bosquejo histórico sobre la novela española: Novelistas posteriores a Cervantes*, ed. C. Rosell y López, 2 vols. Madrid, 1854, vol. 2, pp. xcvii–xcviii, cited in Treviño, p. ix, note 4, my translation.
4 *Novelas de Dª María de Zayas y Sotomayor*, Madrid, Biblioteca de la Mujer, vol. 3; Yllera lists the selections, pp. 110–11.

Zayas's novellas also appeared in translation and adaptation in French, English, German, Italian and Dutch, beginning as early as 1656. The Spanish novella tradition of Cervantes, Zayas and other novella authors played a significant role in the renovation of the French novel. Her novellas also may have marked the English novel tradition, through their influence on the plots and narrative technique of Aphra Behn in the seventeenth century.[5] Between 1656 and 1663, Paul Scarron published, without recognition of her authorship, French adaptations of four Zayas novellas, all from her first volume: "Forewarned but Fooled," "The Miser's Reward," "Just Deserts" and "The Judge of Her Own Case." Scarron changed not only titles but also characters' names; he also eliminated the inserted poetry and added numerous digressions and highlighted those that involved Moors, in tune with the popularity of that theme in France at the time.[6] Scarron's adaptations in turn were translated within a few years of their publication into English and later into German, Dutch, Italian and Russian. The English versions of Scarron's adaptations were repeatedly republished and are readily available online, in Early English Books Online or in Hathi Digital Trust. Other English translations of Zayas stories in the eighteenth century attributed them to Cervantes – probably a strategic "error" made for commercial purposes, as Cervantes was well known to the English public by 1700. Library catalogues generally identify the translations as the work of Edward Ward, but Ana María Murillo makes a good case for the translator being John Stevens. The supposed Ward translation was published in 1709 with the title *The Diverting Works of the famous Miguel de Cervantes*, and again in 1710, entitled *A Week's Entertainment at a Wedding*, and included the frame from Pérez de Montalbán's *Para todos* and two of his stories and a prose version of Calderón's play *Casa con dos puertas, mala es de guardar*, along with three Zayas tales: "The Ravages of Vice," "Traitor to His Own Blood" and "Just Deserts" but not a single Cervantes tale.[7] Zayas's revision of a Cervantes tale as "The Miser's Reward" appeared several times in the nineteenth century in anthologies – without her name, of course. No English translations

---

5   Nieves Romero-Díaz, "Aphra Behn y María de Zayas: En busca de una tradición (im)propia," *Hispanic Journal* 29.1, 2008, pp. 23–35.
6   Yllera, pp. 125–34.
7   Yllera, p. 139 and Ana María Murillo, "Wit, Faithfulness, and 'Improvements' in English Translation Anthologies of Spanish Popular Literature (1700)," *International Anthologies of Literature in Translation*, ed. H. Kittel, Berlin, 1995, pp. 31, 36.

gave her credit until the eight-story, graphically if not grotesquely illustrated book published by John Sturrock in 1963.

In the same years that Scarron published his translations (1656–7), Antoine Le Métel D'Ouville, who had spent seven years in Spain and twelve in Italy before returning to Paris and becoming a playwright, did recognize Zayas as author in his translation of stories from her first volume.[8] He used its title in translation, *Les nouvelles amoureuses et exemplaires*, with the explanatory subtitle "composées en espagnol par cette merveille de son sexe, Doña María de Zayas" (composed in Spanish by that marvel of her sex, Doña María de Zayas). Like Scarron, he included in it "Forewarned but Fooled" and "Just Deserts," but also "Taking a Chance on Losing" and "Aminta Deceived and Honor's Revenge," along with two more novels he attributes to Zayas which are actually by Castillo Solórzano. A French version of all the stories of both volumes, *Nouvelles amoureuses et tragiques de María de Zayas* was published in Paris in 1680, and again in 1711 in Brussels, as well as in a pirated copy. It appeared without the frame story or the translator's name and, as is common in French versions, without the verse segments. It is a free translation, which Yllera characterizes as "softened" by the elimination of daring details and scabrous scenes like one of homosexuality[9] – surely that between the Prince and his servant in D.7, "Marriage Abroad: Portent of Doom." Nevertheless, the heroines' actions were judged scandalous, and in the second volume, the *desengaños* were turned into conventional happy-ending stories. Given all these adjustments, it is more accurate to describe them as adaptations than translations.

Aside from publication statistics, it is difficult to assess just how Zayas novellas were received and read by her Early Modern Spanish public. Detailed critical appreciations of literary works were rare in her day, other than in commentaries on the most canonical poets. Apart from the brief praise bestowed on her by fellow writers like Lope and Pérez de Montalbán, the only other available sources we have are the comments of the two censors – civil and ecclesiastic –who were asked to review and approve the material for publication.[10] Although Zayas's narrators regularly con-

---

8   Frederick de Armas, "Antoine Le Metel, Sieur d'Ouville: The 'Lost' Years," *Romance Notes* 14, 1973, pp. 538–43.
9   Yllera, p. 131.
10 An author or the bookseller who intended to finance publication of his or her work would submit the manuscript to the Council of Castile, or to the equivalent authority in Aragón. That body would refer it to a church official for the ecclesiastical license, and to an expert in the type of material it treated

demn the actions of her heroines' female antagonists, no Spanish censors levied charges of scandalous behavior against either her desiring heroines or their rivals in love. Most censors' approvals were brief and formulaic, reflecting a favorable opinion of the work, usually with a reference to her gender. They could constitute a brief addition to a kind of literary blurb alongside other elements of the book preliminaries. A few do give an idea of the censor's more detailed appreciation, however. Doctor Pedro Aguilón, commissioned by Doctor Juan Domingo Briz, vicar for the archbishop of Zaragoza, to examine the first edition of the *Novelas*, rendered his approval with the standard declaration that the work contained nothing against "our Holy Faith nor good customs," adding to it that her novellas contained "delightful inventiveness and gentle wit, worthy of the talent of such a Lady" [nada he hallado contra nuestra Santa Fe ni buenas costumbres, antes gustosa inventiua y apacible agudeza, digna del ingenio de tal Dama].[11] Perhaps in response to Zayas's demand for courtesy to a woman writer that she makes in the prologue to the *Novelas*, poet and dramatist Joseph de Valdivielso cites the very "foremothers" whom Zayas references: "And even if a license were not due to the Authoress as an illustrious emulator of Corinas, Sapphos and Aspasias, then as a Lady and daughter of Madrid, it seems to me that it cannot be denied to her" [Y quando a su Autora, por ilustre emulación de las Corinnas, Saphos, y Aspasias, no se le deviera la licencia que pide, por Dama, y hija de Madrid, me parece que no se le puede negar].[12]

Ecclesiastic authorities Juan Francisco Ginovés and Pío Vives, authorizing the first and second editions of the *Desengaños* in 1646 and 1648 (published in 1647 and 1649), respectively, praised the didactic value of her fictions. Ginovés, priest of the Church of San Pablo in Zaragoza, credited her works with gender-specific moral correction. He wrote:

> I see it full of examples to reform customs and worthy of being printed, since with it (now that women's idleness has increased the number of useless books), she who occupies herself in reading it will have examples with which to flee the dangers into which some unheeding women rush headlong. This is my view.

---

for the civil license – in the case of a work of fiction, usually to a respected author of similar works. See Olivares, "Introducción," 2017, pp. xvii–xxxiv.

11 María de Zayas y Sotomayor, *Novelas amorosas y ejemplares*, Zaragoza, 1637, Briz: f. q3r; Valdivielso, f. q2r; my translations.

12 María de Zayas y Sotomayor, *Novelas amorosas y ejemplares*, Zaragoza, 1638, f. q2r; Valdivielso, f. q2r; my translation.

[le veo lleno de exemplos, para reformar costumbres, y digno de que se dé a la Estampa, que en él (ya que el ocio de las mugeres ha crecido el número a los libros inútiles) la que se ocupare en leerle tendrá exemplos con que huir los riesgos, a que algunas desatentas se precipitan. Assi lo siento.]

Vives, for his part, saw moral value for both sexes. This friar of the Santa Catalina Martyr Convent in Barcelona wrote:

> I see in it a sanctuary in which the womanish weakness most besieged by flattering importunities can find refuge, and a mirror of that which man most needs for the right ordering of his actions. Therefore, I judge it most beneficial and worthy to be transmitted to the world in print.

> [En él veo un asilo donde puede acogerse la femenil flaqueza más acosada de importunidades lisonjeras, y un espejo de lo que más necesita el hombre para la buena dirección de sus acciones. Y así, le juzgo muy provechoso y digno de comunicarse al mundo por la estampa.][13]

Subsequent Spanish editions of Zayas's collections, published later in the seventeenth and eighteenth centuries, also repeat the licenses and censors' approvals and therefore give no new insight into understanding of her novels, with one exception: the savory appreciation in Friar Vicente Bellmont's approval of a 1712 edition of both volumes:

> I have read what this book contains, and in its entertaining and beneficial *Soirée* that combines the useful with the sweet, in the disenchantments it presents and the novels it recounts (which, although they appear to be fictional stories, reveal much about true events); and having examined it well, I find nothing opposed to the Catholic faith, good customs and privileges of his Majesty; and thus I authorize its license for reprinting; agreeing with the approvals that it has long contained, and applauding the Authoress doña María, who emulates if not surpasses the busy, ingenious Bee in her sting, sweetness and worth.

> [He leído lo que este Libro contiene, y en su Sarao divertido, y provechoso, que mezcla lo útil con lo dulce, en los desengaños que trae, y novelas que refiere (que aunque parecen fabulosos sucesos, muestran mucho de verídicos;) (…) aplaudiendo à la Authora <sic> Doña María, de argumentosa Abeja, que en lo picante, dulce, y provechoso, si no la aventaja, la emula.][14]

---

13 María de Zayas y Sotomayor, *Parte Segunda del Sarao y entretenimiento honesto*, Barcelona, 1647; 1649; Ginovés, f. A2v; Vives, 1649, f. A2r. My translations.

14 Zayas y Sotomayor, *Primera, y segunda parte de las novelas amorosas y ejemplares*, Valencia, 1712. Unnumbered preliminary page. My translation.

Close to the end of the eighteenth century, Zayas would win inclusion in the highly nationalistic appreciation of the Spanish novel by the Jesuit scholar Francisco Javier Lampillas, *Ensayo histórico-apologético de la literatura española contra las opiniones preocupadas de algunos escritores modernos italianos*. There Lampillas wrote,

> The fame that our novella-writers earned among the Italians and the French they owed not to offenses against honest customs but to the delicacy of their moderate affections, to the fertility of their well-made plots and to their stylistic elegance. This paragraph would become endless if I recounted the large number of Spanish Novellas that appeared in those times and that were translated to the most cultured languages of Europe. He who would compare them to the innumerable little entertaining stories that are published every day would scarcely find any invention, denouement, event or plot development that is not in the old Spanish Novellas. Lope de Vega, Juan Pérez de Montalbán, and Alonso Castillo Solórzano all became famous for them, and the erudite Doña María de Zayas, whose Novellas are written so gracefully that seven reprints were made of them within the space of a few years and translated into French, and they were published in Paris in two volumes in 1656, 1680 and 1711.

> [La fama que granjearon nuestros noveladores entre los italianos y franceses no la debieron a la licencia contra la honestidad de costumbres, sino a la delicadeza de sus moderados afectos, a la fecundidad de invenciones bien ordenadas, y a la elegancia del estilo. (...) y la erudita Doña María de Zayas, cuyas Novelas están escritas con tanta gracia, que en el curso de pocos años se hicieron siete reimpresiones, y traducidas en Francés se publicaron en París en dos tomos en los años 1656, 1680 y 1711.][15]

The Literary Canon – Without Zayas

The 1814 publication of her two volumes marked the end of almost two centuries of repeated publication of her novellas in Spain. (One complete edition in Spanish did appear in Paris in 1847, without the "Al que leyere" prologue.)[16] That her last full Spanish publication took place

---

15 Francisco Javier Lampillas, *Ensayo histórico-apologético de la literatura española contra las opiniones preocupadas de algunos escritores modernos italianos*, Madrid, 1789, v. 5, pp. 185–6. My translation.

16 Yllera, pp. 105–7.

just two years after the formulation of the first Spanish constitution, the Constitution of Cadiz of 1812, is not mere historical coincidence. Nor is it a coincidence that 136 years elapsed before her complete tales were published again. In that period, Spain endured more than a century of tumult, sparked when Napoleon forced both Spain's king Carlos IV and his heir Fernando VII to abdicate, then installed his brother Joseph as king. French troops occupied Spain, provoking the War of Independence.[17] While Fernando was imprisoned in France, a *cortes* (a parliament) were called to meet at Cádiz to support the war effort. Instead, the *Cortes*, meeting in Cadiz, a stronghold of liberalism as well as resistance to Napoleon and French domination, drew up a constitution that established a constitutional monarchy, made all citizens equal before the law, and instituted other progressive legislation. Napoleon released Fernando VII, who repealed the Constitution of Cadiz on his return to Spain in 1814, and when it was adopted again in 1820 and 1836, it was repealed each time by conservative reaction. Five more constitutions were undone by similar divides between progressives and conservatives over the next century and a half.

How and why did that prolonged sociopolitical struggle affect the reception of Zayas? Zayas was intimately identified with the aristocracy, which was slowly replaced by a more bourgeois society – but that cultural shift alone does not account for Zayas falling out of fashion. A bourgeois society slowly replaced the traditional oligarchic social structure, bringing cultural changes with it. One of the changes in nineteenth-century Spain, as in other European countries at the time, was the formulation of a national literary canon. As industrial capitalism gained a foothold in Spain, the reading public expanded, primarily in urban areas, along with the meteoric rise of the periodical press in the 1840s. Serialized novels, earlier delivered to subscribers' homes, found a new medium for publication, as *folletines* (serials) published in periodicals. With wider readership, the most successful authors could make a living from their writing. The novel acquired preeminent status in the publishing industry, although many traditionalist commentators considered it a danger to the morals and conduct of impressionable readers, particularly women, the young, and the lower, less educated classes. Some liberal commentators, however, thought that given their power to reach all levels of society, serialized novels could be useful to the social and political interests of the middle

---

17 See Barton, *A History of Spain*, Croydon, 2009, for a concise summary of Spanish history for the period, especially pp. 179–81, 184–6 and 195–7.

classes. At the same time, the number of Spanish women writing novels increased, but they used the form to spread conventional middle-class values, rather than any political subversion or licentiousness.

In the second half of the nineteenth century, the novel gained new critical stature, and this, according to critic Catherine Jagoe, stimulated "a growing desire on the part of a masculine intellectual élite to exert control over novel writing and reading."[18] Men succeeded; all the writers subsequently canonized were men, with the exception of Emilia Pardo Bazán, who was at the time judged to have "masculine" writing traits. Women writers became associated with an idealist mode of writing, previously considered the nobler mode, but then trivialized as realism came into fashion. Benito Pérez Galdós called for a mimetic, national, masculine novel that would accurately represent middle-class society and be perceived as serious, edifying literature, not mere entertainment. Galdós considered the ideal models to be Cervantes and Dickens. Zayas's erasure was not total, however: historian Juan Antonio Llorente, writing in 1822, included Zayas in his list of thirty-seven Spanish authors he thought might have written the original Spanish version of the *Bachilier de Salamanque*, which he considered the model for Alain René Lesage's picaresque version of French society, *Gil Blas de Santillane*.[19] Zayas could have penned the Spanish original, Llorente posited, if she had chosen to write longer, more connected fictions than her novellas. Llorente's statement was enough to pull Zayas's works into a critical discussion that would continue into the twentieth century, so she was not completely forgotten in the shift to realism. Spanish poet, journalist and critic Alberto Lista, in an 1840 essay on the novel, wrote that after Cervantes buried the "monstrous" novels of chivalry, "novel writers dedicated themselves to moral or satirical forms.... There then appeared the novels of Doña María de Zayas, the *Squire Marcos de Obregón*, *The Rogue Justina*, *Guzman de Alfarache*, and many others." He did not distinguish between novels and novellas, nor add adjectives separating high literary forms from low entertainment.

---

18 Catherine Jagoe, "Disinheriting the Feminine: Galdós and the Rise of the Realist Novel in Spain," *Revista de Estudios Hispánicos* 27.2, 1993, p. 230. My summary is largely drawn from her article. See also Greer, *María de Zayas*, pp. 45–53.
19 Juan Antonio Llorente, *Observations critiques sur le roman de Gil Blas de Santillane*, Paris, 1822, p. 196.

Antonio Gil y Zárate's 1844 manual of literature reflected the novel's increased stature, lauding the picaresque novel and Cervantes's works as the two pillars on which Spanish pride in the genre could rest. Of the picaresque, Gil y Zárate says that "Spain had ... the glory of being the creator of this genre of novels, and if the best of them known [*Gil Blas*] is not entirely hers, she at least furnished its materials" [España tuvo ... la gloria de ser la creadora de este género de novelas; y si no es enteramente suya la mejor que se conoce [*Gil Blas*], suministró al menos los materiales].[20] He didn't specifically reject the possibility that Zayas might have furnished those materials, but while naming Zayas as one of their well-known creators, he also demoted all novellas to an inferior classification: "Although their authors show evidence of inventiveness and one can find good prose passages in them, they should in general be considered as entertaining rather than literary works" [aunque sus autores dan prueba de ingenio, y se pueden sacar de ellas buenos trozos de prosa, deben considerarse en lo general como obras de entretenimiento más bien que literarias].

Historian Fernández de Navarrete, despite recognizing the enduring popularity of Zayas's writing with the Spanish public and considering her a "facile poetess, with an uncommon education in human letters," did specifically refute Llorente's assertion that she could have written the model for *Gil Blas*. Writing in the mid-nineteenth century, he calls her a "rare anomaly" in Spain:

> It seems that our customs deny that the women who steal our hearts with their charms should also aspire to capture our understanding with their learning. A literary woman generally appears in the eyes of the masses to have some sort of mannishness that takes away part of the charms of their sex.

Although Fernández de Navarrete concedes that talent has no gender and that many women possess skill in the imaginative arts, he discounts the possibility that any woman writer, even Zayas, could have written *Gil Blas* because

> She lacked observation and that intimate knowledge of scenes of the world that only a man can acquire, and of which a lady is deprived by the retirement and circumspection in which the decorum of her sex requires her to live ... [not entering] the dirty refuge of the vagabond and beggar, the gambling den, nor the brothel of the corrupt courtesan.

---

20 Antonio Gil y Zárate, *Manual de literatura, segunda parte: Resumen histórico de la literatura española*, Madrid, 1854, pp. 243, 244. My translation.

Conclusion: Zayas's Afterlives   171

She does not see the world as it is but as it is offered to her eyes in superficial, controlled acquaintance; men, out of the respect that they deserve, always present themselves before women in a hypocritical pose ... circumstances [that] are bad for writing novels, whose principal merit consists of profound knowledge of the customs of the different classes of society; a knowledge that is acquired less in meditation in the study than in being an actor or at least a spectator of the incidents that are described, or of other identical ones.[21]

Fernandez de Navarrete's patronizing judgment reflects both bourgeois ideology on the nature and proper role of women and the complex role of women in the rise of the novel. The number of women novelists increased substantially in the nineteenth century, but they largely wrote apolitical "educational" novels catering to young ladies and respectable married women.[22] In addition to the new critical establishment that sought to "masculinize" the novel, another reason Zayas novellas ceased to be published for a time may simply have been this wide availability of all the new works by women writers.

Near the end of the nineteenth century, the critic Pardo Bazán countered both the editorial and critical trends in Zayas's reception. In the third volume of her *Biblioteca de la Mujer* series, she included eight Zayas tales and wrote a preface in which she challenges Fernández de Navarrete's evaluation of Zayas and the selection of her novellas he published in *Novelas posteriores a Cervantes*. Zayas was not a poor observer nor timorous in expressing what she saw, in Pardo Bazán's estimation. Zayas wrote with "that frank, dry, rather cynical note" that characterizes picaresque narratives, giving us a distinct literature of the aristocracy:

> What distinguishes the *Novelas* of doña María de Zayas from those of the other classic picaresque authors ... is that the illustrious lady paints the customs of a social sphere we can call aristocratic ... Doña María does not paint common people, and for that in itself her works are a precious document, as they demonstrate to anyone who will take the trouble to compare them with then-popular works that the roguish picaresque spirit was not a phenomenon unique to the lower classes, but diffused among all social spheres.

21 Eustaquio Fernández Navarrete, *Bosquejo histórico sobre la novela española: Novelistas posteriores a Cervantes*, ed. C. Rosell y López, 2 vols. Madrid, 1854, pp. xcvi, xcvii–xcviii. My translation.
22 Jagoe, p. 229–30, 241–4.

[Lo que distingue las Novelas de doña María de Zayas entre las de los demás autores picarescos ... es que la ilustre dama pinta las costumbres de una esfera social que podemos llamar aristocrática... . Doña María no pinta el pueblo, y por lo mismo sus obras son un documento precioso, pues demuestran a todo el que se tome la molestia de cotejarlas con las populares de entonces, que el espíritu picaresco y de bellaquería no era fenómeno peculiar de las clases inferiores, sino que se encontraba difuso en todas las esferas sociales.]

She ranks Zayas's best stories with those of Cervantes and defends her use of magic and the marvelous. Zayas was no more superstitious than writers of Pardo Bazán's day, the critic claimed; Zayas used the marvelous in response to the demands of readers' imaginations. Pardo Bazán regretfully omitted "Forewarned but Fooled" and "Just Deserts," the tales closest to the picaresque mode, citing the "tyranny of custom," the view of the appropriate style then judged appropriate for women writers. She applauds Zayas for her vigorous advocacy of women's rights, and summarizes the pleasure her works afford:

As for me, I can say that doña María leaves on my palate the welcome flavor of Sherry, golden, aromatic, and genuine. I am captivated and enamored by her candor tempered with discretion, her truly feminine wit and vivacity, her poise and dignity as a distinguished lady, and her complete lack of sentimentality and priggishness.

[De mí sé decir que doña María me deja en el paladar el gratísimo sabor del Jerez oro, aromático y neto. Su ingenuidad templada por la discreción; su agudeza y vivacidad propiamente femeniles; su aplomo y señorío de distinguida dama y su completa ausencia de sentimentalismo y gazmoñería, me cautivan y enamoran.] [23]

Around this same time elsewhere in Europe and America, however, many readers had been schooled in restrictive Victorian standards of decency, and they did not share Pardo Bazán's appreciation of Zayas. The American academic George Ticknor, while acknowledging Zayas as a "sturdy defender of women's rights," wrote in 1866 that "Forewarned but Fooled" is "one of the most gross I remember to have read" and criticized Scarron for not mitigating "its shameless indecency" in his French

---

[23] Novelas de doña María de Zayas, ed. Emilia Pardo Bazán, Madrid, c. 1892, pp. 13–14, 16. My translation.

version of the story.²⁴ In 1933 the German scholar Ludwig Pfandl made a similarly extreme condemnation, on both moral and literary grounds. Zayas's tales lacked unity, he asserted, and showed excessive, sadistic realism, obscenity, and repetition of well-known motifs; her work was "a Gothic edifice ruined by Renaissance and Baroque architects" [Un edificio gótico estropeado por arquitectos renacentistas y barrocos]. Arguing with an unnamed "modern American writer" who calls Zayas the first Spanish feminist, Pfandl retorts that in the light of some of the characters in her stories, she is at best an inconsistent feminist. He then wraps up his critique with a rhetorical question: "Can there be anything more common and gross, more unaesthetic and repulsive, than a woman who writes lascivious, dirty, sadistic and morally corrupt stories?" [¿Se puede dar algo más ordinario y grosero, más inestético y repulsivo que una mujer que cuenta historias lascivas, sucias, de inspiración sádica y moralmente corrompidas?]²⁵

The critic whom Pfandl disdained to name was Lena E. V. Sylvania, who raised the issue of feminism in the first monograph dedicated to Zayas, published in 1922, just after women in the United States secured the right to vote. Sylvania classed Zayas "with those who first braved public opinion to assert and maintain, by force of argument, that women have certain rights and that, as human beings, they are not inferior to men." She did concede that Zayas's "sprightly" novellas are "sometimes a little crude, but scarcely objectionable enough to be termed licentious." She described Zayas as an "ardent Christian" and a didactic writer whose occasional crudeness was "justified by the loftiness of her underlying purpose, namely, the enlightenment of her sex, and by her effective protest against the tyranny of man and the warning note she sounds to women to beware of the snares and temptations of the world."²⁶

Professor and literary critic Ángel Valbuena Prat, writing just a few years after Pfandl, in a Barcelona that remained loyal to the Republic after the outbreak of the Spanish Civil War, shifted the terms for judging Zayas's tales from moralistic criteria. With his usual critical acumen, Valbuena Prat credits Zayas with a "finely sensual temperament" and appreciates her tales for their literary merit and psychological insight:

---

24 George Ticknor, *History of Spanish Literature*, 3 vols, Boston, 1866, vol. 3, p. 143.
25 Ludwig Pfandl, *Historia de la literatura nacional española en la Edad de Oro*, Barcelona, 1933, pp. 33, 369, 370. My translation.
26 Sylvania, 1922, pp. 1, 15, 25.

She owes her liveliest successes to amorous themes, in which, on the one hand, she was not afraid of scabrous things, and on the other, filled them with exquisite idealizations. Some elements of her stories, beautiful in literary terms, are also interesting as anticipations of the world of the subconscious, today advanced by the Freudian school.[27]

Valbuena Prat describes at length Jacinta's dreams in her opening novella and delights in the satirical and psychological force of "The Miser's Reward," recognizing its Cervantine model. He also judges Zayas a "true and enthusiastic feminist" who advanced a freer, more modern concept of women than was generally seen in her day. He calls her "distinguished, a refined spirit, and exquisitely erotic, she knew how to give life to realistic scenes and untrammeled tragic adventures that, in my opinion, make her the best successor to Cervantes of the *Exemplary Novels*."

Zayas Recovers a Public

The first complete editions of Zayas's tales since 1814 were published by the literary critic and historian Agustín G. de Amezúa y Mayo in 1948 (*Novelas*) and 1950 (*Desengaños*). He prefaced his edition of the *Novelas* with a substantial introduction, including the limited documents of her life published by Serrano y Sanz and taking issue with many previous criticisms of Zayas. Edwin Place was wrong to dwell on her reuse of plots from earlier novelists, Amezúa argues; with her "naturaleza realista" and inventive talents, she didn't need foreign borrowings. He extends Fernández Navarrete's estimate of her popularity, writing that "with the exception of Cervantes, Alemán and Quevedo," there has scarcely been another writer of entertaining books whose works have gained as many editions as hers" [Con excepción de Cervantes, de Alemán y de Quevedo, no hubo acaso ningún otro autor de libros de pasatiempo cuyas obras lograsen tantas ediciones como ella].[28] He identifies honor and love as her primary themes and exclaims over her "delicious feminism." While recognizing that portions of her tales can be so salacious as to cast doubt on calling them "exemplary," Amezúa objects to Pfandl's severely moralistic critique, noting that censors of her day better understood them as realistic

---

27 Ángel Valbuena Prat, *Historia de la literatura española*, Barcelona, 1937, pp. 105, 106.
28 Amezúa, "Prólogo," p. xxxi. My translation.

reflections of society, yet suggested that they were not appropriate for all readers, who should heed church guidance.

While Amezúa's editions made Zayas's novellas accessible for twentieth-century readers, his critical appraisal stimulated a flurry of rival evaluations, especially in the 1970s, when new readers came to Zayas informed by formalist, structuralist and poststructuralist theories of literature. Novelist and literary critic Juan Goytisolo's provocative essay of 1977 portrayed Amezúa's reading as characteristic of a retrograde nineteenth-century tradition of Spanish literary criticism that ignored the fact that literary works respond more to literary traditions than to social reality. He compared her "crossword-puzzle plots" to those of detective novels and Westerns that employ well-known elements with small variations. What brought Zayas to life for modern readers, Goytisolo believed, was her combination of the erotic with burlesque touches, magic and violence. He concluded: "In a country whose literature has for centuries served as a transmitter – often an admirable one – for the institutionalization of its sexual complexes and frustrations, the novels of María de Zayas alone stand out and still move us with the freshness of her singular and daring challenge" [En un país cuya literatura ha servido desde siglos de vehículo transmisor – a menudo admirable – a la institucionalización de sus complejos y frustraciones sexuales, las *novelas* de María de Zayas se destacan de modo señero y nos conmueven aún con la frescura de su insólito y audaz desafío].[29] Sandra Foa, Alessandra Melloni, Marcia Welles, Salvador Montesa Peydró, Paul Julian Smith, Bruce Gartner, and Lou Charnon-Deutsch also discard the "realist" label for Zayas, from various critical angles.[30] Combining structuralist and feminist approaches, Lou Charnon-Deutsch's insightful article shows how Zayas challenges a sexual economy based on the exchange of women seen as passive, idealized objects, particularly in N. 9, "The Judge of Her Own Case," and D. 1, "Her Lover's Slave." In his detailed, structuralist study of Zayas, Montesa Peydro recognizes the importance of convention in Zayas's stories, while setting them in the context of the social realities of her day. In her pessimism, he claims, Zayas reflects the state of mind of penetrating Spaniards, in which the omnipresence of war and the consciousness of national decline are evident.

29 Juan Goytisolo, "El mundo erótico de María de Zayas," *Disidencias*, Barcelona, p. 109. My translation.
30 For brief summaries of the readings of Foa, Melloni, Wells, Montesa Peydro, Smith, Gartner and Charnon-Deutsch, see Greer, *María de Zayas*, pp. 58–60.

Two other substantial monographs in English were published in 2000 and 2001, almost simultaneously with my own: *The Cultural Labyrinth of María de Zayas*, by Marina S. Brownlee, and Lisa Vollendorf's *Reclaiming the Body: María de Zayas's Early Modern Feminism*. Vollendorf argues that Zayas depicted graphic domestic violence against women to reveal the social underpinnings of gender inequality that facilitated it. She emphasizes that bodies have meaning and that Zayas used those bodies to communicate a clear feminist agenda. That is surely true, particularly of the women whose bodies are said to be yet more beautiful in death than in life, thus serving to figure their perfect innocence of guilt. *Contar* in Spanish means both to narrate and to enumerate. Using either meaning of *contar*, the body count mounts in the *Desengaños*.

Brownlee's monograph analyzes the paradoxical nature of Zayas's novellas, from her opening authorial statement to her closing address to Fabio. Its labyrinthian discourse, Brownlee says, dramatizes the shift from Renaissance clarity to Baroque excess. Drawing parallels between that shift to the Baroque and Postmodernism, in which there is a crisis of legitimacy that makes final meaning impossible, Brownlee underlines the pronounced lack of consensus even among the fictional audience at the soiree. The listeners cannot agree on the meaning of the tales, even though their narrators announced their intents. Without discounting Zayas's pedagogical project of exposing abuses to improve society, Brownlee maintains quite persuasively that Zayas is also a shrewd marketing strategist: she denounces offenses by women as well as men and avails herself of shifting and contradictory subject positions both to elude censorship and to engage a diverse public of varying perspectives. Taking advantage of the new reading market and reading practices, Zayas, in Brownlee's estimation, capitalizes on the popularity of the sensationally lurid tales of monsters and wonders and magic in the growth of the tabloid press; she also cultivates gossip: its lure, its threat to one's reputation, and the pleasure of reading gossip about others. Zayas titillates her readers, Brownlee says, with lurid descriptions of violence and sexual encounters that border on pornography. If there is one weakness to the analysis, however, it is that Brownlee jumps back and forth between Zayas's two volumes rather than consistently registering the changed tone between them, which has now been effectively underlined by Elizabeth Rhodes's monograph on the *Desengaños*. In my opinion, Sander Berg provides a much more thorough and thoughtful study of Zayas's use of the marvelous and miraculous.

Brownlee's stress on the paradoxical nature of Zayas's writing does help explain, nevertheless, the multiplying perspectives that emerge as readership of Zayas continues to increase. For example, Elena Rodríguez-Guridi examines the interplay of religion, medicine and science in her work, and Enrique Fernández looks at the question of subjective interiority and the practice of dissection.[31] Kelsey J. Ihinger brings in feminist disability studies as she treats the issue of blindness and gender.[32] Emre Özmen and Pedro Ruiz Pérez provide a compact analysis of the relationship of heroines' attempts to escape patriarchal domination, suggesting that they mirror those of Zayas's search for recognition of feminine authority in a male-dominated literary field.[33] Like Brownlee and Rhodes, many recent studies stress the Baroque complexity of Zayas's writing style and her visual sensationalism.

Although I do not aspire to give the last word on Zayas, I do believe we should evaluate Zayas's legacy for literary work and women's studies from several angles. Her work and its reception demonstrate the capacity of this talented woman writer to make her place in a masculine literary world, despite being denied access to formal education, and to compete in the literary marketplace of her day. The study of her work calls increased attention to the diversity of Luso-Hispanic writers, female and male, and the importance of paying heed to them, particularly in the study of Renaissance and Early Modern periods, which for so long has been heavily focused on French, Italian and English traditions. The shifting nature of her reception, however, highlights the challenge of avoiding two extremes as readers of later eras engage with Zayas's work. We should pursue neither the impossible goal of understanding her texts with seventeenth-century eyes and ears, nor the opposite mistake, of approaching it only from our own mindset and ignoring how her work was shaped by the dominant ideology and reading practices of her day. From a women's studies perspective, I and many others celebrate this most engaging woman writer, who was popular in her day but was then largely lost to critical view in the nineteenth and early twentieth centuries. We cannot use Zayas as a measure of early feminism, but we can learn from her two volumes to

---

31 Elena Rodríguez-Guridi, "De Eva a Ave: Anatomía médica y crística del cuerpo femenino en los *Desengaños amorosos*," Hispanic Review 87.3, 2019, 265–84; Enrique Fernández, *Anxieties of Interiority and Dissection in Early Modern Spain*, Toronto, 2015.

32 Kelsey J. Ihinger, "'Ojos que no ven': Gender and Blindness in María de Zayas's *Desengaños amorosos*," Journal for Early Modern Cultural Studies 30.1, 2020, pp. 29–58.

33 Emre Özmen and Pedro Ruiz Pérez, "Deseo y autoridad: La tensión de la auotoría en María de Zayas," Criticón 128, 2016, pp. 37–51.

appreciate the complexity of writing as a proto-feminist and to better understand the balancing act that stance demanded in the literary marketplace of patriarchal culture. She ranks as an icon of the Luso-Hispanic world in the best sense of the word icon, not as a two-dimensional symbol, but as a Spanish woman writer of enduring complexity who continues to engage readers today.

Appendix

Plot Summaries

Exemplary Tales of Love – *Novelas amorosas y ejemplares*

Frame story: Friends of **Lisis**, who is ill with a recurring fever, gather to entertain her at Christmastime by telling two stories each night for five nights. Men and woman alternate as narrators; Lisis loves don Juan, who will tell the next-to-last story. **Lisarda**, Lisis's cousin and rival for Juan's love, tells the first story, and Lisis's mother, **Laura**, tells the last. By the end of the volume, Lisis accepts she will not have don Juan and promises another suitor, don **Diego**, that they will be engaged by the new year.

N. 1. Taking a Chance on Losing – *Aventurarse perdiendo*

Narrator: Lisarda

Fabio, a young gentleman from Madrid, climbing Montserrat to visit the monastery, encounters **Jacinta** disguised as a shepherd, lamenting her misfortunes. He realizes she is a woman and entreats her to tell him her story.

When she was a girl of sixteen growing up in Baeza (Andalusia), Jacinta's mother was dead and her father paid attention only to his son. Jacinta dreams of a handsome lover with a cape over his face. When she pulls back the cape, he stabs her in the heart with a dagger. She wakes up in love with this phantom, who later materializes as don **Félix**, a neighbor who had been long off at war. He courts her secretly at night.

Félix's cousin **Adriana** also loves him. At first, he humors her mother's request to court her, but Jacinta demands that he tell Adriana he is already engaged to her. Adriana warns Jacinta's father that his daughter is offending the family honor and kills herself. Jacinta and Félix take refuge in a convent from her enraged father. One night Félix leaves the convent, is attacked by Jacinta's father and brother and kills the brother in self-defense, flees to Naples, then goes to serve in Flanders.

Jacinta's father intercepts all Felix's letters and sends her a forged one that Félix has died. Jacinta takes the nun's habit. Six years later Félix reappears, she breaks her religious vows, and they get a papal dispensation that permits them to marry, but only after a year in which they do not cohabit. During the waiting period, Félix goes off to war in Mamora (Morocco), while Jacinta stays in Madrid with his aunt and the aunt's daughter, **Guiomar**. Jacinta dreams she receives a letter from Félix with a box she expects to contain jewels but in fact contains his severed head. Then she learns that he has drowned at sea. Rather than returning to the convent, she stays with Guiomar and her mother.

She falls in love with Guiomar's friend **Celio** when he boasts of his coldness to another woman's love. At first flattered and attentive, Celio loses interest and leaves for Salamanca. Jacinta follows him but her escort misleads her and robs her. She takes refuge on the mountain of Monserrat, disguised as a shepherd, where Fabio finds her.

Fabio tells Jacinta that Celio treats all women this way, and he has taken orders to join the priesthood. At Fabio's urging, Jacinta leaves Monserrat with him and returns to Madrid, where she enters a convent to live as a secular resident, still in love with Celio and content to see him from afar. Félix's niece Guiomar joins Jacinta in the convent.

N. 2. Aminta Deceived and Honor's Revenge – La burlada Aminta y venganza del honor

Narrator: Matilde

Aminta's father and mother die when she is twelve or fourteen and she is entrusted to her paternal uncle, captain don **Pedro**, in Segovia. It is agreed that Aminta will marry his son, don Luis, a soldier in Italy, on his return. Meanwhile, she has many suitors in Segovia, including "don **Jacinto**," a young man who comes on business with his "sister," a woman who calls herself **Flora**. Flora and **Elena**, a neighboring merchant's widow, help Jacinto seduce Aminta and she goes with him to the vicar, who performs the betrothal ceremony. The newlyweds spend the night in the inn where he and Flora are staying. Jacinto kills Elena to prevent her identifying him, takes Aminta to the house of **Luisa**, a widowed relative, and leaves for Valladolid with Flora. **Martín**, Luisa's son, returns home and they tell Aminta that Jacinto's real name is Francisco, and he is married to a woman in Madrid who has returned to her parents because of his escapades, including those with Flora, his lover. Martín, smitten by Aminta, overhears her crying in her room, breaks open the door to her room, keeps her from to opening her veins and offers to avenge her honor and marry her; she declares that she will avenge herself. Together they follow Jacinto/Francisco to Valladolid, with Aminta dressed as a page and Martín as a muleteer. Still disguised as a page, Aminta serves Jacinto and Flora for a month. Hearing that her uncle don Pedro has died, that her cousin Luis is seeking revenge for her loss and his father's death of shock, Aminta stabs Jacinto and Flora to death and she and Martín depart for Madrid. In the carriage, they change clothes so when the Corregidor encounters them, they go unrecognized. In Madrid, Aminta and Martín marry and live under new names and the widowed doña Luisa comes to live with them.

N. 3. The Miser's Reward – El castigo de la miseria

Narrator: don Alvaro

Twelve-year-old **Marcos** comes to Madrid with his father, a very old poor gentleman from Navarre, and becomes a page in a prince's house. With a miserly lifestyle, Marcos accumulates six thousand ducats by the age of thirty. **Isidora** conspires with her handsome "nephew" **Agustín** and a marriage broker, **Gamarra**, to lure Marcos into marriage. Isidora presented herself as a wealthy thirty-six-year-old widow, but when servant **Inés** wakes them up, Marcos finds Isidora's teeth in his whiskers, her hair on the pillow, and her fifty-five-year-old wrinkles plainly visible; jewels and wedding finery are gone, apparently stolen by the maid **Marcela**, who disappeared. Other creditors come for the silver and clothing he thought were Isidora's; the owner of the house reclaims his property, and Isidora, Agustín and Inés flee with Marcos's money and everything they can carry. Marcos finds no trace of them but meets Marcela, who has him hire a magician (her boyfriend) to conjure up demons to reveal the whereabouts of Marcos's wealth. The "demon" Calquimorro is a tortured cat that attacks Marcos and makes him faint. In a letter, Isidora berates Marcos for his miserliness and says she will happily live as his wife again if he gathers another six thousand ducats. Agustín and Inés embark from Madrid with all the stolen goods, so Isidora is reduced to begging. Her co-conspirators head for Naples, where Agustín becomes a soldier and Inés a courtesan.

Marcos goes out to hang himself and encounters the marriage broker, who says that he plans to do the same rather than be executed in the plaza for gambling away his employer's jewels. He carries rope for both, and Marcos hangs himself, but the other noose is found empty and no trace of Gamarra remains; it is decided the devil drove Marcos to despair. In a revised version of the story, Marcos falls ill from the shock of Isidora's letter and dies.

N. 4. Forewarned but Fooled – El prevenido, engañado

Narrator: don Alonso

Don **Fadrique**, a rich gentleman in Granada, falls in love with **Serafina**, who favors another man. She agrees to marry Fadrique but delays, claiming illness, and one night he sees her come out of the house and give birth in an outbuilding. He saves the baby, has her baptized as **Gracia** and leaves her in a convent to be raised. He sends Serafina a message of rejection and leaves town. Serafina becomes a nun.

Fadrique goes to Sevilla and falls in love with a widow, **Beatriz**, who tells him that, in honor of her dead husband, she won't marry for three years. He gets inside the house one night and sees her going to the stables to care for a dying black man, **Antonio**, her lover. When Antonio dies, she sends Fadrique a note saying she will marry him immediately. He replies suggesting that she mourn her black lover another year, then leaves for Madrid. Beatriz marries another suitor.

With his cousin don **Juan**, Fadrique courts the married **Ana** and her cousin **Violante**. Ana tells Juan to bring Fadrique to take her place in bed with her husband so she can enjoy a night with Juan, and after a fearful night, Fadrique discovers that the "husband" is actually Violante. He carries on an affair with her for months, but she rejects marriage, and then he finds her welcoming into her bed a brother of Ana's husband, who "shoots" at Fadrique with a shoe. When Ana laughs at Fadrique, he beats her and leaves. He goes to Naples and Rome, having affairs with clever, deceitful women. Passing through Catalonia en route to Granada, a **duchess** invites him to enjoy the afternoon with her while her husband is away hunting. When her husband returns unexpectedly, she locks Fadrique in a closet and makes a game of telling her husband she has a lover shut up there, then laughing at her "joke."

Fadrique marries the simple convent-raised Gracia and has her don a suit of armor every night to guard his bed and honor. When he returns from a trip, she tells him how a young man from Córdova showed her pleasanter way for married people to spend the night. Resigned, he lives with her for years and leaves her his fortune on the condition that she become a nun in Serafina's convent. He writes Serafina a letter telling her that Gracia is her daughter, and the two women end their years happily, spending her inheritance building a large convent.

N. 5. The Power of Love – La fuerza del amor

Narrator: Nise

Laura, third child of don **Antonio de Garrafa**, lord of Piedrablanca, four miles from Naples, grows up in Naples with her two brothers; she is particularly close with the younger, **Carlos**. Don **Diego** courts Laura and they marry, but he loses interest and spends more time in the bed of **Nise**, his lover before their marriage. When Laura complains, he abuses her verbally, then physically. Carlos intervenes once and nearly kills Diego, but she stops him. Her father and brothers, pained to see her so abused, move from Naples to their home in Piedrablanca.

Laura asks a sorceress to help her regain her husband's affections. Told to bring her the beard, hair and teeth of a hanged man, Laura goes at night to a roadside chapel between Naples and Piedrablanca, where executed criminals are hung to decompose. While she is there, her brother Carlos wakes up shouting, convinced his sister is in danger. He gallops toward Naples, but the horse stops at the chapel and refuses to budge. Carlos finds Laura and takes her back to Piedrablanca. Don Antonio goes to Naples and complains to the Viceroy. Laura chooses to retire to a convent, although the repentant Diego begs her not to and says he will have Nise put in a convent, but Laura insists. Diego is killed in battle, and Laura becomes a nun.

N. 6. Disillusionment in Love and Virtue Rewarded – El desengaño andando, y premio de la virtud

Narrator: Filis

Don **Fernando**, son of a moderately wealthy widow in Toledo, courts **Juana** promising marriage but puts it off on the pretext of his mother's opposition. Juana's friend **Lucrecia**, an older woman from Rome who has become wealthy practicing sorcery, uses it to take Fernando away from

Juana. Juana appeals to a student from Alcalá for help; he gives her two magic rings with which she can find the truth. A servant borrows the rings, and while she washes clothes with them on, the demons in them escape and beat the student. But they do reveal the truth: Fernando will not marry Juana. She then uses a spell to summon a former suitor, **Octavio**, from purgatory. She will burn eternally in hell, he tells her, unless she reforms. She asks Fernando for a dowry to enter a convent, and he gives it to her.

Fernando marries **Clara**, a merchant's daughter he believes to be rich enough to pay off his large gambling debts, but her father leaves for the Indies with what money there is. Fernando mistreats Clara and goes to Seville with Lucrecia. The marquis don **Sancho** is in love with Clara, but she accepts neither his attention nor his financial help. She leaves her two daughters with Juana in the convent and disguised as a maid, serves Fernando and Lucrecia for a year in Seville. She discovers the secret of Lucrecia's hold over Fernando: a chained and blinded rooster. She frees her husband from the spell. Lucrecia dies by suicide, and Clara takes Fernando back to Toledo, but he dies from the effects of Lucrecia's sorcery. Clara marries Sancho, they live happily and have many children. Her daughters by Fernando, with a dowry provided by Sancho, become nuns in Juana's convent.

N. 7. Just Desserts — Al fin se paga todo

Narrator: don Miguel

A young noble from Madrid in Valladolid with the court of Philip III, don **García,** sees **Hipólita** thrown out of a house, so he takes her to his inn, where she tells him her story. She is married to **Pedro**, the elder of two brothers. The younger brother, **Luis**, who lives next door, also loves and courts her, but she rejects his attentions. After eight years of marriage, she becomes enamored of **Gaspar**, a Portuguese soldier and has a string of comic mishaps as they try to meet. One night when her husband has gone hunting, she takes her bed into the garden to meet Gaspar, but her husband returns and joins her in the garden bed, so Gaspar's only satisfaction is a kiss while her husband sleeps. Then she smuggles her would-be lover into the house, but it catches on fire; another time, he gets stuck trying to climb into the window and flees, window frame and all. In their final misadventure, her husband returns home quickly to "do his necessities," and she hides Gaspar in a trunk. Thinking he has suffocated, she has to enlist Luis to remove the trunk. Gaspar revives, but threats from Luis cure him of further interest in Hipólita. Luis, however, becomes insistent. One night he lets out the horses so that Pedro gets up to retrieve them. Then he sneaks through the attic into Hipólita's bedroom. She thinks Luis is her husband and they make love, then her husband returns with the same in mind; the next day at mass, Luis lets her know he has enjoyed her. Finding the passageway between the houses he used, she sneaks over the next night and kills Luis and, leaving the bloody knife in her house, flees to Gaspar's inn. He beats her and throws her out, where García finds her and shelters her in his own inn. Gaspar leaves for Lisbon, but on the road, a robber kills him. Pedro is charged with the murder of Luis. Hipólita writes the authorities to tell them what happened; Pedro is pardoned and wants her back, but she refuses. He dies within the year, leaving his fortune to Hipólita. She marries García, giving him both wealth and children.

N. 8. Triumph Over the Impossible – El imposible vencido

Narrator: don Lope

Leonor and **Rodrigo**, neighbors in Salamanca, love each other from childhood. Because Rodrigo is a younger son, Leonor's parents instead promise her to **Alonso**, then Rodrigo's parents send him to fight in Flanders. Leonor promises Rodrigo that she will not wed another man for three years. In Flanders Rodrigo discovers that the "phantasm" that haunts a lovely Flemish widow, **Blanca,** with nightly chain rattles is **Arnesto**, a married neighbor enamored of her who hopes thus to gain access to her bedroom. He and his servant helper are executed. Blanca falls in love with Rodrigo, who humors her and cooperates in a bed-switch trick to marry her to a Spaniard who has long loved her.

Leonor's parents, hearing her lament Rodrigo's four-year absence, send a false letter to Rodrigo's parents in which the son announces that he has married a rich Flemish woman. Hearing this, Leonor submits to marriage to Alonso, but never to its consummation. Rodrigo is given a habit of the Order of Santiago and a four-thousand-ducat income for his service in Flanders and goes back to Salamanca to marry Leonor, only to find her already married. Seeing him pass in the street, she falls in a faint. She is declared dead and is buried. Rodrigo, wanting to embrace her, bribes the sacristan to open the tomb. There he prays to Christ and she revives. He smuggles her out, takes her to Ciudad Rodrigo, and summons his parents. On a theologian's advice, they publish the banns and are married in the Salamanca church in the presence of Leonor's parents and Alonso, none of whom react to the names because they are sure she is dead. At the end of the wedding ceremony, Leonor's mother recognizes her. Alonso calls the corregidor to intervene, and Rodrigo's parents appeal to ecclesiastical authorities. The bishop consults a famous professor, who presents the case to his students. They declare in favor of Rodrigo, who is named her true husband, on the logic that she had been forced to break her promise to him, and when she died, the forced marriage was dissolved. Leonor remains as pale as she was in death, but she lives many years happily with her husband. They have one son.

N. 9. The Judge of Her Own Case – El juez de su causa

Narrator: don Juan

Carlos, a gentleman of Valencia, loves **Estela**, but her parents promise her in marriage to an Italian count. **Claudia**, in love with Carlos, dresses as a man and serves as his page. **Amete**, a slave of Carlos's father, also loves Estela. When Amete's wealthy family in Fez arranges his ransom, Claudia helps him kidnaps Estela and he takes her with him to Morocco. In Fez, Claudia renounces her faith and marries Amete's brother.

Estela resists the attentions of Amete, who then mistreats her. She is tricked again by Claudia, who promises to help her escape; when they leave the house, Amete finds them and tries to rape Estela, but **Xacimín**, a Moorish prince, hears her cries and rescues her. He condemns Amete and Claudia to death and gives Estela money, jewels, freedom and help to go where she chooses. Estela goes to Tunis to serve the Emperor Charles V in his war against Barbarroja. She dresses as a man and uses the name Fernando and the emperor gives her a habit of Santiago for saving him in battle. She encounters Carlos, who was jailed on suspicion of having kidnapped and killed her but then escaped and is serving as a soldier. She makes him her secretary but continually questions him about his love for Estela. The emperor names her viceroy of Valencia, and Carlos's case is brought before her. She prolongs his anguish and lets it appear that he will be condemned again but finally reveals her identity. The emperor makes her princess of Buñol and grants the habit of Santiago, Estela's income, and post of viceroy to Carlos. They marry and have beautiful heirs.

N. 10. The Deceitful Garden – El jardín engañoso

Narrator: Laura, Lisis's mother

Two brothers in Zaragoza, the elder and sole heir **Jorge** and the younger, **Federico**, court two sisters, **Constanza** and **Teodosia**. Constanza accepts

Jorge's courtship with restraint, but Teodosia despises Federico and secretly loves Jorge. She tells Jorge that Constanza really loves Federico, and Jorge kills his brother and flees. The girls' father dies, leaving the care of the estate and the daughters in the hands of their mother, **Fabia**.

Two years later the noble but poor **Carlos** arrives in Zaragoza and takes up residence in the house opposite Constanza's. He falls in love with her and befriends the family, cultivating Fabia's affection. Pretending he is mortally ill, he leaves his "fortune" to Constanza, and on his recovery, he marries her. She appreciates him as a considerate husband.

Jorge returns to Zaragoza and again pursues Constanza, who rejects his attentions. Teodosia falls ill and Constanza, recognizing that her sister's love for Jorge is the cause, asks him to marry Teodosia, but he refuses; he wants only Constanza. Exasperated, Constanza tells Jorge that she will respond only if he can create a beautiful garden in front of her window by the next morning. Jorge makes a pact with the devil to give his soul in exchange for the garden. Seeing it the next morning, Constanza asks her husband to kill her to prevent dishonor, but he says he will kill himself instead. Jorge, amazed, grabs Carlos's sword and absolves Constanza of her promise. The devil, not to be outdone, gives up his claim on Jorge's soul. Jorge marries Teodosia and all live happily and have many children. After Jorge dies, Teodosia pens a manuscript recounting the story and revealing that Jorge killed Federico. The testimony is discovered after her death.

Tales of Disillusion – *Desengaños amorosos*

Frame story: Having promised engagement to Diego at the end of the *Novelas*, Lisis's illness is aggravated by don Juan's preference for Lisarda and postpones it. Lisis's friends gather during Shrovetide to entertain her with ten more tales over three nights. All the narrators are women. After Lisis tells the last tale, she retreats to live as a secular resident in a convent, where she is joined by her mother and others. (In the original text, only the first tale has a title. The ones provided here are from the 1716 Barcelona and following editions.)

D. 1. Her Lover's Slave – *La esclava de su amante*

Narrator: "Zelima"/Isabel

"Zelima," a supposedly Moorish slave whose friendship helps Lisis recover her health, reveals that she is really **Isabel Faxardo**, who as a young woman went with her father from Murcia to Zaragoza, where he served during the Catalonian uprising. They lodge in the house of a widow, whose daughter, **Eufrasia**, becomes close friends with Isabel. The widow's son, **Manuel**, courts Isabel and rapes her and then promises to marry her. But Manuel postpones even speaking to her father of marriage and renews an old relationship with **Alejandra**, a married woman. To escape rivalry between Alejandra and Isabel, Manuel sails with the Admiral of Castile, who is going as viceroy to Sicily. **Felipe**, a suitor from Isabel's youth in Murcia who followed her to Zaragoza and serves in her household under the name Luis, warns her of Manuel's plans, and she takes jewels and money and leaves home to follow him. Her father dies from the shock of her disappearance. Isabel dresses as a Moorish slave and has a former servant **Octavio** sell her to the Admiral's majordomo. Felipe in turn follows her. On an outing to an island off Sicily, Manuel, Isabel and Felipe are kidnapped and taken to Algeria, where their captor gives them to his daughter, **Zaida**. Zaida loves Isabel, falls passionately in love with Manuel, and arranges to take all of them back to Spain, and they arrive in Zaragoza six years after they left. Zaida plans to be baptized, and Manuel tells Isabel that he will marry Zaida rather than her. Felipe stabs Manuel to death and flees, Zaida kills herself with his dagger, and Isabel seeks out Octavio and has him sell her again, this time to Lisis's uncle in Valencia. The uncle pursues her, and when "Zelima" tells his wife, **Leonor**, she sends Zelima/Isabel, to her niece Lisis in Madrid. Finishing her story, Isabel announces her wish to become a nun.

D. 2. Most Infamous Revenge – La más infame venganza

Narrator: Lisarda

Octavia and **Juan** are the adult children of a Spaniard who went as a soldier to Milan, where he married and gambled away most of his fortune. **Carlos**, son of a rich senator, courts Octavia and seduces her promising marriage but postpones it because his father wants to marry him to a rich woman. Juan, who has been away studying, returns to Milan when their father is killed in battle. He enjoys gambling and women but keeps Octavia shut up at home with no money. Juan kills a man and flees to Naples which gives Carlos free access to Octavia again; within two years, he tires of her. A friend of Carlos's father dies, leaving his daughter **Camila** extremely rich. She is not as beautiful as Octavia but very virtuous. At his father's urging, Carlos puts Octavia in a convent and marries Camila, then writes Octavia suggesting that she become a nun. Juan returns to Milan and is surprised to find her in a convent; she asks him to avenge her dishonor. He threatens and cajoles her into becoming a nun, then courts Camila as his means of revenge. Camila pays him no attention and says nothing to her husband, believing her own virtue and seclusion will protect her. Juan dons one of his sister's dresses and enters Camila's bedroom, where he tells her of Carlos's relation with Octavia, rapes her at knifepoint and departs, announcing his identity and threatening to kill Carlos too. He and two companions hide in a convent and nothing more is heard of him. Camila goes to a convent and stays there until Carlos's father, persuaded of her innocence, convinces her to come home. Carlos will neither sleep nor eat with her, and after a year, he poisons her. Her entire body except for her head swells to enormous proportions, and she lives thus for six months before hearing a voice announcing her death. Carlos disappears, and the senator remarries to sire more children.

D. 3. (His Wife's Executioner, "El verdugo de su esposa")

Narrator: Nise

Juan and **Pedro**, both sons of Spaniards resident in Palermo, grow up as inseparable friends. When Pedro marries **Roseleta**, Juan stops going to his house, but Pedro insists that he return. Juan does, and he falls in love with Roseleta. He tries to resist temptation but falls ill, suffering that he explains as passion for **Angeliana**, with whom he has already slept and promised to marry. After two months, Juan declares his love to Roseleta and begins to court her. She tells him to stop or she will tell her husband, and when he persists, she shows Pedro the notes his friend has been sending her. Furious, Pedro makes her send a note inviting Juan to their country estate. Pedro leaves town, then doubles back to the estate and hides there.

Leaving Palermo, Juan hears the bells ring the Ave María and stops to pray to the Virgin, asking for her intercession with Christ to protect him and her forgiveness for what he is about to do. Continuing, he passes three robbers hanged by the side of the road. One calls Juan by name, saying that God has miraculously saved his life because he was innocent and asks Juan to cut him down. Together they go to the estate, where the robber insists that Juan hide while he goes to the garden door as if to meet Roseleta. Pedro and servants burst forth firing pistols, shoot the robber and throw him in a well. Juan sees it from his hiding place, and when he comes out, the robber, dripping blood, appears and stops Juan. He was and is dead, he explains, but the Virgin Mary allowed him to appear to Pedro and his servants as Juan, so they think they have killed him and

Juan can escape. Returning home, Juan sees the robber still hanging from his noose, alongside the other two hanged men. In the morning, Juan astounds Pedro and Roseleta by appearing alive. He begs their forgiveness and enters a monastery.

Gossip about the event turns Pedro's love for Roseleta to hate; Angeliana, angry at losing Juan to Roseleta, seeks out Pedro and becomes his lover, flaunting their relationship. Roseleta sends her a threatening note, whereupon Angeliana retaliates by telling Pedro that Roseleta had really been Juan's lover. Together, Angeliana and Pedro plan how to kill Roseleta. Pedro stays away from Angeliana two months, then while Roseleta is being bled for a throat ailment, he removes the bandage as she sleeps, and she bleeds to death. He feigns grief but marries Angeliana within three months. He also tries to kill Juan, but the Mother of God continues to protect him.

D. 4. Too Late Undeceived – Tarde llega el desengaño

Narrator: Filis

Martín is returning to Toledo from Flanders when his ship sinks in a storm. He and a companion are washed ashore on Grand Canary Island and are taken in by **Jaime de Aragón**, owner of a lovely castle. At dinner, Jaime has a small door off the dining hall opened and a beautiful but very thin and roughly dressed blond woman emerges and crawls under the table, where she eats scraps and bones and is served water in a skull. A very ugly **black woman**, richly dressed and bejeweled, is ushered in ceremoniously and Jaime seats her at the table. After the meal, Jaime tells his visitors his story of when he was a young soldier in Flanders and received a mysterious invitation:

Led blindfolded at night by an old servant, he is taken to a luxurious residence, where he is entertained lavishly by a woman whose beauty he can feel but not see. Afterward, she gives him money and jewels and invites him to return for the same favors every night, but he must pledge not to try to see her or learn her identity. After a month, a friend tells him that people are noticing his nightly absences and new wealth and are saying he is a thief. He marks the door of his lover's house with a blood-soaked sponge and talks her into letting him see her beauty. She is Madame **Lucrecia**, the widowed only daughter of a rich and powerful old prince. The next day he courts her openly in the street, breaking his pledge of secrecy, and that evening, six armed men arrive to kill him. Jaime survives and returns to Grand Canary, where the death of his parents leaves him a rich man. But he cannot forget Lucrecia.

At Mass one Holy Week he sees **Elena**, who is a portrait of Lucrecia, but as poor as she is noble, virtuous and beautiful. He marries her and lives happily with her for eight years, until a maid tells him that Elena is having an affair with the handsome young **cousin** who lives with them while studying for the priesthood. Jaime takes the whole household from the city to the country castle, then burns the cousin alive, saving his skull for Elena to use as a drinking vessel as she eats under his table. The maid who told Jaime of the affair is the black woman who enjoys the position of lady of the house.

That night after all have retired, the black woman cries out that she is dying and calls for Jaime. She confesses that she falsely accused Elena. She herself had fallen in love with the cousin, but he rejected her advances and joined Elena in chastising her. Jaime stabs the maid to death, then runs to release Elena, only to find her dead in a saintly pose. He tries to kill himself, and when Martín stops him, he goes mad. Martín goes back to Toledo and marries his cousin.

D. 5. Innocence Punished – La inocencia castigada

Narrator: Laura, Lisis's mother

Inés marries at eighteen, happy to escape the strict seclusion imposed by her brother **Francisco** and his **wife**. Inés lives happily with her husband, seeing the society of her city near Seville. **Diego** falls in love with her, but she is not aware that his courtship is directed at her. A **neighbor** offers to help Diego, borrowing her dress on the pretext of loaning it to a niece for her wedding, then arranges for a prostitute who looks like Inés to wear it. Diego meets her alone, in an almost-dark room, believing he is possessing Inés. After the dress is returned, he speaks to Inés at mass, and when she denies any contact with him, he mentions the dress and the neighbor. She has him come to her house the next day, after her husband has gone to Seville. She calls the corregidor and has him hide while Diego tells his story; the neighbor woman is given two hundred lashes and exiled from the city.

Diego hires a **Moorish sorcerer**, who makes a nude figurine of Inés with a pin through the heart and a candle on her head. When the sorcerer lights the candle, Inés rises from sleep and in a trance comes to Diego's bed, where she stays until he sends her away. Diego enjoys nightly visits from Inés for over a month, although she never speaks, and each morning she thinks that she has been having wicked dreams. One night as she walks through the streets clad only in her shift, she passes the corregidor, making his nightly rounds with his officers and Inés's brother Francisco, and they all witness the effect of Diego's candle-figurine.

Inés, on being awakened, begs the corregidor to kill her, but he refuses and declares her innocent. But her husband, brother and sister-in-law move to a house on the outskirts of Seville, wall her into a tiny space, feeding her only bread and water while her flesh is consumed by vermin and she goes blind in the darkness. After six years, a neighbor hears her lament through the wall and she is rescued. Her family jailors are executed and she enters a convent, where she miraculously regains her beauty, but not her sight.

D. 6. Love for the Sake of Conquest – Amar sólo por vencer

Narrator: Matilde

Esteban, a talented servant for a nobleman, falls in love with **Laurela**, the third daughter of noble, wealthy parents in Madrid. Dressed as a woman and calling himself Estefanía, he secures a position as a maid in her house, where he earns her affection with his musical talent and also draws the eye of Laurela's father and the other servants, men and women alike. "Estafanía" tells everyone that s/he loves Laurela, and that love is a question of souls, not gender. When Laurela visits a neighbor to whom her parents have promised her in marriage, Esteban, sick with jealousy, reveals that he is a man. He convinces Laurela to run away with him, but after one night with her, fearing the consequences, admits that he is the son of a carpenter and is already married. He leaves her at the Santa María church, where her uncle finds her and takes her to his house. The aunt and uncle treat her harshly. A year later, while she is at mass, her father and uncle weaken a wall in her home. The wall falls on her and a maid, killing them. Her sisters enter a convent and after their father dies, her mother joins them.

D. 7. Marriage Abroad: Portent of Doom – Mal presagio casar lejos

Narrator: Luisa, a widow

Four sisters and a **brother** of royal blood are orphaned. The oldest sister marries in Portugal and takes the youngest with her. Her husband sends a page with a letter that falsely implicates her in infidelity, then he kills her. The youngest sister escapes by jumping out a window, she breaks both legs and so spends the rest of her life in bed. The second sister marries in Italy. When she praises the looks of a Spanish captain, her husband strangles her with her own hair while she is washing it and then poisons their four-year-old son.

Before her sisters are killed, the third and most beautiful sister, **Blanca**, is promised by her brother to a **Flemish prince**. She would have preferred to enter a convent but consents, on the condition that the prince come to Spain to court her for a year. He does so, she finds him pleasing yet grows melancholy. After the wedding they go to Flanders and the prince turns quarrelsome. Her father-in-law expresses hatred of her and all Spanish women. She is also mistreated by the prince and his much-favored young page, **Arnesto**. She finds a fast friend in her sister-in-law **Marieta**, whose husband is also cold to her.

Marieta's manservant is mysteriously killed and without investigating, her husband ties her to a chair and strangles her in front of her father, who sentenced her to death. Blanca faints at the sight, and the prince protests as well. Blanca, knowing her turn will be next, distributes her jewels to her Spanish ladies-in-waiting, then sends a letter to her brother in Spain. Four months later, she goes into the prince's bedroom, expecting to find him with another woman but finds him instead in bed with Arnesto, who laughs at her horror. She has the bed taken out to the patio and burned, calls her Spanish confessor, and takes communion. She gives him a chain and rings and asks him to leave and tell her brother she is dying. The next day, Arnesto and her father-in-law bleed her to death, over the protests of the prince. Her brother arrives and, gathering troops, attacks the princes, father and son, and they and many others are killed. The Duke of Alba's punishment of the Flemish is said to be in revenge for Blanca's death.

D. 8. Traitor to His Own Blood — El traidor contra su sangre

Narrator: Francisca

Don Pedro, a proud, cruel and greedy man in Jaén, has a son, **Alonso**, and a **daughter**, **Mencía**. To keep all their wealth for the son, Pedro tries to make Mencía become a nun, refusing to give her a dowry and turning down all suitors. **Enrique**, a wealthy man from Granada, wants to marry Mencía without a dowry, but Pedro refuses his request because his grandparents were commoners. Enrique continues to court her, and they exchange marriage vows. Alonso learns of this from a married woman, **Clavela**, with whom Enrique had previously been involved. Alonso and his father plan to kill Mencía and Enrique. Alonso catches his sister writing Enrique a note, locks her in her room, summons a priest to confess her, and stabs her repeatedly. He sends Mencía's note to Enrique and waits in the street to kill him. When Enrique arrives that night, Mencía's window opens by itself, and he sees her still-bleeding body bathed in light, and her voice warns him that she is dead and pleads that he save himself. He is frozen by the sight, and Alonso and a friend stab him and flee. Enrique survives and becomes a Franciscan monk. He builds a chapel where he has Mencía's still-bleeding body interred.

Alonso goes to Naples, enjoying his father's financial support. He makes friends with an unlicensed priest, **Marco Antonio**, and falls in love with **Ana de Añasco**, granddaughter of a Spanish nobleman. He marries her and they have a son, but when Alonso tells his father, the man disinherits Alonso because he married a poor woman. In hopes of regaining his father's favor, Marco Antonio and Alonso behead Ana at supper in Marco Antonio's garden. They throw her body in the well and bury her head in a cave in the marina, then embark for Spain. The baby son's cries waken his grandmother, and the next day Ana's grandfather identifies her body, laid out in the plaza after a serving woman found it in the well.

Alonso and Marco Antonio stop in Genoa, are arrested for stealing silk stockings, brought back to Naples, and sentenced to death for murdering Ana. Alonso, repentant, asks that they bring Ana's head to beg her forgiveness before his execution. Although six months have passed, the head is still fresh and lovely. When Alonso's father learns of his son's execution, he says that he would rather have his son dead than badly wed and continues playing cards. Shortly thereafter, he dies, and Ana's infant son inherits his fortune.

D. 9. Triumph over Persecution – La perseguida triunfante

Narrator: Estefanía, a nun, cousin of Lisis

King Ladislao of Hungary asks to marry **Princess Beatriz of England** and sends his younger brother **Federico** to arrange the betrothal and bring her to Hungary. Federico falls in love with Beatriz but hides his passion. Ladislao and Beatriz live happily together for a year until he must defend his realm against attack. Before departing, he leaves governing power jointly in the hands of Beatriz and Federico. Federico takes advantage of this to declare his passion and pursue her. After trying in vain to dissuade him, she has a golden cell built and imprisons him in it. The queen rules so well that her vassals do not miss either Federico or Ladislao. A year later, when the returning king nears the city, she frees Federico. He has refused to bathe, shave or change his clothes during his year of captivity, and he tells the king that Beatriz imprisoned him because he refused her sexual advances. The king believes Federico and orders that the queen be taken to the wildest forest, where her eyes are put out and she is left as food for beasts.

Beatriz, praying to God and His Mother, hears steps and a woman's consoling voice. The visitor restores Beatriz's sight, gives her bread, fruit and water, leads her to a meadow and encourages her to persist in her virtuous ways. Beatriz is found by a German, **Duke Octavio**, who takes Beatriz back to his palace, where she lives under the name Rosismunda.

Ladislao, now doubting the truth of Federico's accusation, laments his harshness. Federico goes to look for Beatriz, intending to rape and kill her, but he finds no trace of her. An ugly man dressed as a scholastic appears and says he is a learned magician – a **doctor**, who can help Federico achieve his desires so long as he promises never to confess it, even in the face of death. The prince agrees. The doctor tells Federico that Beatriz is in Germany with her sight restored, but if he rapes and kills her as he planned, he can become king of Hungary. Federico tells Ladislao that he has found the remains of Beatriz's clothes and they are a sign from heaven that she was guilty and has died. The king nevertheless refuses to remarry and names Federico his heir. After a year, Federico and the doctor travel to Germany and, with Federico's appearance transformed by a magic ring, they enter the palace of Duke Octavio. The doctor, making himself invisible, plants treasonous letters in Rosismunda's sleeve, then notifies the duke that he has learned of a plot to kill him. The household is searched and the letters found. She is taken back to the meadow where they found her, and her queenly dress magically reappears, as does Federico, intent on raping and killing her. Beatriz's **marvelous visitor** replaces her with a lion that leaves Federico badly wounded before the doctor saves him.

Her savior takes Beatriz to a shepherd's hut. The **Emperor** and **Empress** pass by and see Beatriz; their six-year-old son loves her on sight. The emperor insists that Beatriz return to the palace and care for the boy, even sleep in the same bed with him. The doctor again reveals her whereabouts to Federico. They go to the emperor's palace, the doctor tells Federico to enter the boy's chamber, put a sleep-inducing herb under Beatriz's pillow and stab the boy to death, then leave the bloody dagger in her hand. When they are thus discovered the next morning, the emperor orders Beatriz beheaded. Beatriz's protectress appears again, taking her from the executioners' hands to a far-away mountain cave. Just as he is about to be buried, the stabbed boy prince revives and calls for his nursemaid Beatriz – or Florinda, as he knows her.

Beatriz lives happily as a hermit in her cave for eight years, and the doctor cannot discover her whereabouts. Then her protectress appears with all the attributes of the Virgin Mary, gives Beatriz men's clothes and herbs, and tells her to go to Hungary, where many are dying from a plague. The herbs will cure anyone, so long as the patient confesses fully – but they are fatal if any sin is not confessed. As she cures all who suffer, her fame spreads and the king sends for her to cure Federico, who is gravely ill. Told the conditions of the use of the herbs, Federico makes the king promise to forgive him for what he is about to say. Over the protests of the doctor, Federico confesses all. King Ladislao is despairing, but Beatriz reveals her identity and is instantly transformed to all her queenly glory. The Virgin appears beside her, while the doctor disappears in an explosion of demonic, sulfurous smoke.

Although Ladislao wants Beatriz to be his queen again, she goes instead to a convent, taking all her ladies-in-waiting with her. Ladislao has her sister Isabel brought from England to marry Federico and then becomes a monk as well.

D. 10. The Ravages of Vice – Estragos que causa el vicio

Narrator: Lisis

During the reign of Philip III, **Gaspar**, a gentleman of the royal chambers, accompanies the king to Lisbon. There he visits the youngest of four sisters, who live in part of a distinguished residence. Entering one night by a side door to which they have given him a key, he hears moaning coming from a cellar and finds the freshly buried body of a young man, dead but still moaning. He has the unidentified man buried and takes it as a divine warning to stay away from such a house.

At Mass, he is struck by the beauty of two sisters, **Magdalena** and **Florentina**. Magdalena is married to **Dionís**, and Florentina lives with them, in such seclusion that Gaspar has no luck approaching her. One night he finds Florentina in the street, nearly dead from sword wounds. He takes her to his inn and has her cared for, and when she regains consciousness, she tells him to take ministers of justice to Dionís's house, where they find a massacre. Florentina tells Gaspar how she wound up bleeding in the street:

Although she and Magdalena were raised as full sisters, they were born of previous marriages of their father and mother. When Dionís courts and marries Magdalena, Florentina also falls in love with him. Eventually she tells him so, and they are lovers for four years, vowing to marry after

Magdalena's death. During Holy Week, Florentina confesses the truth to a priest, who puts the fear of hell in her, and a maid who has been with her from childhood proposes to arrange for Magdalena to die, so that she in her innocence will earn a martyr's crown in heaven. The maid tells Dionís that Magdalena has betrayed him with a young servant and arranges a night-time scene that supports her testimony. Dionís kills the servant and Magdalena, two of her maids, two pages, and three kitchen slaves. Horrified and repentant, Florentina's maid admits her lie and he kills her. Florentina appears and he tries to kill her too, but a black kitchen slave puts herself between them, giving Florentina time to escape. Dionís falls on his sword and she stumbles to the street, where Gaspar finds her.

Hearing this story, Gaspar counsels Florentina to become a nun. She does so, maintaining a friendly correspondence with Gaspar, who returns to Toledo and marries. Although Florentina eventually confesses her own role in the massacre, the king pardons her, and she inherits Dionís's fortune.

Bibliography

Agulló y Cobo, Mercedes, *Noticia de impresores y libreros madrileños de los siglos XVI y XVII*, Madrid, 1976, vol. 2.

Alatorre, Antonio, "El verso esdrújulo en el siglo XVII," *Anuario de Letras* 38, 2000, pp. 423–45.

Alemán, Mateo, *Primera parte de la Vida del pícaro Guzmán de Alfarche*, Barcelona, 1599; *Segunda parte de la vida del pícaro Guzmán de Alfarache*, Barcelona, 1603. Translation by James Mabbe, *The Rogue, or the Life of Guzmán de Alfarache*, London, 1623.

Amezúa, Agustín G. de, "Prólogo," María de Zayas y Sotomayor, *Desengaños amorosos. Parte segunda del sarao y entretenimiento honesto*, ed. Agustín G. de Amezúa, Madrid, 1950, pp. vii–xxiv.

———, "Prólogo," María de Zayas y Sotomayor, *Novelas amorosas y ejemplares*, ed. Agustín G. de Amezúa, Madrid, 1948, pp. vii–l.

Apuleius, *The Golden Ass*, Oxford, 1995.

Arata, Stefano, "Proyección escenográfica de la huerta del Duque de Lerma en Madrid," *Siglos dorados: Homenaje a Agustín Redondo*, Madrid, 2004, pp. 33–52.

Aristotle, *Generation of Animals and History of Animal I, Parts of Animals I*, C. D. C. Reeve, ed. and trans., Cambridge, 2019.

Armstrong-Roche, Michael, *Cervantes' Epic Novel: Empire, Religion, and the Dream Life of Heroes in Persiles*, Toronto, 2009.

Barahona, Renato, *Sex Crimes, Honour, and the Law in Early Modern Spain: Vizcaya, 1528–1735*, Toronto, 2003.

Baranda, Nieves, and Anne J. Cruz, eds., *The Routledge Research Companion to Early Modern Spanish Women Writers*, London, 2018.

Barbeito Carneiro, Isabel, *Mujeres del Madrid barroco: Voces testimoniales*, Madrid, 1992.

Barella Vigil, Julia, "Heliodoro y la novela corta del siglo XVII," *Cuadernos Hispanoamericanos* nos. 529–30, julio–agosto 1994, pp. 203–22.

Barton, Simon, *A History of Spain*, Croydon, 2009.

Bass, Laura R., "Staging Madrid: Urban Comedy for a New Court Capital," Cacho Casal and Egan, *Routledge Hispanic Studies Companion*, pp. 323–42.

Berco, Cristian, "Desire, Fear, and the Inquisition: Male Homoeroticism in Early Modern Spain," Cacho Casal and Egan, *Routledge Hispanic Studies Companion*, pp. 619–31.

Berg, Sander, *The Marvellous and the Miraculous in María de Zayas*, Cambridge, 2019.

Bergmann, Emilie, "The Exclusion of the Feminine in the Cultural Discourse of the Golden Age: Juan Luis Vives and Fray Luis de León," *Religion, Body and Gender in Early Modern Spain*, ed. Alain Saint-Saëns, San Francisco, 1991, pp. 124–36.

Boruchoff, David, "'Competir con Heliodo': Cervantes y la crítica ante una leyenda," *USA Cervantes: 39 Cervantistas en Estados Unidos*, ed. Georgina Dopico Black and Francisco Layna Ranz, Madrid, 2009, pp. 181–210.

Boyer, H. Patsy, "The War between the Sexes and the Ritualization of Violence in Zayas's *Disenchantments*," *Sex and Love in Golden Age Spain*, ed. Alain Saint-Saëns, New Orleans, pp. 123–45.

Brooks, Peter, *Reading for the Plot: Design and Intention in Narrative*, New York, 1985.

Brown, Kenneth, "Context i text del Vexamen d'Academia de Francesc Fontanella," *Llengua i Literatura Catalanes* 2, 1987, pp. 172–252.

———, "María de Zayas y Sotomayor: Escribiendo poesía en Barcelona en época de Guerra (1643)," *Dicenda: Cuadernos de filología hispánica*, Complutense, no. 11, 1993, pp. 355–60.

Brownlee, Marina S. *The Cultural Labyrinth of María de Zayas*, Philadelphia, 2000.

Burns, Kathryn, "Unfixing Race," Greer, Mignolo and Quilligan, *Rereading the Black Legend*, pp. 188–202.

Cabezas, Juan Antonio, *Diccionario de Madrid*, 3rd ed., Madrid, 1989.

Cacho Casal, Rodrigo, and Caroline Egan, eds., *The Routledge Hispanic Studies Companion to Early Modern Spanish Literature and Culture*, London, 2022.

Cadden, Joan, *Meanings of Sex Difference in the Middle Ages: Medicine, Science, and Culture*, Cambridge, 1993.

Calderón de la Barca, Pedro, *El medico de su honra*, ed. D. W. Cruickshank, Madrid, 1981.

———, *The Physician of His Honour*, ed. and trans. Dian Fox, 2nd ed., Oxford, 2007.

Cascardi, Anthony J., "Introduction," *The Cambridge Companion to Cervantes*, ed. A. Cascardi, Cambridge, 2002, pp. 1–10.

Casey, Elena, "The *Cuartanas* of Lisis: The Remissive Etiology of the *Novelas amorosas y ejemplares* by María de Zayas y Sotomayor," *eHumanista* 32, 2016, pp. 570–85.
Casey, James, *Family and Community in Early Modern Spain: The Citizens of Granada, 1570–1739*, Cambridge, 2007.
———, *The History of the Family*. Oxford, 1989.
Castillo Solórzano, Alonso de, *La garduña de Sevilla y anzuelo de las bolsas*, Barcelona, 1644.
Cervantes, Miguel de, *Exemplary Novels*, trans. Edith Grossman, ed. Roberto González Echeverría, New Haven, 2016.
———, *Los trabajos de Persiles y Sigismunda. Historia Septentrional*, ed. Juan Bautista Avalle Arce, Madrid, 1969.
———, *Novelas ejemplares*, ed. Julio Rodríguez-Luis, Madrid, 1994.
———, *The Trials of Persiles and Sigimunda, a Northern Story*, trans. Clark A. Colahan, Berkeley, 1989.
Charnon-Deutsch, Lou, "The Sexual Economy in the Narrative of María de Zayas," *Letras Femeninas* 17, 1991, pp. 15–28.
Coghill, Nevill, "Introduction," Geoffrey Chaucer, *The Canterbury Tales*, trans. Nevill Coghill, London, 1977, pp. 11–18.
Cohen, J. M. "Introduction," *The Life of Saint Teresa of Ávila by Herself*, London, 1957, pp. 11–20.
Connell, Sophia M., *Aristotle on Female Animals: A Study of the Generation of Animals*, Cambridge, 2019.
Coolidge, Grace E., "Aristocracy and the Urban Elite," Baranda and Cruz, *Routledge Research Companion*, pp. 15–26.
Covarrubias Orozco, Sebastián de, *Tesoro de la lengua castellana o española*, Madrid, 1984.
Cruickshank, Don W., *Don Pedro Calderón*, Cambridge, 2009.
Cruz, Anne J., "Las academias: Literatura y poder en un espacio cortesano," *Edad de Oro* 18, 1998, pp. 49–57.
———, "María de Zayas and Miguel de Cervantes: A Deceitful Marriage," *Tradition and Innovation in Early Modern Spanish Studies: Essays in Memory of Carroll B. Johnson*, ed. Sherry Velasco, Newark, 2008, pp. 89–106.
———, "Women's Education in Early Modern Spain," Baranda and Cruz, *Routledge Research Companion*, pp. 27–40.
D'Ouville, Antoine Le Métel, *Les nouvelles amoureuses et exemplaires, composé en español*, Paris, 1656–7.
Dadson, Trevor, "Official Rhetoric Versus Local Reality: Propaganda and the Expulsion of the *Moriscos*," Pym, *Rhetoric and Reality*, pp. 1–24.
Dadson, Trevor J., "'Todos son uno': Moriscos and the Question of Identity in Early Modern Spain," Cacho Casal and Egan, *Routledge Hispanic Studies Companion*, pp. 521–36.

Dandelet, Thomas James, "The Impact of Spanish Imperial Political Culture in Iberia and Europe, 1500–1700," Cacho Casal and Egan, *Routledge Hispanic Studies Companion*, pp. 15–28.
Darnton, Robert, *The Great Cat Massacre and Other Episodes in French Cultural History*, New York, 1984.
De Armas, Frederick A., "Antoine Le Metel, Sieur d'Ouville: The 'Lost' Years," *Romance Notes* 14, 1973, pp. 538–43.
———, *The Invisible Mistress: Aspects of Feminism and Fantasy in the Golden Age*, Charlottesville, 1976.
———, "Psyche's Fall and Magdalene's Cross: Myth and Hagiography in María de Zayas's *Tarde llega el desengaño*," *Estudios en honor de Janet Pérez: El sujeto femenino en escritoras hispánicas*, ed. S. Cavallo et al., Potomac, 1998, pp. 3–15.
Diccionario de autoridades, facsimile ed., Real Academia Española, 3 vols., Madrid, 1979.
Dopico-Black, Georgina, *Perfect Wives, Other Women: Adultery and Inquisition in Early Modern Spain*, Durham, 2001.
Elliott, John H., *Imperial Spain, 1469–1716*, London, 2002.
———, *The Count-Duke of Olivares. The Statesman in an Age of Decline*, New Haven, 1986.
Escabias, Juana, "Ana María Caro Mallén de Torres: Una esclava en los corrales de comedias del siglo XVII," *EPOS: Revista de filología* 28, 2012, pp. 177–93.
Eslava, Antonio de, *Noches de invierno*, ed. Julia Barella, Madrid, 2013.
Espinosa, Juan de, *Diálogo en laude de las mujeres*, Albolote, Granada, 1990.
Evans, Geraint, "Masculinities and Honour in *Los comendadores de Córdoba*," *A Companion to Lope de Vega*, ed. Alexander Samson and Jonathan Thacker, Woodbridge, 2018, pp. 199–213.
Fariña Busto, María Jesús, "María de Zayas y Sotomayor: A propósito de algunos sonetos incluidos en las *Novelas y Desengaños Amorosos*," *Monographic Review* 13, 1997, pp. 53–63.
Fernández Guerra, Matías, *Parroquia madrileña de San Sebastián: Algunos personajes de su archivo*, Madrid, 1995.
Fernández Navarrete, Eustaquio, "Bosquejo histórico sobre la novela españoola," *Novelistas posteriores a Cervantes*, 2 vols., Madrid, 1854.
Fernández, Enrique, *Anxieties of Interiority and Dissection in Early Modern Spain*, Toronto, 2015.
Feros, Antonio, *El duque de Lerma: Realeza y privanza en la España de Felipe III*, Madrid, 2002.
———, *Kingship and Favoritism in the Spain of Philip III, 1598–1621*, Cambridge, 2000.
Ferrer Vals, Teresa, dir., *Diccionario biográfico de actores del teatro clásico español*, Kassel, 2008.

Foa, Sandra, *Feminismo y forma narrative: Estudio del tema y las técnicas de María de Zayas y Sotomayor*, Valencia, 1979.
Folger, Robert A., "From Lazarillo to 'otro Lazarillo': The Picaresque Novel in Golden Age Spain," Cacho Casal and Egan, *Routledge Hispanic Studies Companion*, pp. 291–304.
Forcione, Alban K., *Cervantes Christian Romance: A Study of Persiles y Sigismunda*, Princeton, 1972.
Francomano, Emily C., "The Early Modern Foundations of the *Querella de las mujeres*," Baranda and Cruz, *Routledge Research Companion*, pp. 41–59.
Friedman, Edward H., "Enemy Territory: The Frontiers of Gender in María de Zayas's *El traidor contra su sangre* and *Mal presagio casar lejos*," *Essays on Golden Age Spanish Literature for Geoffrey L. Stagg in Honor of His Eighty-Fifth Birthday*, ed. Ellen M. Anderson and Amy R. Williamsen, Newark, 1999, pp. 41–68.
———, "María de Zayas's *Estragos que causa el vicio* and the Feminist Impasse," *Romance Languages Annual* 8, 1997, pp. 472–5.
———, *The Antiheroine's Voice: Narrative Discourse and the Transformations of the Picaresque*, Columbia, 1987.
Fuchs, Barbara, "The Spanish Race," Greer, Mignolo and Quilligan, *Rereading the Black Legend*, pp. 88–98.
Gagliardi, Donatella, "Dos testamentos inéditos de María de Zayas (Nápoles, 1656 y 1657)," *eHumanista* 40, 2018, pp. 561–86.
Gamboa, Yolanda, *Cartografía social en la narrativa de María de Zayas*, Madrid, 2009.
Garber, Marjorie, *Vested Interests: Cross-Dressing and Cultural Anxiety*, New York, 1992.
Gartner, Bruce, "María de Zayas y Sotomayor: The Poetics of Subversion," PhD diss., Emory University, 1989.
Gil y Zárate, Antonio, *Manual de literatura, segunda parte: Resumen histórico de la literatura española*, Madrid, 1854.
Gil-Olse, Juan, "La tradición de la amistad femenina en *La traición en la amistad* de María de Zayas," *Bulletin of Hispanic Studies* 93.4, 2016, pp. 361–83.
Gossy, Mary S., "Skirting the Question: Lesbians and María de Zayas," *Hispanisms and Homosexualities*, ed. Sylvia Molloy and Robert McKee Irwin, Durham, 1998, pp. 19–28.
Goytisolo, Juan, "El mundo erótico de María de Zayas," *Disidencias*, Barcelona, 1977, pp. 68–115.
Greer, Margaret R., "A Tale of Three Cities: The Place of the Theatre in Early Modern Madrid, Paris and London," *BHS* 77, 2000, pp. 391–417.
———, "María de Zayas and the Dukes of Alba," *"Los cielos se agotaron de prodigios": Essays in Honor of Frederick A. de Armas*, ed. Kerry Wilks and Christopher Weimer, Newark, 2017, pp. 225–34.
———, "María de Zayas and the Female Eunuch," *Journal of Spanish Cultural Studies* 2.1, 2001, pp. 41–53.

———, *Maria de Zayas Tells Baroque Tales of Love and the Cruelty of Men*, University Park, 2000.

———, "Spanish Golden Age Tragedy: From Cervantes to Calderón," *A Companion to Tragedy*, ed. Rebecca Bushnell, Malden, 2005, pp. 351–71.

———, "The Politics of Memory in *El Tuzaní de la Alpujarra*," Pym, *Rhetoric and Reality*, pp. 113–30.

———, "Volume Editor's Introduction," Zayas y Sotomayor, *Exemplary Tales*, pp. 1–42.

Greer, Margaret, and Elizabeth Rhodes, "Note on the Translations," María de Zayas y Sotomayor, *Exemplary Tales of Love and Tales of Disillusion*, ed. and trans., Margaret R. Greer and Elizabeth Rhodes, London, 2009, pp. 39–42.

Greer, Margaret, Walter D. Mignolo, and Maureen Quilligan, "Introduction," *Rereading the Black Legend*, pp. 1–24.

Greer, Margaret, Walter D. Mignolo, and Maureen Quilligan, eds., *Rereading the Black Legend: The Discourses of Religious and Racial Difference in the Renaissance Empires*, Chicago, 2007.

Grieve, Patricia E., "Embroidering with Saintly Threads: María de Zayas Challenges Cervantes and the Church," *Renaissance Quarterly* 44.1, 1991, pp. 86–106.

Gurumbe: Canciones de tu memoria negra, created by Miguel Angel Rosales, Canal Sur TV with the collaboration of the Consejería de Cultura, Junta de Andalusia, 2016.

HarperCollins Bible Dictionary, revised ed., Paul J. Achtemeier, general ed., San Francisco, 1996.

Harris, A. Katie, "The Sacromonte and the Geography of the Sacred in Early Modern Granada," *Al-Qantara: Revista de estudios árabes* 23.2, 2002, pp. 517–43.

Hegstrom, Valerie, "Introduction," María de Zayas y Sotomayor, *La traición en la amistad / Friendship Betrayed*, ed. Valeria Hegstrom, trans. Catherine Larson, pp. 13–35.

Henrich, Joseph, *The WEIRDest People in the World: How the West Became Psychologically Peculiar and Particularly Prosperous*, New York, 2020.

Ife, B. W., *Reading and Fiction in Golden-Age Spain: A Platonist Critique and Some Picaresque Replies*, Cambridge, 1985.

Ihinger, Kelsey J., "'Ojos que no ven': Gender and Blindness in María de Zayas's *Desengaños amorosos*," *Journal for Early Modern Cultural Studies* 30.1, 2020, pp. 29–58.

Ireton, Chloe L., "Black Africans' Freedom Litigation Suits to Define Just War and Just Slavery in the Early Spanish Empire," *Renaissance Quarterly* 73, 2020, pp. 1277–319.

Jagoe, Catherine, "Disinheriting the Feminine: Galdós and the Rise of the Realist Novel in Spain," *Revista de Estudios Hispánicos* 27.2, 1993, pp. 225–48.

Jameson, Frederic, "On 'Cultural Studies'," *Social Text* 34, 1993, pp. 17–52.
Jordan Gschwend, Annemarie, and K. J. P. Lowe, eds., *The Global City: On the Streets of Renaissance Lisbon*, London, 2015.
Kagan, Richard L., *Students and Society in Early Modern Spain*, Baltimore, 1974.
Kaminsky, Amy J., "Dress and Redress: Clothing in the *Desengaños amorosos* of María de Zayas y Sotomayor," *Romanic Review* 79.2, 1988, pp. 377–91.
King, Margaret L., and Albert Rabil Jr., "The Other Voice in Early Modern Europe: Introduction to the Series," María de Zayas, *Exemplary Tales*, pp. ix–xxviii.
King, Willard F., *Prosa novelística y academias literarias en el siglo XVII*, Madrid, 1963.
Lagreca, Nancy, "Evil Women and Feminist Sentiment: Baroque Contradictions in María de Zayas's 'El prevenido engañado' and 'Estragos que causa el vicio'," *Revista Canadiense de Estudios Hispánicos* 28, 2004, pp. 565–82.
Lampillas, Francisco Javier, *Ensayo histórico-apologético de la literatura española contra las opiniones preocupadas de algunos escritores modernos italianos*, Madrid, 1789, vol. 5.
Laqueur, Thomas, *Making Sex: Body and Gender from the Greeks to Freud*, Cambridge, 1990.
Lara Alberola, Eva, "El conde-duque de Olivares: Magia y política en la corte de Felipe IV," *Studia Aurea* 9, 2015, pp. 565–94.
La vida de Lazarillo de Tormes: Y de sus fortunas y adversidades (1654), ed. Alberto Blecua, Madrid, 1972.
Lazarillo de Tormes and The Grifter, ed. and trans. David Frye, Indianapolis, 2015.
Lehfeldt, Elizabeth A., *Religious Women in Golden Age Spain: The Permeable Cloister*, Aldershot, 2005.
León, Fray Luis de, *A Bilingual Edition of Fray Luis de León's La perfecta casada: The Role of Married Women in Sixteenth-Century Spain*, ed. and trans. John A. Jones and Javier San José Lera, Lewiston, 1999.
Leoni, Monica, "María de Zayas's *La traición en la Amistad*: Female Friendship Politicized?" *South Atlantic Review* 68.4, 2003, pp. 62–84.
Llorente, Juan Antonio, *Observations critiques sur le roman de Gil Blas de Santillane*, Paris, 1822.
MacKay, Ruth, *Life in a Time of Pestilence: The Great Castilian Plague of 1596–1601*, Cambridge, 2019.
Maravall, José Antonio, *Teatro y literatura en la sociedad barroca*, Barcelona, 1990.
Mariscal, George, *Contradictory Subjects: Quevedo, Cervantes, and Seventeenth-Century Spanish Culture*, Ithaca, 1991.
Martín, Adrienne Laskier, *Cervantes and the Burlesque Sonnet*, Berkeley, 1991.
Martín García, Alfredo, "Divorce and Abuse in 16th, 17th and 18th Century Spain," *Procedia: Social and Behavioral Sciences* 161, 2014, pp. 184–94.

Martínez de Portal, María, "Estudio preliminar," *Novelas completas de María de Zayas*, ed. María Martínez de Portal, Barcelona, 1973, pp. 9–30.

Masson de Gómez, Valerie, "The Vicissitudes of the *Capitolo* in Spain," *Pacific Coast Philology* 16.1, 1981, pp. 57–65.

Matos-Nin, Ingrid E. "Lisis o la remisión de la enfermedad del amor en las novelas de María de Zayas y Sotomayor," *Letras femeninas* 32.2, 2006, pp. 101–16.

Melloni, Alessandra, *Il sistema narrativo di María de Zayas*, Torino, Quaderni Iberoamericani, 1976.

Menocal, María Rosa, *Ornament of the World: How Muslims, Jews, and Christians Created a Culture of Tolerance in Medieval Spain*, Boston, 2002.

Menton, Seymour, "El gato emblemático," *La Gaceta* 232, pp. 37–9.

Merrim, Stephanie, *Early Modern Women's Writing and Sor Juana Inés de la Cruz*, Nashville, 1999.

Moll, Jaime, "Diez años sin licencias para imprimir comedias y novelas en los reinos de Castilla: 1625–1634," *Boletín de la Real Academia Española* 54, 1974, pp. 98–103.

———, "Escritores y editores en el Madrid de los Austrias," *Edad de Oro* 17, 1998, pp. 97–106.

Montesa Peydro, Salvador, *Texto y contexto en la narrativa de María de Zayas*, Madrid, 1981.

Morby, Edwin, "The *Difunta pleitada* Theme in María de Zayas," *Hispanic Review* 16, 1948, pp. 238–42.

Murillo, Ana María, "Wit, Faithfulness, and 'Improvements' in English Translation Anthologies of Spanish Popular Literature (1700)," *International Anthologies of Literature in Translation*, ed. H. Kittel, Berlin, 1995, pp. 30–9.

Nalle, S. T., "Literacy and Culture in Early Modern Castile," *Past and Present* 125, pp. 65–96.

Nirenberg, David, *Communities of Violence: Persecution of Minorities in the Middle Ages*, Princeton, 1996.

———, "Race and the Middle Ages: The Case of Spain and Its Jews," Greer, Mignolo and Quilligan, *Rereading the Black Legend*, pp. 71–87.

O'Brien, Eavan, *Women in the Prose of María de Zayas*, Woodbridge, England, 2010.

Olivares, Julián, "Introducción," María de Zayas y Sotomayor, *Honesto y entretenido sarao (Primera y segunda parte)*, ed. J. Olivares, Zaragoza, 2017, vol. 1, pp. xi–cvi.

———, "Introducción," María de Zayas y Sotomayor, *Novelas amorosas y ejemplares*, Madrid, 2000, pp. 11–150.

Olivares, Julian, and Elizabeth S. Boyce, *Tras el espejo la musa escribe: Lírica femenina de los Siglos de Oro*, Madrid, 1993.

Osuna Rodríguez, Inmaculada, "Literary Academies and Poetic Tournaments," Baranda and Cruz, *Routledge Research Companion*, pp. 153–67.

Özmen, Emre, and Pedro Ruiz Pérez, "Deseo y autoridad: La tensión de la autoría en María de Zayas," *Criticón* 128, 2016, pp. 37–51.
Pardo Bazán, Emilia, "Breve noticia," *Novelas de Dª María de Zayas y Sotomayor*, Madrid, Biblioteca de la Mujer, vol. 3, [c.1892], pp. 5–16.
Parker Aronson, Stacey L., "Monstrous Metamorphoses and Rape in María de Zayas," *Revista Canadiense de Estudios Hispánicos* 29.3, 2005, pp. 525–47.
Parker, Geoffrey, *The Army of Flanders and the Spanish Road, 1567–1659*, Cambridge, 1972.
Parker, Geoffrey, *Europe in Crisis 1598–1648*, 2nd ed., Oxford, 2001
———, *The Dutch Revolt*, rev. ed., London, 1985.
Pérez de Montalbán, Juan, *Para todos, exemplos morales, humanos y divinos. En que se tratan diversas ciencias, materias y facultades. Repartidos en los siete días de la semana. Y dirigidos a diferentes personas. Y con algunas adiciones nuevas en esta quinta impresión*, Madrid, 1635.
Pérez de Montalbán, Juan and María de Zayas y Sotomayor, *The diverting Works of the famous Miguel de Cervantes... Now first translated from the Spanish. With an introduction by the author of the London-Spy*, London, J. Round et al., 1709.
Perry, Mary Elizabeth, *The Handless Maiden, Moriscos and the Politics of Religion in Early Modern Spain*, Princeton, 2005.
Pfandl, Ludwig, *Historia de la literatura nacional española en la Edad de Oro*, Barcelona, 1933.
Piedra, José, "Nationalizing Sissies," *¿Entiendes?, Queer Readings, Hispanic Writings*, Durham, 1995, pp. 370–409.
Pierce, Leslie, "An Imperial Caste: Inverted Racialization in the Architecture of Ottoman Sovereignty," Greer, Mignolo and Quilligan, *Rereading the Black Legend*, pp. 27–47.
Pym, Richard J., *Rhetoric and Reality in Early Modern Spain*, ed. Richard J. Pym, London, 2006.
———, "Tragedy and the Construct Self: Considering the Subject in Spain's Seventeenth-Century *Comedia*," *Bulletin of Hispanic Studies* 75.3, 1998, 273–92.
Rhodes, Elizabeth, *Dressed to Kill: Death and Meaning in Zayas's Desengaños*, Toronto, 2011.
———, "Skirting the Men: Gender Roles in Sixteenth-Century Pastoral Books," *Journal of Hispanic Philology* 11.2, 1987, pp. 131–49.
Rigolot, François, "Magdalenes's Skull: Allegory and Iconography in *Heptamerón* 32," *Renaissance Quarterly* 47.1, 1994, pp. 57–73.
Rodríguez de Ramos, Alberto, "La biografía de María de Zayas. Una revisión y algunos hallazgos," *Analecta: Revista de la Sección de Filología de la Facultad de Letras, Universidad de Málaga*, 37, 2014, pp. 237–53.
Rodríguez del Padrón, Juan, "El libro de las donas," *Obras de Juan Rodríguez del Padrón*, ed. A. Paz y Meliá, Madrid, 1884, pp. 85–127.

Rodríguez-Garrido, José A., "El ingenio en la mujer: *La traición en la amistad* de María de Zayas entre Lope de Vega y Huarte de San Juan," *Bulletin of the Comediantes* 49.2, 1997, pp. 357–73.

Rodríguez-Guridi, Elena, "De Eva a Ave: Anatomía médica y crística del cuerpo femenino en los *Desengaños amorosos*," *Hispanic Review* 87.3, 2019, 265–84.

Rojas Zorrilla, Francisco, "La difunta pleitada," *Comedias varias nunca impresas, Parte Veinte*, Madrid, Imprenta Real, 1663, pp. 185–225.

Romero-Díaz, Nieves, "Aphra Behn y María de Zayas: En busca de una tradición (im)propia," *Hispanic Journal* 29.1, 2008, pp. 23–35.

Romero-Díaz, Nieves, *Nueva nobleza, nueva novela: reescribiendo la cultura urbana del barroco*, Newark, 2002.

Rosell, Cayetano, ed., *Novelistas posteriores a Cervantes*, 2 vols., Madrid, 1851–4.

Rowe, Erin Kathleen, "Enslaved and Free Black Africans in Early Modern Spain," Cacho Casal and Egan, *Routledge Hispanic Studies Companion*, pp. 537–52.

Samson, Alexander, "Distinct Drama? Female Dramatists in Golden Age Spain," *A Companion to Spanish Women's Studies*, ed. Xon de Ros and Geraldine Hazbun, Woodbridge, Suffolk, 2011, pp. 157–72.

San Juan, Juan Huarte de, *Examen de ingenios para las ciencias*, ed. Guillermo Serés, Madrid, 1989.

Sánchez Ortega, María Helena, "Sorcery and Eroticism in Love Magic," *Cultural Encounters: The Impact of the Inquisition in Spain and the New World*, ed. Mary Elizabeth Perry and Anne J. Cruz, Berkeley, 1991, pp. 58–92.

Scarron, Paul, *Les nouvelles tragi-comiques*, Paris, 1655–7.

———, *Le Roman comique*, Paris, 1657.

———, *Scarron's novels: viz. The fruitless precaution. The hypocrites. The innocent adultery. The judge in his own cause. The rival brothers. The invisible mistress. The chastisement of avarice. The unexpected choice. Done into English, with additions. By J. D. Esquire*, London, 1700.

———, *The comical romance: and other tales, done into English by Tom Brown of Shifnal, John Savage and others; with an introduction by J. J. Jusserand*, London, 1892.

———, *The comical romance, or, A facetious history of a company of stage-players: interwoven with divers choice novels, rare adventures, and amorous intrigues / written originally in French by the renowned Scarron; and now turned into English by J. B.*, London, 1665.

Serés, Guillermo, "Introducción," Juan Huarte de San Juan, *Examen de ingenios para las ciencias*, pp. 11–131.

Serrano y Sanz, Manuel, *Apuntes para una biblioteca de escritoras españolas desde el año 1401 al 1833*, 2 vols., 1905, vol. 2, 583–620.

Smith, Paul Julian, *The Body Hispanic: Gender and Sexuality in Spanish and Spanish American Literature*. Oxford, 1989.

Soufas, Teresa S, "The Gendered Context of Melancholy for Spanish Golden Age Women Writers," in *Spanish Women in the Golden Age: Images and Realities*, ed. M. S. Sánches and A. Saint-Saëns, Westport, 1996, pp. 171–84.
Stroud, Matthew D., *Fatal Union: A Pluralistic Approach to the Spanish Wife-Murder Comedias*, Lewisburg, 1990.
Sullivan, Henry W., *Grotesque Purgatory: A Study of Cervantes's* Don Quixote, *Part II*, University Park, 1996.
———, *Tirso de Molina & the Drama of the Counter Reformation*, Amsterdam, 1981.
Sylvania, Lena, *Doña María de Zayas y Sotomayor: A Contribution to the Study of Her Works*, New York, 1922.
Taylor, Scott K., *Honor and Violence in Golden Age Spain*, New Haven, 2008.
Teresa of Avila, *The Life of Saint Teresa of Avila by Herself*, trans J. M. Cohen, London, 1957.
The New English Bible, with the Apocrypha, Oxford Study Edition, New York, 1976.
Thompson, Peter E., *The Triumphant Juan Rana: A Gay Actor of the Spanish Golden Age*, Toronto, 2006.
Ticknor, George, *History of Spanish Literature*, 3 vols. Boston, 1866.
Timoneda, Juan de, *El patrañuelo*, Valencia, Juan Mey, 1567.
Tinhorão, José Ramos, *Os negros em Portugal: Uma presença silenciosa*, Lisbon, 2019.
Treviño Salazar, Martha Elizabeth, "Estudio y edición de la *Parte segunda del Sarao y entretenimiento honesto* (1647) de María de Zayas y Sotomayor," PhD diss., Universitat Autónoma de Barcelona, 2018.
Valbuena Prat, Ángel, *Historia de la literatura española*, Barcelona, 1937.
Vega, Lope de, *Laurel de Apolo*, ed. Antonio Carreño, Madrid, 2007.
———, *Los comendadores de Córdoba*, Comedias de Lope de Vega, Parte II, vol. 2, ed. José Enrique Laplana Gil, Lleida, 1997, pp. 1023–171.
Velasco, Sherry, "Listening to Lesbians in Early Modern Spain," Cacho Casal and Egan, *Routledge Hispanic Studies Companion*, pp. 584–600.
Vélez de Guevara, Luis, *La mayor desgracia de Carlos V*, ed. William R. Manson and C. George Peale, Newark, 2002.
Vilches, Elvira, "The Character and Cultures of Credit in Early Modern Spanish Texts: Matters of Trust, Belief, and Uncertainty," Cacho Casal and Egan, *Routledge Hispanic Studies Companion*, pp. 124–39.
Vives, Juan Luis, *The Education of a Christian Woman* (De institutione foemimnae Christianae, 1524, 1538), ed. and trans. Charles Fantazzi, Chicago, 2007.
Vollendorf, Lisa, *Reclaiming the Body: María de Zayas's Early Modern Feminism*, Chapel Hill, 2001.

———, "The Future of Early Modern Women's Studies: The Case of Same-Sex Friendship in Zayas and Carvajal," *Arizona Journal of Hispanic Cultural Studies* 4, 2000, pp. 265–84.

Weber, Alison, "The Cultural Labyrinth of María de Zayas," Review, *Renaissance Quarterly* 54.4, 2001, 1606–7.

Welles, Marcia, *Persephone's Girdle: Narratives of Rape in Seventeenth-Century Spanish Literature*, Nashville, 2000.

Wilkerson, Isabel, *Caste: The Origins of Our Discontents*, New York, 2020.

Williamsen, Amy R., "Women Playwrights," Baranda and Cruz, *Routledge Research Companion*, pp. 187–202.

Wright, Elizabeth R., "Iberia's Atlantic Households: How Slavery and Diaspora Powered a 'Golden Age' of Empire (1444–1640). In progress.

———, *The Epic of Juan Latino: Dilemmas of Race and Religion in Renaissance Spain*, Toronto, 2016.

Wunder, Amanda, "Innovation and Tradition at the Court of Phillip IV of Spain (1621–1665): The Invention of the *Golilla* and the *Guardainfante*," *Fashioning the Early Modern: Dress, Textiles and Innovation in Europe 1500–1800*, ed. Evelyn Welch, 2017, pp. 111–33.

Yllera, Alicia, "Introducción," María de Zayas y Sotomaryo, *Parte segunda del Sarao y entretenimiento honesto [Desengaños amorosos]*, Nueva edición revisada, Madrid, Cátedra, 2021, pp. 9–178.

Zayas y Sotomayor, María de, *A Shameful Revenge: And Other Stories*, trans John Sturrock, illus. Eric Fraser, London, The Folio Society, 1963.

———, *Exemplary Tales of Love and Tales of Disillusion*, ed. and trans. Margaret R. Greer and Elizabeth Rhodes, Chicago, 2009.

———, *Honesto y entretenido sarao (Primera y segunda parte)*, ed. Julian Olivares, 2 vols., Zaragoza, 2017.

———, *La traición en la amistad / Friendship Betrayed*, ed. Valerie Hegstrom, trans. Catherine Larson, London, 1999.

———, *Novelas amorosas y exemplares*, ed. Julián Olivares, Madrid, 2000.

———, *Novelas de doña María de Zayas*, Emilia Pardo Bazán, ed., Madrid, c1892.

———, *Parte segunda del sarao y entretenimiento honesto [Desengaños amorosos]*, Nueva ed., revisada, Alicia Yllera, Madrid, 2021.

———, *Primera, y segunda parte de las novelas amorosas y ejemplares*, Valencia, 1712.

———, *The Disenchantments of Love: A Translation of the* Desengaños Amorosos, trans. H. Patsy Boyer, Albany, 1997.

———, *The Enchantments of Love. Amorous and Exemplary Novels*, trans H. Patsy Boyer, Berkeley, 1990.

General Index

Academies, literary 10-11, 12
Aguilón, Pedro 9, 165
Alba, 3rd Duke of, Fernando Álvarez de Toledo 193
Alemán, Mateo 60, 64, 162, 174
　Guzmán de Alfarache 60
　See also Mabbe, James
Alpujarras, revolt of 114
Amezúa y Mayo, Agustín de 7, 118, 162
　editions of Zayas 174, 175
　Zayas as realist 162, 175
Anderson, Ellen M. 30 n.16
Anne of Austria, queen of France 148
Aragon 9, 11, 13, 82, 107, 164 n.10
aristocracy 4, 19, 21, 60, 96, 109, 160, 168, 171
　and military service 20
　residence patterns 160
Aristotle 144
Armstrong-Roche, Michael 59, n.29

Bandello, Matteo 50, 57
Baranda, Nieves 6 n.9, 117
Barbeito Carnero, Isabel 14 n.22, 118, 122
Barton, Simon 79 n.1, 168, n.17, 113 n.39
Bass, Laura 21 n.36, 108 n.29, 157 n.28
Behn, Aphra 163
Bellmont, Friar Vicente 2 n.2, 167

Berg, Sander 124 n.11, 129 nn.18, 20, 130, 131, 134, 135, 138, 139, 176
Bergmann, Emilie 24 n.3
Bernini, Gian Lorenzo, "Ecstasy of Saint Teresa" 121
Bible 40 n.32, 145
　Genesis 145
Boccaccio 50, 57
　Decameron 1, 20, 42, 44
　De claris mulieribus 148
Boruchoff, David 59 n.29
Botello, Miguel de 8
Boyce, Elizabeth S. 51
Boyer, H. Patsy xv, xvi, 17 n.30, 18 n.32, 34 n.23, 49 n.8, 54, 56, 63, 68, 74, 75, 78, 143, 153
Briz, Juan Domingo 9, 165
Brown, Kenneth 11 n.19, 13 n.21
Brownlee, Marina S. 176, 177
Burgos 33, 34
Burns, Kathryn 112

Cádiz 114, 168
　Constitution of Cadiz 168
Calderón de la Barca, Pedro 43 n.40, 57
　Casa con dos puertas, mala es de guardar 163
　El médico de su honra (The surgeon of his honor) 95-6, 138, 160
　La vida es sueño (Life Is a Dream) 131

Canary Islands 15, 101
Cantigas de Santa María 125
Carasa, Ana de, sister of María de Carasa 5, 6
Carasa, María de, mother of author María de Zayas y Sotomayor 4, 160
Cardona, Juana de, godmother of author María de Zayas y Sotomayor 4
Carew, Richard 145
Carlos IV, King of Spain 168
Caro de Mallén, Ana 8, 148
Carvajal, Mariana de 20, 34 n.23
Carreño, Antonio 2 n.1, 161 n.1
Carreño de Miranda, Juan 2, 3
Casamayor, Inés de 10, 21
Casey, Elena 47
Casey, James 101, 102, 113 n.39, 114
Castile 19
   Council of Castile 9
Castillo de Solórzano, Alonso de 2 n.1, 57, 163, 167
Castro, Francisco de (count of Castro, duke of Taurisano, viceroy of Sicily, 8th count of Count of Lemos) 106
Castro, Pedro Fernández de, 7th Count of Lemos 125
Castro, Vaca y Quiñones, Pedro de, archbishop 126
Catalonia 11, 13, 122, 182
   Revolt of 13, 15, 37, 78, 81–2, 85, 188
Catherine of Aragón, Queen of England 24, 58
Catholicism xiv, 125, 131
Cervantes, Miguel de 8, 22, 125, 160, 162, 163, 169, 170, 172, 174
   "Colloquy of the Dogs" 62
   "The Deceitful Marriage" ("El casamiento engañoso") 57, 60, 62, 68, 69
   La destruición de Numancia 129
   Don Quixote 8, 10, 25
   "The Man Who Was Recklessly Curious" 57, 86, 137
   Novelas ejemplares 22, 25, 49, 50
   "Rinconete y Cortadillo" 60
   Los trabajos de Persiles y Sigismunda 59

Charles V, King of Spain 37, 38, 148, 186
Charnon-Deutsch, Lou 175
Chaucer, Geoffrey, *Canterbury Tales* 45, 58
   Nevill Coghill, translator 58
Cinzio (Giovanni Battista Giraldi) 50
class 50, 96, 97, 102, 108, 112, 116, 127, 152, 153, 154, 156, 159, 169, 171
clothing 83, 108–12, 116, 158, 191, 195
commoners 1, 19, 21, 24, 98, 107, 193
convents 13, 30, 31, 33, 47, 48, 71, 75, 77, 80, 84, 88, 94, 105, 106, 112, 117, 124, 135, 143, 152, 154, 156, 159, 160
   Immaculate Conception 122, 124
   refuge from human justice or paternal violence 28, 119–20, 126, 180, 189
   Santa Catalina Mártir, Barcelona 12, 166
schools 6, 7
Covarrubias Orozco, Sebastían de 46, 58, 112, 129, 146
crossdressing 18, 26, 33, 38, 53, 97, 109–10
Cruickshank, Don W. 81 n.6, 96 n.6, 138 n.39
Cruz, Anne J. 6 n.9, 11 nn.17, 18, 70 n.16, 117, 145 n.6, 155 n.26

Darnton, Robert, *The Great Cat Massacre* 68
death 1, 4, 6, 8, 9, 13, 15, 16, 26, 28–32, 35–6, 40–1, 44, 71–2, 74, 78, 84, 86, 88–9, 93, 98, 99, 100, 101, 104, 106, 111, 115, 116, 129, 130, 133, 136–8, 153, 155, 156, 159
   beauty in death 139, 142, 176
   certificates of 13, 21, 124, 161
De Armas, Frederick A. 87 n.16, 164 n.8
Defoe, Daniel, *Moll Flanders* 60
Desengaño 17, 87, 143, 148
desire xiv, 11, 12, 22, 25–7, 29–31, 33, 36, 42, 44, 50, 51–4, 72, 75, 78, 80, 88–9, 91–2, 96, 100, 127, 133, 152, 156, 169

disillusion, disillusionment   10, 53, 79, 80, 118

Elliott, J. H.   20 n.36, 76 n.26, 81 n.6, 126 n.12, 127
England   16, 24
Eslava, Antonio de, *Noches de invierno*   45, 47
Esquer, Pedro de   9, 25, 124
Evans, Geraint   102 n.14
exemplary, exemplarity   6, 22–5, 32, 44, 174

faith   16, 19, 115, 117, 122, 124, 125, 130, 131, 165, 166
Fariña Busto, María Jesús   51 n.10
feminism   xiv, 116, 159, 174, 175, 176, 177
Ferdinand II, King of Spain   125
Fernández, Enrique   177
Fernández de Navarrete, Eustaquio   162, 170, 171
Fernando VII, King of Spain   168
Feros, Antonio   76 n.26, 85 n.13
Fez   15, 38, 110, 111, 127, 128
fiction, fictional   16, 19, 39, 46, 48, 51, 52, 59, 62, 66, 78, 139, 146, 152, 162, 165, 166, 169, 176
  distrust of   23–5
Flanders   15, 18, 20, 28, 35, 36, 37, 40, 101, 105, 127, 135
Florence   1, 20
Foa, Sandra   175
Fontanella, Francesc, *Vejamen*   11, 12, 13, 21, 33
Fontanella, Josep   12
Forcione, Alban   59 n.29
France   16, 18, 41, 82, 85, 145, 148, 163, 168
Frazer, James George   132
free will   27, 129–31, 139, 145
Friedman, Edward   30 n.16, 60 n.31, 91

Gagliardi, Donatella   15
Gálvez, Countess of   15
Gamboa, Yolanda   124
Garber, Marjorie   108 n.30
Gartner, Bruce   175

Gil y Zárate, Antonio   170
Ginovés, Juan Francisco   165, 166 n.13
Góngora   55, 161
González Echevarría, Roberto   22 n.1
Goytisolo, Juan   175
Granada   41, 70, 74, 75, 101
  relics unearthed there   126
Grasa, Laura   14
Greek romance   45, 59
Grieve, Patricia   58
Grossman, Edith   22, n.1

hagiography   45, 58
Harris, A. Katie   126 n.116
Hegstrom, Valerie   157
Henrich, Joseph   101
Henry VIII, King of England   24
hidalgo   17, 63
Hijar, duke of, Jaime Fernández de Híjar, Silva, Pinós, Fenollet y Cabrera   10
honor, dishonor   26, 27, 28, 29, 30, 32, 34, 39, 42, 62, 70, 75, 84–5, 86, 91, 94–5, 99, 102–4, 107, 116, 121–2, 133, 138, 151 n.16, 154, 156, 174
Huarte de San Juan, Juan   145–7, 148

Ife, B. W.   23
Ihinger, Kelsey J.   177
Isabel Clara Eugenia, infanta   148, 149
Isabella, Queen of Spain   125
Italy   16, 18, 20, 35, 45, 54, 85, 97, 100, 133, 145, 164

Jews, Judaism   16, 23, 117, 124–5
Juana Inés de la Cruz   xiii, 2, 160
Juan Rana *see* Pérez, Cosme

Kagan, Richard L.   19 n.2
Kaminsky, Amy   112 n.35
King, Margaret L.   6 n.9

Labadía, Juan de   41
Lagreca, Nancy   91–2
Lampillas, Francisco Javier   167
Larson, Catherine   157
Le Métel D'Ouville, Antoine   164
Lemos, 7th Count of (Pedro Fernández de Castro)   5, 7, 10, 105, 106, 161

General Index

Lemos, 8th Count of *see* Francisco de Castro
Lemos, Countess of 15
Lerma, sargento Antonio de 106
Lerma, Duke of, Francisco Gómez de Sandoval y Rojas 7, 75–6, 78
Lesage, Alain René, *Gil Blas de Santillane* 169
Lesbos 2, 13
letrados 19
Lisbon 50, 77, 90, 114
Lizau, Matías de 10
Llorente, Juan Antonio 169
López, Ana, godmother of Isabel de Zayas 4
López de Úbeda, Francisco, *La pícara Justina* (The Spanish Jilt) 60
love xiii–xiv, 1, 10, 12, 15, 20, 23–5, 27–33, 37–44, 47, 62, 89–92; 120; *see also* Appendix, plot summaries
   love poetry 51–4
   queer love 12–13, 33–7
Luna, Álvaro de 148
Luna, Miguel de 126

Mabbe, James, translator, *The Rogue, or the life of Guzman de Alfarache* 60
Madrid 2, 4–9, 10, 13, 18, 19, 21, 32, 46, 50, 63, 65, 70, 72, 73, 76, 78, 84, 94, 108, 122, 124, 158, 161, 165
   literacy rates, Early Modern 6–7
   made capital of Spain 19
   religious buildings
      San Jerónimo, church 126
      San Sebastián, church 4
   streets, plazas, market
      Calle de Atocha 4
      Calle de la Cabeza 4–5, 14
      Calle del Olivar 14
      Paseo del Prado 107, 108, 158
      Plaza Mayor 5
      Rastro 5
magic xiv, 1, 67–9, 87–8, 117, 131, 134
   and the devil 40, 44, 129, 140–1
   in first volume 132, 136
   and foreigners 135
   gender divide 133–5
   and Moors 104, 128–9, 139
   in second volume 136–41
Malagón, Marquise of (Magdalena Ulloa) 13, 14
Mamora, La (Mehdya) 15, 21, 29, 180
Mantuan Succession, war of 85, 86
Maravall, José Antonio 95
Margarita of Austria, Queen of Spain 148
marriage xiv, 4, 21, 23, 27, 29, 32, 34, 35, 37, 41, 59, 62–3, 65, 69–70, 77–8, 84, 89, 90, 98, 99, 100, 132, 135–6, 153–5, 156, 158
   cousin marriage 28, 100–2
   marriage law 27, 41, 83, 85, 135–6
   parents right to arrange 27, 28, 32, 38
   sacrament 27
   vows of 40–1
Martín, Adrienne 55
Mary I, Queen of England 24
Matos–Nin, Ingrid 47
Mayorazgo 21
Medina, Lucas de, husband of Jerónima Zayas 4
Melloni, Alessandra 175
Menocal, María Rosa 124 n.11
Mignolo, Walter 112 n.36
Molera, Theodora, Sor 13
Molina, Tirso de 131, 158
   El burlador de Sevilla (attributed) 136
Moll, Jaime 9, 19, n.35
Montesa Peydro, Salvador 175
Montferrat, Marquisate 85
Montserrat 32, 93, 108, 122, 154
   Virgin of Montserrat 122, 123
Moors xiv, 4, 28, 29, 38, 41, 83, 87, 88, 102, 104, 110, 112, 114, 127, 128–9, 135, 139, 163
Moriscos 114, 125, 126, 128
   expulsion from Spain 105, 127
   and peace treaty with Dutch rebels 127
Moses 94–5
mothers 5, 7, 17, 27, 28, 29, 30, 40, 42, 43, 63, 75, 82, 85, 99, 100, 104, 106, 121, 124, 136, 137, 139, 140–1, 148, 155, 156, 159
   importance in Zayas stories 63

Murillo, Ana María 163
Murillo, Bartolomé Esteban, "The Immaculate Conception of Los Venerables" 121
Muslim 23, 59, 83, 93, 113, 117, 124, 125, 127, 129

Napoleon 168
Navarre, Marguerite de 57
　Heptameron 87 n.16
Netherlands 16, 24, 40 n.33, 145, 148
Narcissus 27, 53, 108
Nirenberg, David 125 n.11

Olivares, Count–Duke of 9, 78, 81 n.6, 82, 108, 125, 131 n.25
O'Brien, Eavan 152
Olivares, Julián 9 n.14, 10, nn.15, 16, 13 n.21, 47 n.4, 51 124 n.11, 165 n.10
Olmedo Tufiño, Alonso 41
One Thousand and One Nights 45
Osuna, 3rd duke of, Pedro Téllez–Girón; Viceroy of Sicily, 1611–16; of Naples, 1616–20 67, 106, 132
Ovid 24
Özmen, Emre 177

Padilla, María de 134
Pardo Bazán, Emilia 38, 169, 172, 173
　publisher of Zayas novellas 162, 171
　on Zayas's picaresque of the aristocracy 60, 171
Paris 24, 164, 167
Parker, Geoffrey 37 n.27, 40 n.33, 85 n.13, 127 n.15
patriarchal culture, society 13, 26, 27, 31, 75, 91, 105, 144, 152, 159, 177–8
patriarchy 139
Pedro I, King of Castile 134, 138
Pérez, Cosme 33
Pérez de Montalban, Alonso 6
Pérez de Montalban, Juan 6, 8, 10, 55, 57, 157, 162, 167
　praise for María de Zayas 10, 165
　Para todos 163
Pérez Galdos, Benito 169
Pfandl, Ludwig 173

Philip II, King of Spain 4, 15, 19, 148
Philip III, King of Spain 4, 5, 7, 15, 50, 77, 90, 105, 127, 148, 158
Philip IV, King of Spain 9, 15, 78, 148
picaresque tales 45, 60, 170–2
　Guzmán de Alfarache, see Alemán, Mateo
　La garduña de Sevilla (The Stone marten of Seville) 60
　La hija de Celestina (Celestina's daughter) 60
　La pícara Justina – see López de Úbeda
　La vida de Lazarillo de Lazarillo de Tormes (The Life of Lazarillo de Tormes) 60, 64
Pierce, Leslie 112 n.36
Plato 23, 140
Portugal 4, 35
　revolt of 15, 37, 79, 91, 113, 145
Pym, Richard 125 n.11

Quartan fever 47, 80, 119
Quevedo, Francisco de 60, 162, 174
　El buscón 60, 64
Quilligan, Maureen 112 n.36
Quintana, Francisco de 8

Rabil, Albert Jr. 6 n.9
race xiv, 112
　and skin color xiv, 113–16
　and slavery 112–14
religion 96, 112, 114, 117, 132, 177
　religious division 19, 93, 117
Rhodes, Elizabeth xiv, 53 n.15, 55, 58, 74, 86, 88, 89, 96, 122, 137, 138, 139, 151–4, 176
　Dressed to Kill 79 n.1, 85 n.12, 177, 178
Ribera, José de 12
Robles, Luisa de 41
Rodríguez-Garrido, José A. 148
Rodríguez de Ramos, Alberto 6 n.7, 122
Rodríguez-Guridi, Elena 177
Rodríguez-Luis, Julio 22 n.1
Romero-Díaz, Nieves 19–20
Ruiz Pérez, Pedro 177

Salamanca 30, 40, 114, 135, 136

San Sebastián, parish, church   4, 5, 13, 14
Saint-Saëns, Alain   34 n.23
saints   24, 58, 60, 122
　Paula of Avila, Saint (Santa Paula Barbada)   12
　Teresa of Ávila, Saint   58, 122, 125, 160
　　canonization   120
　　The Interior Castle   120
　　Life   120
　Thäis, Saint   88
　Theodora of Alexandria, Saint   88
Sánchez, Francisco   5
Sánchez, Luis, godfather of Isabel de Zayas   4, 5, 6 n.7, 8
Sánchez Coello, Alonso   149
Sánchez Ortega, María Helena   132, 133, 134
Santa Cruz, 2nd marquis of, (Álvaro de Bazán y Benavides)   106
Santiago, Order of   5, 16, 40, 124, 161
Santoyo, Diego de, godfather of author María de Zayas y Sotomayor   4
Sappho of Lesbos   2, 12, 13, 35, 125, 165
Savoy, duke of (Charles Emmanuel)   85, 106
Scarron, Paul   163, 164, 172
Segovia   97, 100
Serrano y Sanz, Manuel   4 n.5, 7, 8, 11, 121 n.9, 124, 157, 174
Seville   8, 20, 65, 71, 88, 109, 114, 116, 148
sex, sexual   xiv, 9, 10, 11, 12, 21, 25, 26, 32, 38, 69, 72, 88, 91, 96, 100, 103, 115, 129, 159, 175, 176
　extra-marital   154
　sexual difference   144, 146
Shakespeare, William, *Romeo and Juliet*   136
Sicily   15, 37, 83, 106
Smith, Paul Julian   91, 175
Spain   18, 24, 30, 94, 97, 101, 134
　economic distress   16, 159
　education in   6, 19
　Empire of   4, 15–16, 37, 79
　literacy in   6, 49, 168
　literary tradition   xiii, 1, 56, 58, 60, 169, 170
　nobility in Early Modern Spain
　　traditional concept   97–9, 107, 152–4
　　urban   19–20, 46, 95, 107–8
　pessimism in 17th century   15, 48, 79
　social mobility in   18–19, 97
　story setting   27
　wars   16, 82, 85, 127, 139, 168
Stevens, John   60, 163
Sturrock, John   164
storytelling, oral   xiv, 45, 47, 48, 112, 126
suicide   28, 32, 132
supernatural   5, 68, 11, 136
Sylvania, Lena E. V.   118, 173

Thirty Years' War   16
Ticknor, George   172
Timoneda, Juan de   44, 50
Toledo   12, 91, 101, 135
Treviño, Elizabeth   4 n.5, 6 n.7, 13 n.21, 14 n.23, 15 n.24, 122, 162
Tunis   38
Tunisia   15

Vega, Lope de   8, 35, 55, 69, 148, 157, 158, 160
　El caballero de Olmedo   136
　Los comendadores de Córdoba   55, 102
　La difunta pleitada (attributed to)   136
　La gatomaquia   69
　Laurel de Apolo   2 n.1, 13
　"The fortunes of Diana"   57
Valbuena Prat, Ángel   173, 174
Valdés, Juan de   13, 14, 21, 122
Valdivielso, Joseph de   9, 165
Valencia   38, 39, 74, 84, 110
Virgin of Montserrat   123
Vives, Juan Luis   24, 58
　Education of a Christian Woman   24, 58
Vives, Pío   12, 165–6
Vollendorf, Lisa   34 n.23, 176

Weimer, Christopher   40 n.33
Welles, Marcia   83 n.9, 175
Whitenack, Judith   139
Williamsen, Amy R.   30 n.16

Wilkerson, Isabel 112 n.36
Wilks, Kerry 40 n.33
women, Early Modern
  deemed inferior 1, 144–7
  education 6, 7, 24
  literacy rates 6, 49
  La querella de las mujeres 145–6, 152
  writers 6
Wright, Elizabeth 113

Yllera, Alicia 8, 47 n.4, 85, 118, 157 n.28, 161, 162 n.4, 163 nn.6, 7, 164, 167 n.16

Zaragoza, Bartolomé de 14
Zayas, María de, widow of Juan de Valdés 13, 14
Zayas, María de, widow of Francisco de Vargas Machuca 15
Zayas y Sotomayor, Fernando de, father of author 4, 5
Zayas y Sotomayor, Isabel, younger sister of author 4, 14, 161
Zayas y Sotomayor, Jerónima, sister of author, 4, 161
Zayas y Sotomayor, Luisa, paternal grandmother of author 5
Zayas y Sotomayor, María de (author)
  baptism 4
  birth 4
  and convent of the Immaculate Conception 122, 124
  converso ancestry, possibility of 124–5
  defender of women's worth 1, 58, 61–2, 72–3, 80, 86–7, 91, 144, 152
  education 6–7, 21, 150
  father *see* Fernando de Zayas y Sotomayor
  feminism, proto–feminism 116, 159, 173, 174, 176, 177
  foremothers list
    Argentaria 148
    Aspasia 148
    Barahona, María de 148
    Cenobia 148
    Contreras, Eugenia de 148
    Cornelia 148
    Diotima 148
    Eudocia 148
    Ribadeneira, Isabel de 148
    Themistoclea 148
    See also Isabel Clara Eugenia; Anne of Austria, and Ana Caro de Mallen
  godparents of *see* Santoyo, Diego, and Cardona, Juana de
  mother, *see* Carasa, María de
  praises by contemporaries 2
  publication 1, 7, 8–10, 12, 67–8, 161–4, 167, 174
    censors 2, 164–6
    death certificates 13–14
    editions 9–10, 161, 162, 174
    literary models 1, 45–60
    and Olivares reform program 9
    modern 174–5
    paused, nineteenth century 162, 167–9, 174
    reception 1–2, 38, 162, 164–7, 169–77
    title choice 9, 15, 46
  residence
    Barcelona 8, 11, 13
    Madrid 7
    Naples (alleged) 7–8
    Valladolid (alleged) 7
    Zaragoza (alleged) 7, 8, 13
  Tenth Muse 2, 6
Zayas y Sotomayor, Luisa de, grandmother of author 5
Zúñiga, Inés de, Countess of Monterrey 2–3

Index of Zayas's Works

Novellas

frame tale   1, 10, 31, 48–9, 50, 56, 80–1, 100, 112, 119, 143, 156
Prologue ("To the Reader")   xiv, 7, 10, 13, 61, 79, 143–4, 148
N. 1 ("Taking a Chance on Losing")   25–32 33, 80, 83. 93, 100, 101, 105, 110, 119, 122, 126, 143, 156, 159
N. 2 ("Aminta Deceived and Honor's Revenge")   32, 62, 84, 91, 94, 97, 99, 100, 101, 103, 108 110, 154, 156
N. 3 ("The Miser's Reward")   8, 28, 62–67, 69–70, 86, 132
N. 4 ("Forewarned but Fooled")   2, 87, 100, 109, 114–15, 116, 119, 120, 154, 155
N. 5 ("The Power of Love")   30, 33, 80, 87–8, 94, 99, 100, 105, 124, 130, 133, 134, 135, 156
N. 6 ("Disillusionment in Love and Virtue Rewarded")   28, 94, 97–8, 103, 104, 124, 134, 155, 156
N. 7 ("Just Desserts")   27, 45, 75, 94, 99, 114, 154–5
N. 8 ("Triumph over the Impossible")   28, 39–41, 78, 89, 98, 99, 114, 130, 135, 155
N. 9 ("The Judge of Her Own Case")   37–9, 42, 48, 50, 110, 127, 156, 175
N. 10 ("The Deceitful Garden")   39, 40, 42-4, 80, 90–2, 99, 136, 155, 156

Desengaños

D. 1 ("Her Lover's Slave")   28, 52, 59, 80–4, 94, 99, 100–1, 103–4, 110, 127, 156
D. 2   54, 81, 84, 98, 102–3, 120, 136
D. 3   57, 86, 120, 137, 156
D. 4   3-4, 28, 32, 57, 81, 86–7, 88, 100, 103, 114, 115–16, 124, 130, 153
D. 5   80, 87–9, 99, 104, 110, 111, 119, 128, 135, 139, 156
D. 6   12, 18, 33–5, 36, 52, 97, 159
D. 7   12, 18, 35–7, 40 n.33, 81, 94, 101, 130, 153, 164
D. 8   5, 19, 21, 28, 89, 98, 99, 100, 106, 111, 120, 130, 137, 138, 139, 156
D. 9   58, 88–9, 94, 104, 111, 118–19, 121, 140
D 10   50, 55, 80, 90–1, 96, 98, 105, 114, 139, 156
play (*Friendship Betrayed*)   157–9

Characters' names

(Not included are a handful of significant characters only named by rank, color, or religion, as is the Duchess in N. 4, the Flemish prince in D. 7, the black servant in D. 4, a Moorish sorcerer in D. 5, or the doctor / devil in D. 9. Titles for Tales of Disillusion D. 2 through D. 10 are those provided by subsequent editors, not Zayas herself. See also these and other character names listed in Plot Summaries in the Appendix.

Adriana (N.1: "Taking a Chance on Losing") 28, 100–2, 154, 156
Agustín (N. 3: "The Miser's Reward") 65–7, 70
Alejandra (D. 1: "Her Lover's Slave") Alejandra 83, 156
Alonso (N. 8: "Triumph over the Impossible") 40–1
Alonso (narrator, N. 4, "Forewarned but Footed") 70, 74, 75, 87, 109, 115, 116
Alonso (D. 8: "Traitor to His Own Blood") 89, 98–9, 100, 106
Álvaro (narrator, N. 3: "The Miser's Reward") 62–6, 69, 70, 132
Amete (N. 9: "The Judge of Her Own Case") 38, 110, 127–8
Aminta (N. 2: "Aminta Deceived and Honor's Revenge") 32, 62, 84, 91, 94, 97, 99, 100, 104, 108
Ana (N. 4: "Forewarned but Fooled") 72–3, 109
Ana de Añasco (D. 8: "Traitor to His Own Blood") 89, 99, 106, 111
Angeliana (D. 3: "His Wife's Executioner") 139, 156
Antonio (N. 4: "Forewarned but Fooled") 115, 116
Antonio Garrafa (N. 5: "The Power of Love") 99, 10
Arnesto (N. 8: "Triumph Over the Impossible") 185
Arnesto (D. 7: "Marriage Abroad: Portent of Doom") 35–6, 37

Bernardo (D. 6: "Love for the Sake of Conquest") 36
Beatriz (N. 4: "Forewarned but Fooled") 71–3, 88, 114–15, 116
Beatríz (D. 9: "Triumph Over Persecution") 58, 94, 104, 111, 118, 121, 140–1, 154
Belisa (*Friendship Betrayed*) 158
Blanca (N. 8: "Triumph over the Impossible") 155
Blanca (D. 7: "Marriage Abroad: Portent of Doom") 35–6, 37, 94, 101, 153
Camila (D. 2: "Most Infamous Revenge") 84–5, 86, 99, 103, 120, 130, 136–7
Carlos (N. 5: "The Power of Love") 105, 133–4
Carlos (N. 9: "The Judge of Her Own Case") 38, 110, 127–8
Carlos (N. 10: "The Deceitful Garden") 17, 43–4, 155
Carlos (D. 2: "Most Infamous Revenge") 54, 84, 85, 98–9, 103
Celio (N. 1: "Taking a Chance on Losing") 29–31, 53, 94, 129
Clara (N. 6: "Disillusionment in Love and Virtue Rewarded") 17, 96, 99, 104, 134–5, 156
Claudia (N. 9: "The Judge of Her Own Case") 38, 53, 103, 110, 127–8, 156
Clavela (D. 8: "Traitor to His Own Blood") 156
Constanza (N. 10: "The Deceitful Garden") 17, 42–4, 155
Devil (N. 10: "The Deceitful Garden") 40, 42, 44, 67, 90, 115–16, 129, 132–3, 134–5, 136, 139, 140, 155
Diego (N. 5: "The Power of Love") 33, 105, 106, 133, 156
Diego (D. 5: "Innocence Punished") 87–8, 104, 128, 129, 156
Diego (fame tale) 39, 47, 79, 80, 81
Dionís (D. 10: "The Ravages of Vice") 90–1, 96–7, 103
Elena (D. 4: "Too Late Undeceived") 88, 101, 115, 116

Enrique (D. 8: "Traitor to His Own Blood")   19, 21, 98, 130, 139
Enrique (D. 6: "Love for the Sake of Conquest")   33, 35
Estefanía (narrator, D. 9: "Triumph over Persecution")   118, 119, 121
Estefanía / Esteban (D. 6: "Love for the Sake of Conquest")   12, 18, 33–5, 36, 52, 97, 159
Estela (N. 9: "The Judge of Her Own Case")   38–9, 110, 127–8
Eufrasia (D. 1: "Her Lover's Slave")   82, 100
Fabia (N. 10: "The Deceitful Garden")   43, 155
Fabio (N. 1: "Taking a Chance on Losing")   26–7, 29, 30–1, 32, 84, 93–4, 108, 110, 122, 154
Fabio (frame tale)   31–2, 176
Fadrique (N. 4: "Forewarned but Fooled")   56, 70–5, 87, 100, 109, 115–16, 154
Federico (N. 10: "The Deceitful Garden")   43, 44, 155
Federico (D. 9: "Triumph Over Persecution")   94, 104, 111, 140–1
Felipe (D. 1: "Her Lover's Slave")   59, 81, 83–4, 94, 99
Félix de Ponce de León (N. 1: "Taking a Chance on Losing")   27–9, 30, 31, 51, 88, 93, 100, 101, 105, 119–20, 126–7, 154, 156, 158
Fenisa (*Friendship Betrayed*)   158–9
Fernando (N. 6: "Disillusionment in Love and Virtue Rewarded")   17, 98, 134–5, 156
Filis (narrator, N. 6: "Disillusionment in Love and Virtue Rewarded")   156
Filis (narrator, D. 4: "Too Late Undeceived")   86, 124, 130
Flora (N. 2: "Aminta Deceived and Honor's Revenge")   32, 62, 110, 156
Florentina (D. 10: "The Ravages of Vice")   55, 90–2, 96–7, 140, 156
Francisca (narrator, D. 8: "Traitor to His Own Blood")   89, 106
Francisco (N. 2: "Aminta Deceived and Honor's Revenge")   32, 94, 100, 103, 110, 154
Francisco (D. 5: "Innocence Punished")   99
Gamarra (N. 3: "The Miser's Reward")   65, 67, 132
García (N. 7: "Just Desserts")   45, 76, 77–8, 155
Gaspar (N. 7: "Just Desserts")   70, 77, 94, 114, 155
Gaspar (D. 10: "The Ravages of Vice")   50, 90–1, 139–40
Gracia (N. 4: Forewarned but Fooled")   71, 75, 119, 154
Guiomar (N. 1: "Taking a Chance on Losing")   29, 30
Hipólita (N. 7: "Just Desserts")   45, 75–8, 114, 154
Inés (N. 3: "The Miser's Reward")   65–7, 70 n.16
Inés (D. 5: "Innocence Punished")   87–9, 99, 104, 110, 111, 119, 128, 129, 139, 156
Isidora (N. 3: "The Miser's Reward")   65–8, 69–70, 128, 132, 133
Jacinta, (N. 1: "Taking a Chance on Losing")   26–33, 51, 53, 81, 84, 88, 93, 94, 100, 102, 105, 108, 110, 119, 126, 127, 129, 143, 154, 156, 158, 174
Jacimin, Moorish prince (N. 9: "The Judge of Her Own Case")   38, 110, 128
Jacinto (N. 2: "Aminta Deceived and Honor's Revenge")   32, 62, 94, 97, 100, 103, 110, 154, 156
Jaime (D. 4: "Too Late Undeceived")   87, 88, 101, 103, 115–16, 153
Jorge (N. 10: "The Deceitful Garden")   42–4, 136, 155
Juan (N. 4: "Forewarned but Fooled")   72–3
Juana (N. 6: "Disillusionment in Love and Virtue Rewarded")   124, 134–5, 156
Juan (frame story and narrator, N. 9, "The Judge of Her Own Case")   10, 39, 42, 47, 48, 53, 80, 100, 156

Juan (D. 2: "Most Infamous Revenge")   84–5, 86
Juan (D. 3: "His Wife's Executioner")   86, 103, 137–8
Ladislao (D. 9: "Triumph Over Persecution")   118
Lisarda, (frame story and narrator of N. 1: "Taking a Chance on Losing")   25, 47, 53, 62, 80, 84, 85, 100, 103, 156, 159
León (*Friendship Betrayed*)   158–9
Liseo (*Friendship Betrayed*)   158–9
Lisis (frame story and narrator of D. 10: "The Ravages of Vice")   1, 10, 15, 17, 20, 31, 39, 42, 46–9, 53, 79–81, 84, 86, 90, 91, 97, 100, 107–8, 110, 112, 118, 124, 138, 143, 155, 156, 157
Laura (N. 5: "The Power of Love")   7, 30, 33, 94, 99, 100, 105–6, 124, 130, 133, 156
Laura (Lisis's mother and narrator of N. 10 "The Deceitful Garden")   42, 44, 155
Laura (*Friendship Betrayed*)   158
Laurela (D. 6: "Love for the Sake of Conquest")   33–6
Leonor (N. 8: "Triumph over the Impossible")   40–1, 78, 114, 130, 135, 136, 155
Lisarda (frame-story and narrator, D. 2: "Most Infamous Revenge")   10, 25, 39, 47, 53, 62, 80, 84, 85, 100, 103, 156, 159
Lope (narrator, N. 8: "Triumph over the Impossible")   40
Lucía (*Friendship Betrayed*)   158
Lucrecia (N. 6: "Disillusionment in Love and Virtue Rewarded")   134–5, 156
Lucrecia, Madame, Princess of Erne ("Fourth Tale of Disillusion")   153
Luis (N. 2: "Aminta Deceived and Honor's Revenge")   100, 101
Luis (N. 7: "Just Desserts")   77, 155
Luisa (narrator, D. 7: "Marriage Abroad: Portent of Doom")   18, 36

Magdalena (D. 10: "The Ravages of Vice")   90–1, 103
Manuel (D. 1: "Her Lover's Slave")   52, 82–4, 127
Marcela (N. 3: "The Miser's Reward")   65–7
Marcia (*Friendship Betrayed*)   158–9
Marco Antonio (D. 8: "Traitor to His Own Blood")   106
Marcos (N. 3, "The Miser's Reward")   8, 16–7, 63–8, 69–70, 86, 128, 132–3
María (D. 7: "Marriage Abroad: Portent of Doom")   94, 153
Marieta (D. 7: "Marriage Abroad: Portent of Doom")   35, 101
Martín (N. 2: "Aminta Deceived and Honor's Revenge")   32, 94, 100–1, 154
Martín (D. 4: "Too Late Undeceived")   101, 114, 115, 116
Matilde (narrator, N. 2 "Aminta Deceived and Honor's Revenge")   62, 99
Mencía (D. 8: "Traitor to His Own Blood")   19, 21, 89, 98, 99, 100, 120, 130, 138, 139–40
Miguel (narrator, N. 7: "Just Desserts")   45, 75, 78, 114
Nise, (narrator, N. 5: "The Power of Love")   30, 99, 106, 156
Nise, (narrator, D. 3: "His Wife's Executioner")   57, 86, 137, 138
Octavia (D. 2: "Most Infamous Revenge")   54, 84–5, 98–9, 103
Octavio (D. 1: Her Lover's Slave")   83, 84
Octavio (N. 6: "Disillusionment in Love and Virtue Rewarded")   134
Pedro (N. 2: "Aminta Deceived and Honor's Revenge")   99, 108
Pedro (D. 3: "His Wife's Executioner")   120, 138, 139
Pedro (N. 7: "Just Desserts")   77–8, 154–5
Pedro (D. 8: "Traitor to His Own Blood")   98–100, 120, 138
Rodrigo (N. 8: "Triumph Over the Impossible")   114, 130, 135, 155

Roseleta (D. 3: "His Wife's
    Executioner") 86, 130, 137–8, 156
Sancho (N. 6: "Disillusionment in Love
    and Virtue Rewarded") 96, 98,
    103, 104
Sarabia (N. 1: "Taking a Chance on
    Losing") 28
Serafina (N. 4: "Forewarned but
    Fooled") 56, 70–1, 73, 75, 120,
    154
Teodosia (N. 10: "The Deceitful
    Garden") 43–4, 155, 156
Vicente (N. 4: "Forewarned but
    Fooled") 56, 70

Violante (N. 4: "Forewarned but
    Fooled") 72–3, 100, 109, 154
Virgin María (D. 3 "His Wife's
    Executioner") 137
Virgin María (D. 9: "Triumph Over
    Persecution") 104, 121, 131, 137,
    140
Zaida (D1: "Her Lover's Slave") 57, 83
Zelima / Isabel (D. 1: "Her Lover's
    Slave") 47, 59, 80, 81, 84, 110,
    114, 127

TAMESIS

Founding Editors
†J. E. Varey
†Alan Deyermond

General Editor
Stephen M. Hart

Advisory Board
Andrew M. Beresford
Zoltán Biedermann
Celia Cussen
Efraín Kristal
Jo Labanyi
María E. López
José Antonio Mazzotti
Thea Pitman
Julius Ruiz
Alison Sinclair
Isabel Torres
Noël Valis

www.ingramcontent.com/pod-product-compliance
Lightning Source LLC
Chambersburg PA
CBHW081825230426
43668CB00017B/2384